BIBLICAL ECONOMIC POLICY

Ten Scriptural Truths
for Fiscal *and* Monetary
Decision-Making

by
DAVE ARNOTT
and **SERGIY SAYDOMETOV**

Deep River
B O O K S

Table of Contents

Chapter 1: Christianity and Economics: Two Dismal Sciences . . 7

The Christian Worldview: Creation, Fall, Redemption

Creation

Fall

Redemption

"Imagine" That: A Christian Worldview Case Study

Input and Output

Chapter 2: The Ten Commandments of Biblical Economics . . . 41

1. People Should Be Free

2. Work Is Good

3. Don't Steal

4. Don't Covet

5. Use Honest Measures

6. Trade Is Good

7. Love Your Neighbor as Yourself

8. Take Care of Widows and Orphans

9. Be a Good Samaritan

10. Honor Those in Power

Chapter 3: International Trade 83

Free Trade or Managed Trade?

Should the Government Institute Tariffs?

The Bible and Balance of Trade

Should the Government Allow Outsourcing to Low-Wage Nations?

Are Free-Trade Agreements and Trading Blocs Biblical?

Chapter 4: Government Policies 107

The Benevolent Social Planner

Should the Government Set a Minimum Wage?

Does Rent Control Lower the Housing Cost for the Poor?

Should Saving Be Encouraged?

Chapter 5: Markets Work 121

In a Fallen World, Should Regulations Be Increased or Decreased?

Lowering the Cost of Food: Government Dictate or Free-Market Competition?

Chapter 6: Taxes 133

What Is the Purpose of Taxes?

What Is the Proper Level of Taxes?

Is It Better to Tax Corporations or Individuals?

Chapter 7: Production 145

Policies That Promote Production

Scarcity vs. Abundance

Chapter 8: Unemployment 167

Should the Government Encourage Work?

What Causes Unemployment?

Should the Government Pay Unemployment Insurance?

Chapter 9: The Monetary System 187

Is Borrowing and Lending Biblical?

What Is the Correct Interest Rate?

Should the Federal Reserve Increase the Money Supply?

Is a Strong Dollar Good for America?

Should There Be Active or Passive Monetary Policy?

Chapter 10: Inflation. 209

What Does the Bible Say about Inflation?

Chapter 11: Fiscal Policy 219

Should the Government Practice Stimulus Spending?

Should the Government Have Debt?

Should There Be Active or Passive Fiscal Policy?

Chapter 12: Income Inequality 231

Are the Rich Paying Their Fair Share of Taxes?

Should the Government Redistribute Wealth?

Should the Government Attempt to Provide Equality of Income?

Chapter 13: Social Economics 253

Is Social Security a Biblical Role for the Government?

Should the Government Pay Agricultural Subsidies?

Should Genetically Modified Crops Be Banned?

Should Population Be Controlled by Abortion?

Should College Be Free?

Should the Government Provide Healthcare as a Right?

Should the Government Provide Incentives for Renewable Power?

Chapter 14: Conclusion: Biblical Economic Policy in the Twenty-First Century **271**

The Economy in the Twenty-First Century

The Role of the Church

The Role of the Christian

The Role of the Government

The Role of the Nation

Christianity and Capitalism in the Twenty-First Century

Appendix: Life Is Better Now Than Any Time in History **289**

Notes and Sources **293**

Chapter 1

Christianity and Economics:
Two Dismal Sciences

Christianity is dismal, because we "look through a glass darkly." Economics is dismal, because it's about human behavior.

Economics is about how humans make choices of production and distribution of products and services in scarce environments. You would think that self-interested (fallen) people would make choices that serve themselves at the expense of others. They do. But that's the providential thing about free market economics: When fallen people make self-interested choices, they serve others. The idea comes directly from Adam Smith's *The Wealth of Nations*: "the person intends only his own gain, and he is in this, as in many other cases, led by an invisible hand to promote an end which was no part of his intention." Or more simply stated, "Individuals serving their own interest, provide for the interest of all."[1] While it sounds dismal, we're going to call it providential—and even refer to it as "the divine hand," although Adam Smith never used that term.

At its core, stewardship is about making choices, and making choices is the science of economics. Making decisions that please God is our goal as God's stewards.[2] At its bottom, economics is about us—what we choose; what we value; what we represent in language and symbols; how

7

we interact with each other in a market; and especially how we produce, exchange, and distribute goods, services, risk, and wealth.[3] It's about how we go about our lives. We are called to "go." For some of us, that means to professionally go be a missionary, pastor, or evangelist. For the rest of us, it can mean "as you go" about our daily lives. Our lives are economic. We continually make exchanges in a scarce environment. Your choice to read this book prevents you from doing something else. Economists call that "opportunity cost."

Economics is dismal because, as a social science, it tries to predict human behavior. Good luck with that.

Let's differentiate "hard sciences" from "social sciences." The iceberg represents what we can see and measure above the water (hard sciences) and what is more difficult to see and measure below the water (social sciences). If you see the top of an iceberg, you know it's supported by a

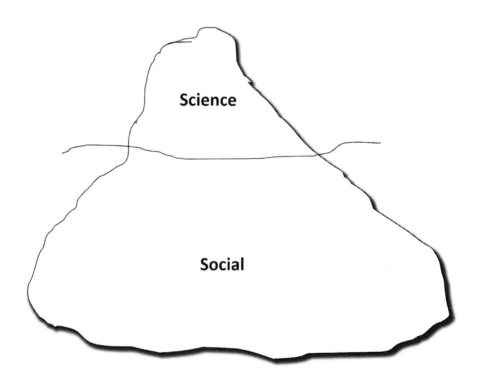

large portion of the iceberg underwater. In social sciences, like economics, we're trying to measure "underwater" concepts.

In the classroom, Dave shows the iceberg diagram, and writes the concept "love" below the water. Groups of students are assigned to suggest "above-water" measures of love in a marriage that adhere to the rules of science: Constructs must be measurable and replicable— meaning, when you see one and I see one, we both count it as one. The best answers are "The size of the diamond" and "number of children." You're probably thinking, "Those are terrible measures!" Welcome to the dismal science.

In economics we say people have needs. How do they satisfy those needs? Well, the interesting thing is, needs have never changed. We don't care if you believe the world is six thousand or millions of years old; human needs have never changed. All the needs satisfied by the smartphone (that has been interrupting your reading of this book) were the same needs that humans had when they first appeared on earth. How they *satisfy* those needs has changed. That's what economists try to predict in our dismal science. Mark Twain was right: "Predictions are difficult, especially those about the future." They are difficult, and dismal.

In his important book *Human Action*, Ludwig Von Mises defines economics as the science of purposeful human action.[4] In our context, economics is the science of making God-pleasing decisions. Normative economics explain how the economy *should* work. The Good Samaritan story is a good example. "When gas prices go up, people should drive less" is another. These are economic predictions that look forward, trying to predict future behavior. When gas prices go up, people *do* drive less. How much? That's econometrics, which is beyond the scope of this book. We will concentrate mostly on direction in this book, not specific data measurement.

Dave often walks across the front of his classroom and says, "Your seventh-grade physical science teacher walked across the front of the classroom like this and asked you which direction she was pushing the earth." The answer is pretty simple, and is a good way of teaching Newton's third law of motion about equal and opposite forces. The teacher was obviously pushing the earth backward from the direction she was walking.

Economic "pushes" are like that. We know how poverty is alleviated and wealth is created. What is so perplexing, and so maddening, is how many Christian thinkers seek to eradicate the remaining poverty while largely ignoring the known and well-trod path.[5] Economists know what causes *The Wealth of Nations,* and *The Poverty of Nations.* Why we continually practice more poverty than wealth is a main theme of this book.

Positive economics looks back and says, "When people accept the Good Samaritan story as Jesus told it, they respond more kindly to the poor and injured." When a measure is produced that verifies it, you have positive economics. A measure showing that people reduced their driving by five percent as a result of the last gas price increase is positive economics. So, economics can be seen as a hard science when you look back, because the data is irrefutable. But it's typically seen as a soft (dismal) science because it tries to look forward.

Harvard economist and textbook author Gregory Mankiw served in the George Bush administration. In a March 2019 interview, he was asked by Dallas Federal Reserve Bank president Robert Kaplan, "What is the biggest misunderstanding that politicians have about economists, and that economists have about politicians?" His answer: "Politicians ask us questions we can't answer." Those are the predictions about the future: What will be the response to tax cuts, tariffs, etc.? "And they don't ask us questions that we *can* answer, like the effects of rent control." The biggest misunderstanding that economists have about politics? "How hard it is to change policy."[6] He was making the point that economics is dismal because politicians want us to predict the future, which is quite hard to do. We're better at predicting the past.

Christian economics is about making biblical choices among the many opportunities presented to us. We cannot pursue every good idea that comes along. Economists are the ultimate party poopers. We have to be. Someone has to remind caring, enthusiastic Christians that we simply cannot pursue every single good idea that comes along.[7] So which opportunities should we pursue? How should we behave? That's what this book is about. In chapters 3–13 we relate biblical truths to specific economic policies.

Christianity. The study of Christianity is dismal also. What did God intend? Well, if we knew that, we would be God. That's why our "Ten Commandments of Biblical Economics" is not very accurate. That assumes we know what God meant. We don't. We're fallen, foolish humans, stumbling around the broken earth, trying to figure out how to redeem it. There is no escape from the task of interpretation; we read and apply the Bible as fallible and finite human beings who will disagree with each other until our Lord returns.[8]

There's no such thing as an egotistical believer. We see things through a glass darkly. That's why Joe Galindo[9] suggested we have "an abundance of advisors." The more views we have on a Christian subject, the better chance we have of getting to the truth. We expand this idea in the Christian Worldview section of this chapter.

All this may come as a disappointment to any who hoped we would be able to give definitive "Christian answers" to economic problems. But Jesus never promised us that Christian discipleship in a fallen world would be easy: the Christian who wishes to comment on economic issues has no shortcuts available, no answers that he can read off directly. Submission to the Scriptures, intellectual humility, a willingness to listen to other Christians, and openness to the guidance of the Holy Spirit are the qualities required.[10]

The father of the scientific method, Francis Bacon, said it this way, "A little philosophy inclineth men's minds to atheism, but depth in philosophy bringeth men's minds about to religion."[11] Keep learning, you'll get closer to God. That's where he wants you, closer to him, knowing more about the bountiful world he made. He wants you to help him re-create in wonderful, amazing ways you can't even imagine.

So we have two dismal sciences: Christianity and economics. Thanks for joining us on an adventure to match up what we know with what we don't know, as we travel this journey to seek answers about some of the most difficult questions that face us.

The Christian Worldview: Creation, Fall, Redemption

There are 2.2 billion Christians in the world, because their worldview fits reality.

The fall. You can't understand economics separate from the fall. If people are not fallen, there is no scarcity, and there's no economics. We believe that in the creational garden of Eden, there was no scarcity, because the world was made perfect by God. Economics starts with the fall. If the fall is the problem, what's the cure? Redemption. Not only spiritual redemption by the acceptance of Jesus Christ as our personal Savior, but redemption of the world through the use of God's viceroys—us!

Everyone has answers to three questions:

Where did we come from?

What's our condition?

What's the cure?

In the Christian worldview, our answers are: creation, fall, redemption. Every good story has a creational beginning, a fallen middle, and a redemptive end. Every episode of *I Love Lucy* started with sweet music, and a loving caress between Lucy and Ricky. That's creation. Then Lucy would do something crazy to create a mess, often involving her friend Ethel. That's the fall. Somewhere between acts two and three, Ricky would utter his famous line, "Lucy, you got some 'splaining to do!" She "splained," asked for forgiveness, and the story ended with redemption. Every good story has those three elements. Why?

As Christians, we believe God imprinted that three-part outline on our hearts. We look for it in stories. When stories end badly, we are disappointed. When the "savior" defeats the bad guys and the good guys

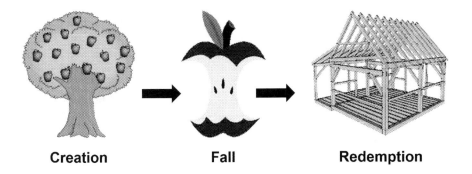

| Creation | Fall | Redemption |

win, we turn off the TV, or close the book, with a great deal of satisfaction. Who cares about worldview? Well, just about every action you take is based on your worldview assumptions. Our colleague at Dallas Baptist University (DBU), Davey Naugle, says it this way in *Worldview*: "Since nothing could be of greater final importance that the way human beings understand God, themselves, the cosmos, and their place in it, it is not surprising that a worldview warfare is at the heart of the conflict between the powers of good and evil. Consequently, an in-depth look at a concept that plays such a pivotal role in human affairs seems particularly worthwhile."[12]

The modern world tells kids that they are nothing more than a random collection of atoms, and that their lives are accidental and have no meaning. Then we send them to self-esteem classes. Wouldn't we save a lot of retraining if we just told them that their lives have meaning and purpose because they were beautifully made by their Creator who has a creational intention for their lives?

In the Narnia series, C. S. Lewis puts it this way: "For what you see and hear depends a good deal on where you are standing: It also depends on what sort of person you are." Your worldview is where you "stand."[13] Your perspective is driven by your worldview. Our worldview is the spectacles through which we see and interpret reality, shaping the way we relate to God, self, others, and creation on both the personal and systematic levels.[14]

Do you see humans as created beings who are hands and minds to work? Or do you see them as mouths to feed? That determines your view of humans and whether there should be more of them, or fewer. This worldview understanding drives your economic view of people. Is an increasing population better for the world, or worse? The concept of rational economic man is consistent with the biblical view of fallen man, which may explain why the concept has proved so enduring in the history of economic analysis.[15]

In soccer, you can't touch the ball with your hands. In basketball, you can't touch it with your feet. It's important to understand what sport you're playing. If you adopt the wrong set of rules, you will see the world in a very different manner. We believe the reason the Christian worldview is so popular is because it fits reality. More than 2 billion Christians believe in creation, fall, and redemption. They're playing basketball with their hands and soccer with their feet. But so often, we see people economically playing soccer with their hands and basketball with their feet.

It doesn't work. In *Redeeming Capitalism* Kenneth Barnes cites a study from the National Employment Law Project which shows no historic correlation between minimum wage increase and overall employment levels.[16] That seems impossible. He is suggesting that when you raise the price of something (labor) people *don't* buy less. The world doesn't work that way.

To start his macroeconomics class, Dave asked a student named Caitlin how much she paid for the coffee she was drinking. Then he asked another student, Cayden, "If the price of coffee goes up, will Caitlin buy more or less?" Cayden correctly answered "less." He had been studying economics for forty-five seconds and he knew more than the National Employment Law Project. Cayden was playing basketball with his hands; the NELP was playing with their feet. Cayden was expressing his understanding of our fallen nature: people will serve their own best interest by buying more coffee when the price goes down, and less when it goes up. You don't have to intrinsically know the Christian worldview, nor economics, to understand what Cayden does.

Dave had cataract surgery on his right eye twenty-five years ago, but still has not had the other eye fixed. The right side of his classroom looks like a white sheet of paper, the left side like a manila folder, kind of dull. So when you ask for Dave's perspective on a paint color, he will ask, "Which eye are you asking me about? I have two very different views of the world." Those who adopt the Christian worldview see the world as created perfect by God and messed up by human sin—and know that we have a command from God to help Him redeem it. Those who disagree with any of those three parts of the Christian worldview will "see" the world very differently.

Everyone has a worldview. When Bart Simpson was asked to say grace before dinner, he mumbled, "Dear god. We paid for all this stuff ourselves, so thanks for nothing!" That's a worldview. It's sometimes called the "Three-chapter gospel:" Creation, fall, redemption. And without it, economics can't exist. We refer to this concept often throughout the book.

Creation

If God is dead, Malthus was right. He was wrong. Creation was more than a seven-day event. It continues. Each time a baby is born, creation continues.

God made the world perfect. In the garden of Eden, there was work to do, but it was not painful. Adam and Eve named animals and plants, they tended the garden, and everything was fine. "God created the world in perfect harmony and flourishing, and he was pleased," writes Ann Bradley in *Be Fruitful and Multiply*.[17] Nothing was scarce, so there was no economics. Work only became difficult after the fall, as has everything humans have touched. But more about that later.

"God's daily work of preserving and governing the world cannot be separated from His act of calling the world into existence," writes Albert Wolters in *Creation Regained*.[18] Those who believe God created the world, then flicked it off his thumb with his index finger into space, are deists.

They believe there *is* a God, but that he's not with us anymore. Christians who believe there is a guiding and guarding God, who still functions in the world, make very different economic assumptions from those deists who believe we're out here on our own. If you believe God only created the world in seven days, and then left us, you will support more active monetary policy, as explained in chapter 9. If you believe there is a God who is active in our lives (creation continues), then you will favor making some decisions by man, and some hand-in-hand with God.

This gets us quickly into the politics of economics. The key question is, "When do *we* make decisions, and when do we rely on *God's providence?*" Well, if there is no active God, man has to make all of them. The phrase "God or government" comes to mind. There is clearly something wrong with the world, which is explained in the next section. If there's no God around anymore, it's pretty easy to assume that humans are going to have to make all the decisions. Human ingenuity, creativity, inventiveness, and entrepreneurial zeal are the engines that have improved the human condition. Those humans were made in the image of God, and thus are image-bearers as they co-create with God, a better world for their fellow humans. This is the antithesis of what atheists believe, as represented by the Club of Rome, who thinks that humans are the *enemy*![19] Creative humans make the world better, not worse.

In the story of creation, God brought order out of chaos. A gardener does something similar when he creatively uses the materials at his disposal and rearranges them to produce additional resources for mankind.[20] Humans were poor for thousands of years. In Jesus' time, estimates are that about 95 percent of the population was in slavery. Then in 1776, James Watt perfected the steam engine and the world got richer. That great leap ahead in technology and living standards—the scientific revolution—came about because Christianity views man as the creative steward of a rational creation, a creation that we can explore and understand because we are made in the image of a rational God who formed the cosmos.[21] That "leap ahead" gives title to Nobel Prize-winning economist Angus Deaton's book *The Great Escape*.[22] We escaped poverty by the creative nature we inherited from God.

What's our role in all this? Jim Denison says it this way, "You are on this planet for a reason. God did not make you because the world needs another human to add to the 7.7 billion already here. He made you because he has a purpose for you that no one else can fulfill. Stay faithful to the last word you heard from God and open to the next. If you will ask your Father to use you today, he will use you today. And whether you see the results or not, eternity will never be the same."[23] One of Jay Richards's top ten ways for alleviating poverty is, "Encourage belief in the truth that the universe is purposeful and makes sense."[24] In economic terms, we were created to please God. We do so by producing and distributing goods and services that our neighbors demand.

We human beings are creatures made in the image of God, placed in the context of scarcity, and given a capacity to reason, create, and transcend.[25] Workers are precious resources created in the image of God who must be able to consider prayerfully, for themselves, issues of calling, stewardship, leisure, and labor.[26] Adam Smith (a deist) believed in God, so he saw this invisible hand as God's providence over human affairs, since it creates a more harmonious order than any human being could contrive. Even though Friedrich von Hayek did not see God's providence in the market, he too marveled at what he called its "spontaneous order."[27] So both of these economists are observing order. As Christians, we attribute that to God's order.

We believe God is "still around," guarding and guiding. He appointed us his viceroys, but he's still active in our economic lives. When Dave mentioned to his wife Ginger that he was struggling with the idea that "creation is an ongoing concept," she simply replied, "Sure. Every time a baby is born, creation continues." Simple as that. The capacity for altruism and the desire to work come from the creational nature.[28] We were created to work, and to do work that serves our neighbors.

In *The Second Machine Age*[29] Erik Brynjolfsson and Andrew McAfee correctly point out that truck drivers will be unemployed by self-driving trucks. Then, they incorrectly assume that demand for problem-solvers is fixed, because they claim the government needs to support these unemployed truck drivers. Economists call this structural unemployment. But Brynjolfsson and McAfee are not operating under Christian worldview assumptions. We assume that fallen humans have unlimited needs, and that humans made in the image of God have unlimited creativity. When those two concepts are interceded by policies that promote production, truck drivers will use their "image of God" creativity to solve human needs that creates more value for society than they did while driving a truck.

If we want to see all of the seven billion-plus people on planet Earth flourish, we need to ask, what is the alternative? The answer features the word *sustainability*. Very well, but does anyone really know what that involves? Isn't thinking that we are even capable of knowing this just one more example of the hubris that regularly gets us into trouble? We submit that it is impossible for anyone or any group to know the limits of our terrestrial resources and imprudent to attempt to restrict responsible exploration and use of them. In the 1970s Americans were told we would run out of oil and gas; in 2013 we were told that it is entirely possible for North America to become energy self-sufficient. New discoveries, new technologies, greater efficiencies, alternative sources of energy—the list goes on, and no one knows what the future will bring. We will only find out when we give permission to free and resourceful people to keep trying. For any group or state to arbitrarily impose limits to this human activity would be to consign the poorest of the poor to their permanent fate. All Christians should find this unacceptable. There is a deep irony in this attempt to curtail human creativity and resourcefulness.[30]

Dave was shopping the close-out aisle at Walmart and dropped a to-go coffee mug in his basket. Later, he realized it was designed with a device on the bottom that prevented tip-overs. It has become one of his favorite classroom examples. Tipping coffee cups is a problem in a fallen world. A creative human solved the problem. There are unlimited problems to be solved and unlimited creativity to solve them. When mediated by policies that promote production—where people are rewarded for solving problems—there should never be an unemployed person. "No one ever made an ounce of earth," is the first line in Fred Gottheil's textbook *Principles of Economics*.[31] He continues, "Economists accept as fact that every resource on the face of the earth is a gift of nature." And as Hugh Welchel said, "God made something out of nothing. Our call is to make something out of something."[32]

A Hallmark gift bag reads, "We create ourselves as we go." That's a very humanistic worldview that Christians reject. We did not create ourselves. God created us. And he created us for a reason: for our lives to have meaning. Our purpose in life is to discover what God intends for us.

God creates, humans discover. We discover God's creation when we "positivize" it. The whole of creation is crying out to be positivized.[33] God creates, humans discover. In economics, we discover what God had in mind. The German-based company BASF has a TV advertisement that proclaims, "We create chemistry." In the Christian worldview, we believe they "discover" chemistry. The label on a bottle of Ozarka water reads, "Made in Texas." Really? They *made* the water? Maybe they "discovered" the water. Dave drives by Midlothian High School every day. There is a marble diagram designed into the floor of the main hallway that reads, "MISD: Creating a better future, one student at a time." We know what they mean, so we're not going to show up at a school board meeting and make a fuss. But we understand that God *created* the world; we simply *discover* what He wants us to do with it. A better statement might be: "Discovering a better future for our students." That would keep the slogan in line with the Christian worldview.

Creative destruction is rooted in creation, not the fall. Humans are created in the image of God; thus, the seed of creativity we all enjoy causes us to create new and better ways of producing value for our fellow humans. There have been eleven recessions since World War II. Each of the ten low points at the bottom of the cycle are higher than the previous nadir.

Why? Because we inherited creativity from our Creator. We contemplate our ideas in the sunlight of heaven, Acton observed, and apply them in the darkness of earth.[34] The next section is about how Christians should deal with that darkness.

Fall

Most economic myths stem from a denial of the fallen nature.

Without the fall, there's no scarcity. Without scarcity, there's no economics. You have to understand the fall to understand economics. In *The Virtues of Capitalism*, Austin Hill and Scott Rae recount being at a summer seminar when the leader asked, "What's not scarce?" One of them answered, "Salvation."[35] We agree. Dave starts his classes by observing what happened when his second through seventh grandchildren were born. Dave and Ginger didn't have to manufacture more love, nor spread around the scarce element of love, so that must not be scarce either. If salvation is because of God's love for us, then salvation is based in love. Therefore, love is the only thing in the world that is not scarce? Seems like it.

Everything else is scarce, and it became so when Adam ate the apple. The fallen nature cursed everything, and economics began. At a recent meeting with Josh McDowell, Dave noticed how he spent a few minutes explaining how a phone-sized modem could be set on the dashboard of a car and people near it could get free Wi-Fi, and a link to the gospel message. Then Josh spent forty-five minutes railing at the curse of pornography that was being spread on smartphones. God made both the modem and the smartphone for good purposes, but fallen humans can choose to use them for good or evil. Josh explained how the modem was being used for good and the same-sized smartphone was being used for evil. That's true of just about everything. Wolters writes, "Anything in creation can be directed either toward or away from God: That is, directed either in obedience or disobedience to His law."[36]

Marxism was doomed to failure because it did not take into account human sinfulness and our need for spiritual redemption.[37] In *Joy at Work*, Dennis Bakke explains, "After Adam and Eve broke their relationship with God, all of life, including work, became more difficult and troublesome. For some, that is where the story ends. Mundane daily work is seen as an obligation, a burden, or even pure drudgery, rather than the joyous experience it was meant to be."[38] Humans flourish when they find God's creational intent for their work, which is redeeming a broken world. Work and change did not arise from our fall into sin. The fall simply turned work into toil, since the ground would resist our efforts to cultivate it.[39]

In April 2019, Facebook CEO Mark Zuckerberg called for more federal and even global oversight and governance of his company(ies). The online blog Morning Brew (which likes to abbreviate names) wrote it this way, "Zuck said he agrees with lawmakers that Facebook has too much power over what constitutes free speech."[40] If the Facebook employees are not fallen, why would they need to be governed? Free speech was the reason Facebook was so popular. It's fascinating when one of the most powerful CEOs in the world admits his own employees are fallen. Europe's General Data Protection Regulation went into effect in May of 2018, and Zuckerberg thinks it should become a global law. The fallen nature of producers is evidenced by their activity in Washington, DC, clamoring for more "rent" for their stakeholders. We address this fallen nature in many chapters of this book, citing the fact that America's four richest counties are all suburbs of Washington, DC.[41]

Agnostic Jew David Horowitz explains it this way, in a radio interview: "The big problem we face in the world is us. And I think every Christian knows that. That we are sinners, that one of the protestant ideas is salvation by faith. We are so flawed in our beings, so prone to sin and temptation, that none of us deserves to get to heaven and that we can only get there by divine grace. It's a very profound idea." He may understand the Christian worldview better than many Christians. He continues, "Why do we have a system of checks and balances?

Because the founders didn't trust the people, they felt they had to be restrained."[42] You can't understand economics without understanding the fallen nature of humans. And there's more from Horowitz's book *Dark Agenda: The War to Destroy Christian America*, "It is the Christian view: The post-Edenic world is a fallen place, irreparably damaged by the corruption of human hearts, so that no human agency can heal it."[43] We'll discuss later in the book how some believe government can save men and women.

God made fermentation so glucose could be broken into carbon dioxide and ethanol. That's how alcohol is made. It's been shown that a glass of wine might be good for you. The same alcohol is often used for evil. Twenty-three thousand people die each year in drunk-driving accidents in the United States alone. Maybe humans, created in the image of God, will perfect autonomous vehicles, and drunk driving will be eliminated, because there will be no more drivers. We would see that as a redemption of the fall. But more about that soon.

What should we do about the fallen nature of humans? Confusion arises when people see evils and mistakenly assume that getting rid of the free market will somehow magically solve the problem of fallen people. Only a little reflection should reveal the error. Moving to a command-and-control economy doesn't remove lust and selfishness from the human heart. Those vices go right on thriving—only now they are fed and cared for by some arm of the state.[44] The history of centralized government reflects the fall, and the truth of Lord Acton's proverb: "Power corrupts and absolute power corrupts absolutely."[45]

Roman Montero tries to make a case for current-day Christian socialism in *All Things in Common*: "This is why people are willing to give what they can and take only what they need, the assumption is that the individuals involved are socially bound together."[46] Montero is right: Where people are bound, you can practice socialism, as my wife and I do in our home, where we are bound. To assume we are bound by being Americans—or more precisely, by being in America—is to assume that our fellow Americans are not fallen. They are. I am. You are.

"Nothing is secular," says Arthur Brooks. His point is that the sacred-secular divide that the Greeks first introduced and is so popular in modern culture is not God's idea. Duality is dangerous, because it encourages us to keep our Lord in his glass-stained box for Sunday. That's not how the Christian worldview works, and it's not how economics works. Everything is economic (except for love) and everything is sacred. Trying to make the sacred secular is not biblical. It's a nice tradition to pray before eating a meal. But if you're thanking God for providing food, there are equally good reasons for thanking Him before you start your car, turn on your computer, or open this book. He provided all of them for you. All of them were made for a sacred purpose, but can be used for secular ends.

This sacred-secular split is explained by the famous Abraham Kuyper quote, "There is not a square inch in the whole domain of our human existence over which Christ, who is Sovereign over all, does not cry: Mine!" That's been a favorite quote of our colleague at Dallas Baptist University, Davey Naugle, who authored the definitive book on Christian worldview, titled *Worldview.*[47] His dog is named Kuyper.

Western culture was inherited from the Greeks and Romans. Centuries before Christ, they believed in a division of the soul and the body. They determined that the soul was positive while the body was evil. This split later led Christians to honor monastic withdrawal from the world as the highest form of devotion.

This pervasive secular idea has encouraged Christians to adopt the culture that splits Sunday's churchgoing from their weekday work. The Christian worldview does not support that split. That's what this book is about: trying to determine how we integrate our Christian worldview and biblical understanding with our economic behaviors.

Obamacare assumed that people would rise above their self-interest and buy insurance, even though it was cheaper to simply pay the fine and buy the insurance once you got sick. Self-interested consumers paid the fine—and when they bought the insurance, found that the group of insured people contained too many sick people and not enough healthy folks. When the Obamacare plan was announced, everyone who under-stood the Christian worldview knew it would not succeed because it denied the fallen nature. Economics is rife with these examples, leading us to proclaim, "Most economic failures are caused by a misunderstand-ing of the fallen nature."

One of our bright DBU students asked us what should be done about the "gentrification" of neighborhoods—when a neighborhood moves upscale and former tenants and homeowners can no longer afford to live there. If you assume the improvement of neighborhoods is from the fall, you will wage war against it. If you assume it's from creation, you will encourage it. It's quite clear: improving a neighborhood is part of creation, so we should encourage it. Now, what should be done to aid families who get displaced is a more difficult question, and we appreciate that one of our students is in the neighborhood trying to help. This is a good applica-tion of the Christian worldview and economics. When you can determine whether an effect is part of creation or the fall, you know how to proceed.

The Christian worldview seems unique in its assumption that cre-ation and the fall are distinct events. All other belief systems seem to fall into the trap of blaming God for human mistakes. That's what makes the Christian worldview so powerful in economics. God made a perfect world; it's us humans who have messed it up. The I-ching diagram, so popular for its yin-and-yang elements, says that the good is enfolded in the bad and the bad is enfolded in the good. As the wheel turns, the two get mixed up. The Christian worldview rejects that idea. The fall is a parasite on, not a part of, creation.[48]

Understanding of the fallen nature encourages Christians to reject state-controlled or centrally controlled economies, which would concen-trate power in the hands of a few sinful individuals. Instead, we should support an economic system that would disperse that power and protect us from greed and exploitation.[49] We must look to the economic system that takes men and women on their worst days and can, more often than not, get them to act in the interest of others.[50] That system is a mostly free-market economy, as we explain many times in this book.

The same people who resolutely oppose economic growth tend to resist any curtailment in the growth of the state's power to intervene and to redistribute wealth. Christians who take the reality of sin seriously ought to do the exact opposite: encourage economic development and growth while advocating and working for a curtailment of state power and the accumulation of national debt. In other words, we should trust free people more and powerful people—or those lusting after power—less.[51] Chapters 3–13 rely on this assumption many times.

Government-controlled economies have attempted and continue to attempt to transform human behavior through manipulation and the elimination of trade, and the consequences are dire: great suffering and early death. Capitalism, rather than trying to change the sinner's heart, takes it as it is and uses a system of incentives to encourage service. The result is greater flourishing, better-protected environments, increased wealth and well-being, and the near-eradication of abject poverty.[52] Free economies do a far better job than socialist economies at giving greedy people socially useful ways to get rich.[53] Fallen people can be induced to serve others, when the inducements are right.

Throughout this book, we will keep the fall in mind. We will generally follow Lord Acton's maxim of "Power corrupts, and absolute power corrupts absolutely." As government gets bigger, it becomes more corrupt. As the eminent philosopher Reinhold Niebuhr wrote, big centralized governments are inevitably immoral, since people are capable of moral good only in small communities. According to Niebuhr, human beings are too self-serving and limited in imagination to treat people outside their sphere of personal contacts with the kind of care and respect those people deserve.[54]

In *Roaring Lambs*,[55] Bob Briner asked why his fellow parishioners in a small Free Methodist church in South Dallas didn't encourage him to take his writing skills to Hollywood as a teenager. The obvious answer is, "It's a den of thieves. It's Sodom and Gomorrah." Briner reasonably asked, "If Christians abandon an industry, how can it be redeemed?" Good question. We are not supposed to abandon politics, business, entertainment, nor economics. It's just that the "double-dismal" science of Christian economics makes interpretations rather difficult. It doesn't mean we should give up and let the secular world take over. We should analyze and try to determine God's creational intent for the economic lives we have together in macroeconomics.

Nothing will be perfect in a fallen world. In *Money, Greed, and God* Jay Richards writes, "Can't we build a just society? The answer: we should do everything we can to build a *more* just society and a more just world. And the worst way to do that is to try to create an egalitarian utopia."[56]

As Christian economists, we are wary of utopian plans that promise perfection. We believe our calling is to gently redirect our world. We don't believe in violent overthrow, and we don't believe in destroying an existing environment. A Christian called to be the economic czar of Cuba or North Korea would not destroy the existing system; he would merely redirect the scarce resources that God put there. That's because we believe God had a perfect intention, and the call of fallen humans is to make it better by gently changing the economic system.

Friedrich von Hayek, one of the greatest economists of the twentieth century and a Nobel Prize-winner, wrote *The Road to Serfdom*.[57] Perhaps the most significant connection between von Hayek and Christianity can be found in their common understanding of human nature. Von Hayek started with a simple premise: Human beings are limited in their understanding. The Bible would say we are fallen creatures living in a fallen world.[58] There is little point in advocating for a secular society, economic structures which presuppose the existence of a closely knit community of love, as in the early church in Jerusalem. That would be foolish utopianism. Instead we have to look for a second-best.[59]

The central point is not our greed, but the limits to our knowledge. The market is a higher-level order that vastly outstrips the knowledge of any and all of us. So free-market capitalism doesn't need greed. At the same time, it can channel greed, which is all to the good. We should *want* a social order that channels proper self-interest as well as selfishness into socially desirable outcomes.[60] That's the problem with free-market capitalism's opposite, socialism: it doesn't fit the human condition. It alienates people from their rightful self-interest and channels selfishness into socially destructive behavior like stealing, hoarding, and getting the government to steal for you. That's because capitalism discourages miserliness and encourages its near opposite: enterprise.[61] The goal of capitalism is not to change people, but to protect us from human sinfulness.[62] That's the whole point of freedom that we discuss in the next chapter: it always involves costs—that is, trade-offs. To choose one path is to foreclose the opposite path, which economists call "opportunity cost." Even God accepted trade-offs. He chose to create a world with free beings, one that allowed those beings to turn against him. And they did. But their freedom didn't *cause* them to choose the bad—it just *allowed* them to. So too with a free economy. Critics notice all the vice present in free societies. But it is only in free societies that we can fully exercise our virtue. Charity is charity, for instance, only if it's not coerced.[63]

Utopian Ideas Deny the Fallen Nature

Can't we build a just society? The answer: we should do everything we can to build a *more* just society and a more just world. And the worst way to do that is to try to create an egalitarian utopia.[64] The world is not perfect, and we can't make it that way. But we can make it better.

Society makes opportunity cost trade-offs. Environmental pollution provides a good example. The optimal level of pollution cleanup for a society is not zero. Neither is it 100 percent. The optimal level of pollution cleanup lies at the point where we decide additional cleanup is not worth the time, trouble, and money. We should clean up our environment until things are "good enough," and then move on to more urgent tasks.[65] A normative understanding of our economic life must be rooted in creation and not in eschatology. . . . but as a check on perfectionist utopianism, not as a template for radical transformation of our social order.[66] Recognizing that heaven on earth is impossible, we do not pursue utopian schemes.[67] When an economist hears the phrase "win-win," our economic antennae start to quiver.

In *The Red Sea Rules*, Robert Morgan writes that the first rule is, "Realize God intends for you to be where you are."[68] You are called to re-create the economic situation you're in. God put you there for a reason, and it's your calling to figure that out. Ann Bradley adds, "You are the only *you* there ever was or ever has been."[69] In the movie of the same name, *The Blues Brothers* famously shouted, "We're on a mission from God." Are you?

"We are called to be Christian Economists, not a Christian who is an economist," writes Arthur Holmes in *The Idea of a Christian College*.[70] The title is taken from *The Idea of a University* by Cardinal John Henry Newman. Seen in this light, the Christian worldview is the ballast that holds up the road we live on. When we see the world through our Christian worldview lens—creation, fall, redemption—we find answers to our questions about how to distribute scarce goods in a fallen world. We will never create full *shalom* in this current age.[71] It's not a perfect world, and we can't make it perfect. We have to settle for marginal improvements.

Here's a story that demonstrates our belief about providence: Almost all men marry women shorter than them—Milt was a five-foot-tall student at the University of Chicago in 1932. As an atheist, he considers it a coincidence that he met a woman shorter than he was, named Rose, in one of his first economics classes. The Christian worldview looks at the same situation and calls it "providence" that Milt and Rose met in that class. When Rose married Milt, her last name changed to Friedman, and thus the most influential husband-wife economics team of the twentieth century was created. God intended Milton and Rose Friedman to be in the same classroom at the University of Chicago in 1932. They were not Christians, but in the Christian worldview, we believe God used them to re-create His world through their economic research and teaching.

We should encourage an orientation to the future and the belief that progress—but not utopia—is possible in this life.[72] Left to ourselves, things tend toward disorder, a loss of spiritual life, and a decline in vitality,[73] because we have a fallen nature. Christians believe we need to find a way for fallen people to serve one another. That happens in free-market systems.

The Christian worldview assumes there *is* perfection in creation, but that we can't find it, because we're fallen humans with limited understanding of the world he created.

Redemption

Most religions believe you behave to be saved. Christians believe we are saved to behave.

This direction of causality is important. We need to make it clear that we don't redeem the world to earn our salvation—we redeem the world because we're saved. In *The Cure*,[74] John Lynch, Bill McNicol, and Bruce Thrall describe two different rooms: the room of good intentions, and the room of grace. Their thesis is, "You're saved. Start acting like it!" That's how the Christian worldview sees behavior. Your salvation is secure, now go out and redeem the world. When it speaks of the kingdom, the New Testament uses verbs like receive, inherit, enter, and work. We are called to enter into it by faith in Christ alone and to pray that we may be enabled more and more to submit ourselves to the beneficent rule of God in every area of our lives.[75]

This makes a clear distinction between the economic thinking of the Christian worldview and others. We don't believe we can make things perfect. Thus, utopian plans are not in our wheelhouse. We can't do it. During class, Dave praised the Trump administration's renegotiation of the NAFTA deal with Mexico and renamed it "The United States, Mexico, Canada Agreement." A bright student asked, "But it will require that a higher percentage of autos be made with expensive US labor, increasing the cost to the consumer." Professor Arnott agreed, and made the Christian worldview application, "It's not perfect, but it's better."

To Lord Acton, the world exhibits the hand of providence—the action of Christ—not by being good but by becoming better, not by its perfection but by its improvement.[76] That's what we do as Christian economists. To quote Alex Haley, "We find the good and praise it." We know there is no perfection in a fallen earth, but we claim redemption when we make it better. That's our role—not utopian dreams of perfection, but incremental improvement.

The search for second-best solutions should not, however, be allowed to erode our perception that they are only second-best and not fully consistent with what God requires. In pursuing the possible, we must not forget the ideal, and there should be an element of sadness and repentance that our solutions must fall so far short of the ideal.[77]

Redemption, above all, applies to all of life. Not only are we redeemed from our sin (personal), we are brought into a new community—the body of Christ (corporate). Our redemption, though, extends beyond the personal and corporate to the whole cosmos. God's ultimate goal is the "restoration of all things."[78] This means that our calling is to take God's creation and try to figure out what he wants us to do to "redeem" it.

Dennis Bakke, in *Joy at Work*, explains it this way: "Joy will be difficult to experience. It requires that we understand that the major purpose of work is to use the resources of the created world to serve our needs and the needs of others. The purpose of business is to steward resources with a goal of creating products and services beneficial to people."[79] Ultimately, wealth is created as people obey the cultural mandate to subdue the world and make it useful for human beings.[80] Thus, we poor, foolish humans are stumbling around in God's perfect creation, continually asking the question, "What did God have in mind?" How do we use these scarce resources to create value for ourselves and our fellow humans? God intended humans to flourish, but we struggle to do so because of our fallen nature.

God did not have to include us in his redemptive mission, but because of his love for us, he requires us to help further his kingdom until Christ returns. We can only experience true joy when we do what God has ultimately designed us to do. God did not create us to run around engaging in useless, time-consuming activities to await his return. Instead, he created us to use our gifts to serve his creation, bring him glory, and contribute to greater human flourishing. In doing this, we help bring about a state of affairs that is closer or more aligned with the way things were supposed to be as we anticipate his return.[81]

The work flowing from God's vocational call on our lives is an extension of God's work of maintaining and providing for His creation. But even more than that, it is reweaving *shalom*. It is a contribution to what God wants done in the world.[82] Christ's redemption of our lives allows us to be more and more what we are created to be.[83]

We are enjoined to participate in ways framed by the revelation of God's work in the creative and renewing work of world-making and remaking. And it is in the divine nature of this work that vocation is imbued with great dignity.[84] We must see our work within the larger perspective of God's plan for the restoration of His creation.[85]

While God made the world "perfect," he left it incomplete. This means that while the world was created to be without defect, God called humans to interact with creation, to make possibilities into realities, and to be able to sustain ourselves via the fruits of our stewardship.[86] We are called to be stewards of the earth. Stewardship comes from the Greek word *oikonomia*, which appears in the New Testament. It is a Greek compound word translated as "the management of household affairs, stewardship, and administration." Of course, this is where we get the term "economics."[87]

Economics is a young discipline. If Adam Smith was our founder when he wrote *The Wealth of Nations*[88] in 1776, the study of economics is only 244 years old. But we usually talk about the "modern era" of economics starting when John Maynard Keynes wrote *The General Theory* in 1936.[89] Friedrich von Hayek wrote *The Road to Serfdom* in 1944.[90] We have very little data. There have only been eleven recessions since World War II, and that's the time period in which we've been making significant economic observations. We tell our students that models may get better in their lifetime, as the study of economics advances.

Are you beginning to see how the fall is important to our view of redemption? If you assumed humans were not fallen, you would expect perfect economic decisions. The fall. That's it. When you understand the fall, economics starts to make sense.

But more about redemption. So, what does this thing called redemption look like? In Dave's hometown of Midlothian, Texas, many of his neighbors work at one of the three cement plants in "The Cement Capitol of Texas." As workers dig out limestone that was left by a receding ocean millions of years ago, they subject it to a three-thousand-degree Fahrenheit furnace and turn it into cement. As a result, we have homes to live in, roads to drive on, and office buildings to work in. That's how fallen humans redeem God's creation to produce human flourishing. In the same way, Daniel's approach to life in Babylon as a public servant meant that he sought to use his gifts through his vocational calling to transform the culture around him.[91] He used the resources available to him to help create a better life for his neighbors.

Hugh Welchel says it this way: "Milton Friedman said the purpose of a business is to increase value for the owners. Our owner is God."[92] So we "serve our owner" when we create value for our fellow humans. It is no use seeking salvation in institutions, programs, and projects. We shall save ourselves only if more and more of us have the unfashionable courage to take counsel with our own souls and, in the midst of all this modern hustle and bustle, to think of ourselves as the firm, enduring, and proved truths of life.[93] We should not accept the idea that the state can transform people from the outside. Only the gospel can change people from the inside and so that they become new creatures, as stated in 2 Corinthians 5:17.[94]

God's creational intent was for you to have a perfect physical body. You don't, because you eat too many donuts and cookies. You join with God's creational hand when you re-create your body. You call it recreation. That's a powerful metaphor for understanding how we work hand in hand with God to bring redemption to the world. When you stop a fight between your small children, you're re-creating their relationship. When you teach a kid how to play soccer, you're re-creating his ability. When you teach Sunday School, you are contributing to God's re-creational intent. This compound word "re-creation" is powerful, because it contains our purpose and direction as Christians: To recreate the world, using the resources God has provided and the image of God creativity born in us.

Fred Gottheil, in his economics textbook, says, "[After creation,] Resources were there for the taking. And we took! We learned how to extract natural resources from the earth, how to fish them out of the waters, and how to harvest them from the land. We transform iron ore into steel, crude petroleum into plastic, trees into furniture, rays of the sun into energy, sand into glass, limestone into cement, and water flow into electricity. We are continually discovering newer techniques for transformation."[95] We re-create the earth that God created.

When Dave worked in pro tennis, there was a theme of "being in the flow," or "being in the zone." This comes from a guy named Mihaly Csikszentmihalyi. It meant the player felt he could hit the ball anywhere he wanted in any situation. Abraham Maslow called it "self-actualizing." In the movie *Chariots of Fire* Eric Liddell exclaimed, "When I run, I feel God's pleasure." That's what work feels like when we are in line with God's creational intent. We're in the flow of God's intention for our lives. We're re-creating the world, hand in hand with the very creator of the universe.

"A city that is set on a hill cannot be hid" (Matthew 5:14, KJV). Ronald Reagan adapted it to say, "America is a shining city upon a hill whose beacon light guides freedom-loving people everywhere." Blair Blackburn authored the book *A City on a Hill*[96] about the Christian and patriotic emblems on the DBU campus where we teach. God built the hill. We built the city. That's how we work hand in hand with God.

Wolters writes:

> In connection with our theme of re-creation it is particularly striking that all of Jesus' miracles (with the one exception of the cursing of the fig tree) are miracles of restoration- restoration to health, restoration to life, restoration to freedom from demonic possession. Jesus' miracles provide us with a sample of the meaning of redemption: a freeing of creation from the shackles of sin and evil and a reinstatement of creaturely living as intended by God.[97]

As Christian economists, we simply ask "What economic policies re-create the world?" How can we act as his viceroys and marshal scarce resources that clothe the poor, feed the hungry, employ the indigent, and provide for widows and orphans? The market is, as von Hayek said, "probably the most complex structure in the universe." It deserves our admiration. And yet very few Christian critics have fully understood it. Fewer still have thought of it as a stunning example of God's providence over a fallen world. It is just what we might expect of a God who, even in a fallen world, can still work all things together for good.[98]

So that's what we will continue to ask in this book: "What did God intend?" We are going to seek God's creational intent for taxes, for minimum wage, and thirty-eight other meaningful macroeconomic questions.

In Christian worldview terms, we try to encourage human flourishing by redeeming the economy. That means, bringing it into alignment with God's original creational intent. As fallen humans, we have trouble communing with the everlasting, sovereign, eternal God, but we try. Some of the economic rules are easier to discern than others. Some are quite clear, while others remain "behind a glass darkly." Thanks for joining us as we try to interpret God's creational intent for the economy.

"Imagine" That: A Christian Worldview Case Study

When John Lennon sang "Imagine no possessions," he added more to his possessions than any other song he possessed. Here's a Christian worldview analysis of this popular song.

Imagine there's no heaven.

Heaven and hell are the original representations of good and bad. If there's no good nor bad, how would we determine that "Imagine" is a good song, and that others are bad? If we can't determine good from bad, how would we know which songs to listen to—and why would we be listening to "Imagine"?

It's easy if you try. No hell below us. Above us only sky. Imagine all the people living for today.

This is hilarious! If John Lennon was "living for today," why did he record the song? And if we're "living for today," why are we denying his command by listening to a song he recorded in 1971? We're aware of the idea of mindfulness, and some of that is okay. But think about it: if you're really "living for today," you're saying, "I was taught in the past how to be 'in the present' in the future." Confused? Us too. Think about it: When were you taught to be mindful? Answer: In the past. When are you going to be mindful? Answer: In the future. Why would a student "living for today" get out of bed and be in Dr. Arnott's 8:00 a.m. Economics class? Don't you think that during a break from recording the song, this occurred to someone? Do you suppose that they all broke out laughing hysterically about spending the entire day, investing themselves in the future, by recording a song that instructs them to "live for today"?

Imagine there's no countries, it isn't hard to do.

If there were no countries, who would John Lennon turn to when he wanted to enforce his copyright to the song "Imagine"?

Nothing to kill or die for, and no religion too.

"No religion." We tried that, in John Lennon's lifetime. There was no religion in China when Chairman Mao's cultural revolution killed 60 million people, mostly by redistributing food. That was between 1958 and

1961, just ten years before Lennon recorded the song. The Soviets had no religion, which allowed Josef Stalin to kill 40 million in John Lennon's lifetime. Maybe Lennon didn't read the newspapers. In an interview conducted in September 1980, three months before his death, Lennon told *Playboy* journalist David Sheff: "People always got the image I was anti-Christ or antireligion. I'm not. I'm a most religious fellow." If John Lennon didn't follow his own advice, why should we?

Imagine all the people living life in peace.

In this book, we write about the "three-chapter gospel"—meaning creation, fall, redemption. Many people see it as a "four-chapter gospel," adding restoration, when Christ returns. Then John Lennon will be correct; that's when all the people will live life in peace. We hold no disagreement with the four-chapter gospel. But think about it: if we're all "living life in peace," we wouldn't need a song encouraging us to do so, and we wouldn't listen to "Imagine." Imagine that!

You, you may say I'm a dreamer, but I'm not the only one.

I suppose he's right: There are a lot of people who write, record, and listen to songs that make no sense. He's not the only one. By the way, that's why there are 2.2 billion Christians in the world: the Christian worldview of creation, fall, and redemption *makes* sense. It fits reality. That's how the world is.

I hope someday you'll join us, and the world will be as one.

We agree with John Lennon: In restoration, the fallen nature will be replaced by the rule of Christ. But in the meantime, we live in a fallen world, so the world won't "be as one."

Imagine no possessions, I wonder if you can.

This is the best line. By possessing the copyright to *Imagine*, John Lennon gained more possessions than any other song he possessed. Don't you think there were howls of laughter among the recording crew? You have to wonder how Lennon sang this line without busting out laughing!

No need for greed or hunger.

Lennon's wish has almost come true in 2020. In January of this year, it was reported that worldwide poverty has fallen to 8.6 percent. That's astounding. *The New York Times* ran an article on January 6, 2019, titled, "Why 2018 Was the Best Year in Human History!" *The Great Escape* by Nobel Prize-winning economist Angus Deaton explains how humans escaped thousands of years of destitution-level poverty; his first line is, "Life is better now than almost any time in history." In *Enlightenment*, Steven Pinker predicts the end of global poverty in his lifetime. And in the documentary film *The Pursuit* Arthur Brooks states, "Two billion people have been pulled out of starvation level poverty. . . . What did that?"

In other sections of this book, we will answer Brooks's question. For now, the short answer is: the market. People possessing goods and trading them—which is the exact opposite of what John Lennon called for.

A brotherhood of man.

Yes, like Cain and Abel. That kind of brotherhood. Because, that's the kind you can expect in a fallen world. John Lennon did not understand the fall, but he practiced it. The Beatles were only together seven years when, in September of 1969, John Lennon told the group he was leaving. That kind of brotherhood. Milton Friedman said, "Most economic myths are based on the incorrect assumption of zero-sum economics." Friedman was an atheist. We're Christians, so we say that most economic myths are based in a denial of the fallen nature.

Imagine all the people sharing all the world.

If Lennon meant "Sharing free-market capitalist ideas," he was right. But we think he meant sharing goods. There is a volume of data that shows he was wrong. Just one for now: US President Lyndon Johnson declared a "War on Poverty" in 1965. In the ensuing fifty years, an estimated five trillion dollars was spent—and the poverty level remained unchanged. "Sharing all the world" doesn't improve people's economic condition. What does? "Policies that Promote Production," as we explain in Chapter 7. Later in the book, we will cite *When Helping Hurts*, *Poverty Inc.*, *Poverty Cure*, and many other publications that show how Lennon was wrong.

You, you may say I'm a dreamer, but I'm not the only one. I hope someday you will join us. And the world will live as one.

Lennon was right: It was a dream. When the many others who dream with him, wake from their dreams, they will find what the rest of us know when we're awake, which is: the free market encourages fallen people to serve one another.

Input and Output

The current split in the Supreme Court is over originalism and progressivism. Originalists say the purpose of the court is to compare the new law with the existing constitution to see if it fits. We call that "input." Progressives say the purpose of the court is to measure the effect on society. We call those "outcomes." In *Last Call for Liberty*[99] Os Guinness warns that a living constitution brings death, because the humans who breathe life into it are fallen. We follow his advice: inputs (like freedom) are more important than the outcomes. If the ends justify the means, there is no limit to human error.

In Christian economics, the "constitution" is the Bible. We have attempted to summarize the biblical economic teachings in our "Ten Commandments of Biblical Economics." Throughout the book, we will use those commandments as the input, in an attempt to determine what God wants us to do in the economic realm. We also will look at the outcomes, or what effects that decision will have on our society.

Economists tend to look too much at the output. When analyzing socialized medicine, most economists will point out that when you increase demand and decrease supply—which socialized medicine has proven to do—there will be a shortage. That's the outcome measure. But as Christians, it seems we should be more concerned about the input measure, i.e., What did God intend for us to do? If we find that God commanded us to have socialized medicine, we should lobby for it, no matter what the cost. We should do what's right, not "what works." Christians are commanded to do what's right and bear the cost. A tenacious focus on outcomes (as in redistribution to achieve income parity) inevitably leads to treating people unfairly—unequally—by taking from one who has worked and produced superfluous wealth, and giving to one who has not.[100] The plain truth is that no nation can achieve material, cultural, and moral greatness unless it offers extensive freedom of choice to workers, consumers, producers, and voters. Freedom is a worthy objective in itself.[101] That is: freedom, which we will dig into further in chapter 2, is a worthy input that is often disregarded in economic analysis.

This hits at the heart of the political-economic divide. Politicians do what gets them elected, not what's right. Throughout the book, we will point out numerous flagrant economic mistakes made by politicians. When they do, we will ask, "Ignorance or malfeasance?" Often, the answer is "malfeasance." You have to think that someone in the Oregon legislature knew that rent control would lower the quality and quantity of housing when they enacted their economically foolish plan in March 2019. Why did they do it? Malfeasance. They knew the input was wrong; they did it to garner votes. They assumed the Oregon voters were too economically ignorant to figure it out. We get to watch and see what happens, but any economist who can draw demand-and-supply curves knows what will happen.

"Capitalism is the tool for Shalom."[102] *Shalom,* in this sense, means more than just peace. It means human flourishing that is consistent with God's creational intent. But what did he intend? That's what we explore in the next chapter.

Chapter 2

The Ten Commandments
of Biblical Economics

God communicates His creational intent to us through the Bible, His written word for Christians. As we have searched the Scriptures, we have found Ten Commandments of Biblical Economics. We explain those ten commandments in this chapter; then in chapters 3–13, we consider how they can be used to evaluate the appropriateness of economic systems. While not endorsing a particular economic system, the Bible has important principles regarding human nature, private property rights, and the role of government. We assert that biblical principles of economic activity are consistent with political, economic, and religious freedom, and that they can be used to evaluate economic systems.[103]

Perhaps it is better to speak of certain key biblical *principles* relevant for economics than to speak of "biblical economics." The best we can do is to evaluate particular economic systems as being more or less consistent with biblical teaching,[104] which is our intent in this book. It must be conceded that in the mind of God at least there is a set of principles for the social and economic life of his creatures. Furthermore, the whole point of revelation is to give us an insight into his purposes for men.[105] If the New Testament told us more about Jesus' activities before his ministry, we would learn a lot about economics from his behavior.

We know this much: Jesus produced and distributed scarce furniture for about fifteen years before his ministry began. So he participated in the economy, both as a supplier and a demander.

In social science research, there's something called the GAS trade-off. All theories favor either *generalizability*, *accuracy*, or *simplicity*, at the cost of the others. On the horns of this dilemma, we have chosen generalizability and simplicity as strengths, realizing we will suffer from accuracy along the way. Trying to draw conclusions about forty different economics concepts means we're seeking the general side of the equation, using a simple formula. We have attempted to capture scriptural teaching about economics in the ten commandments of biblical economics. The Bible does not prescribe a particular form of government or a particular economic system. But the biblical perspective does contain principles conducive to political, economic, and religious/moral freedom.[106] The Bible does not endorse a particular system, but it does have key principles about human nature, private property rights, and the role of government. These can be used to evaluate economic systems.[107]

1. People Should Be Free

The crossroads of Christianity and economics is freedom. We believe that God, the greatest being ever conceived of, gives humans the choice to accept or reject His invitation of salvation. That's a big concept to understand and accept. It's a great deal of freedom. The predominant note of the New Testament is not political freedom but freedom in Christ from bondage to sin, the Law, Satan, the old man, and death. Liberty is the highest ideal of man, the reflection of his divinity.[108] It is not that political freedom or freedom from slavery was unimportant but that there was an even deeper bondage that had to be overcome first.[109] Yet, we still can draw from these religious freedoms, that God intended economic freedoms as well.

The famous painting of Jesus standing at the door titled "Light of the World," by William Holman Hunt, is based on the scripture from Revelation 3:20, "Behold, I stand at the door, and knock: if any man hear my voice, and open the door, I will come in to him, and will sup with him, and he with me." The main point of the famous painting is this: There's no door handle on Jesus' side of the door. We are free to open the door, or keep it closed. If God gave us the freedom to accept or reject His invitation, we have to believe he wants us to have as much freedom as possible in our economic lives. As Christians, we are not free to seek any end that satisfies our individual needs. We make a free, conscious decision to be guided by a "multitude of advisors" in making free choices. Don't miss the point: We make a choice to limit our own freedom, and take direction from other Christians to whom we choose to give power.

Friedrich von Hayek was an atheist, so he made his case for economic freedom using a moral argument. If government assumes our moral responsibility, then we are no longer free moral agents.[110] If Christians really want to help the poor, they will, among other things, support economic freedom.[111] What about freedom and the poor? "The biggest poverty-reduction measure of all is liberalising markets to let poor people get richer."[112]

In *Dark Agenda: The War to Destroy Christian America*, self-described agnostic Jew David Horowitz writes about "the Augustinian view that human beings are flawed and sinful by nature, and, therefore, can only be saved by God's grace. This led logically to the American idea that government requires a system of checks and balances to restrain the devious impulses and desires of its citizens and officials."[113] In free-market economies, flawed suppliers to markets are checked by their competitors: Coke by Pepsi, Walmart by Target, and General Motors by Ford. Consumers are only economically free when they have the freedom to choose from among competing suppliers. Antitrust legislation is intended to maintain competition in markets. If you didn't believe suppliers were fallen, you would give *them* the freedom to have a monopoly. But, since we believe they are fallen, we institute laws to maintain competition, so consumers have freedom. Thus, freedom flows from an assumption of the fallen nature, as we explained in chapter 1.

In a free economy in which wages, costs, and prices are left to the free play of the competitive market, the prospect of profits decides what articles will be made, and in what quantities—and what articles will not be made at all. If there is no profit in making an article, it is a sign that the labor and capital devoted to its production are misdirected: the value of the resources that must be used up in making the article is greater than the value of the article itself.[114] In a controlled economy, socialists take the opposite view and pose as humanitarians and sometimes even as Christians but their system strangles personal freedom.[115] This is based in the important Christian Worldview presented in chapter 1. If people are fallen, you don't want to give them a monopoly. You don't want businesspeople nor the government to have a monopoly. Competition and antitrust legislation prevent monopolies in free-market economies. But in socialist economies, monopolies are encouraged, and even mandated. People do not flourish under monopolies.

So how *does* a human being flourish? The argument of Christians ranging from Augustine to Aquinas is that we do so *in the process of free choice*.[116] In economics, we often ask the question about the degree of freedom people should have. We believe people are fallen, so we have to institute some rules. But how many? And which ones? This is the road we travel as Christian economists, trying to determine what level of freedom the Bible commands us to enact. But we're pretty confident that God wants us to have as much freedom as possible, because he gave us the freedom to accept or reject his offer of salvation.

That is an important and recurring theme for us in Christian economics. In *Money, Greed and God*, Jay Richards lists as one of his ten rules for the Christian economy: "Encourage economic freedom: Allow people to trade goods and services unencumbered by tariffs, subsidies, price controls, undue regulation, and restrictive immigration policies. Too often, even fans of capitalism neglect the entrepreneur, focusing on free markets rather than free men and women."[117]

Markets don't exist without people. If you want to get existential about it, markets don't exist at all; they are simply the exchanges made by humans. Markets happen when men and women freely trade what they have for what they don't have. That's the only route to increased wealth and human flourishing. To quote Richards again, "Without freedom, there can be no free creativity."[118] He's right, by definition. How can there be *controlled* creativity? By its nature, creativity has to be free. As Christians, we believe that's what God intended. If God creates, and we are in His image, then we have inherited the freedom to be creative from our maker.

Most people in free societies produce more resources than they consume. This is the Achilles heel of the misanthropic strain of modern environmentalism: free societies allow human beings to be fruitful and multiply rather than merely consume. If they didn't, market economies would shrink. Instead, over the long run, they grow. Man, not matter, is the ultimate resource. As the Chinese proverb says, "If you want one year of prosperity, grow grain. If you want ten years of prosperity, grow trees. If you want one hundred years of prosperity, grow people."[119]

Political and economic freedom are fellow travelers. It's hard to find one without the other. History indicates that when China stepped through the door of free-market capitalism by joining the World Trade Organization in 2001, the political camel got its nose in the tent. While it's taking longer to gain political freedom than most people expected, it's easy to predict that wealthy Chinese citizens will use their economic might to pry open the political door as well. The American experiment is based on the assumption that religious freedom leads to political and economic freedom. A free-market system, far from encouraging wrongful behavior, does better than any other economic system at deterring such wrong behavior by bringing legal and economic sanctions against corporate wrongdoers.[120] Thus, in an economy where competitors are relatively free, wrongful behavior is punished and positive behavior is encouraged.

For all the fancy left/liberal blather about diversity, unity without God soon becomes enforced unity, which is another name for coercion and uniformity and the totalitarian suppression of real diversity. Thanks to political correctness, the process is well underway in America, and there is no greater need than the need to defend and expand the remaining spheres of freedom.[121] This leads us to our first of ten commandments of biblical economics: people should be free.

Free-market capitalism refers to an economic system with rule of law and private property, in which people can freely exchange goods and services[122] to enrich themselves and others. Since our impulse is to be as free and independent as we can, freedom is the last thing that should be taken for granted. Because of the fall, we are in bondage to sin. True freedom necessitates the Spirit's work to change our heart and redirect our lives, which will otherwise give way to entropy.[123] So it's freedom that enables and encourages the economic flourishing that God intends for us.

In *Defending the Free Market*, Rev. Robert Sirico writes about the important freedom to own private property, "Every scheme of redistribution that has defied the right to private property has created more poverty. The right to private property is not absolute, but it is a basic human right. When and where that right is respected, people and whole societies flourish."[124] They flourish because they are rewarded for expressing the creative image of God to create greater value for their neighbors. Thus, freedom is the core tenant of "policies that promote production," which we mention later in this chapter.

Karl Marx called for the abolition of private property in a book that has been copyrighted. Bernie Sanders exercised his freedom of speech to comment, "You don't necessarily need a choice of twenty-three underarm spray deodorants." Yet he has exercised his freedom to own three houses. He purchased the last one, a vacation lake house, for $575,000. Interesting how folks use their own freedom to limit the freedom of other people. And as a side note, it should be added that there is greater economic freedom and flourishing in a country that provides twenty-three deodorants than in a country that restricts its consumers to only one. When asked about his fortune, Bernie Sanders bragged that he made it by selling books—in a free-market economy that he opposes.

Religious freedom was the stalk from which political freedom grew in Colonial America. It caused the US Revolutionary War. Only a decade and a half later, the French Revolution did the opposite: it threw out religion. The difference between those two revolutions is chronicled in *Last Call for Liberty* by Os Guinness: "At the core, the deepest division is rooted in the differences between two world-changing and opposing revolutions, the American Revolution of 1776 and the French Revolution of 1789, and their rival views of freedom and the nature of the American experiment."[125] It's easy to tie France's disdain for religion in their revolution to the political and economic upheaval they are facing today. Without a religious rudder, the country embraces a relativism that threatens both its economic and governance systems.

In the movie *Braveheart*, Mel Gibson plays the part of William Wallace. He gives a rousing speech to the Scots before the battle of Stirling in 1297 with the question, "What will you do without freedom?" Good question. In economic terms, he was asking them how they would farm to feed themselves, and how they would produce and distribute goods to enrich each other. He rouses the clans to fight, then rides over to his second-in-command, who asks, "Fine speech. Now what do we do?" The answer is obvious: Fight for your freedom.

Among Jay Richards's "Ten Ways to Alleviate Poverty" is, "Encourage economic freedom: Allow people to trade goods and services unencumbered by tariffs, subsidies, price controls, undue regulation, and restrictive immigration policies."[126] Free people make themselves and their neighbors richer by seeking their own self-interest.

In *The Tragedy of American Compassion*, Marvin Olasky writes, "The goal of charity workers, therefore, was not to press for governmental programs, but to show poor people how to move up while resisting enslavement to the charity of governmental or private masters. Charity leaders and preachers frequently spoke of freedom and showed how dependency was merely slavery with a smiling mask. . . . Freedom could be grasped only when individuals took responsibility."[127] To speak of freedom with government control is an oxymoron. "Free" is not the same as "freedom." As a matter of fact, accepting free goods reduces freedom.

Economic freedom is so taken for granted that Americans are not frightened by socialist politicians nor their calls for the New Green Deal. They have no knowledge of what it's like to live in a socialist state. George Santayana famously said, "Those who cannot remember the past are condemned to repeat it." In *The Commanding Heights*, Daniel Yergin and Joseph Stanislav quote Lilia Shevtsova, author of *Yeltsin's Russia*, saying in 1998, "My kids, they don't know what socialism is. They ask me 'Mom, what was socialism?'"[128] That was only nine years after the end of the most painful epic socialism has ever produced.

Americans need real people who have lived through socialism to tell us how it condemns people to poor living standards and prevents human flourishing. Where do we find these people?

This book is coauthored by Dave Arnott and Sergiy Saydometov, but we're making an unusual departure for a few lines, directly from Dave:

> The Soviet satellite countries gained their freedom from Communist socialism in 1990. That was thirty years ago. Anyone who was fifty at that time is now eighty, so there are few of them capable of revealing the socialist lie. The prime age for storytellers is someone who was between the ages of ten and forty during the end of the Soviet era in 1990. The people with the longest time to tell those stories would be ten-year-olds from that era. The most populous country under Soviet rule was the Ukraine, with a population of 45 million. So, if we could find someone from the Ukraine who was around the age of ten in 1990, we would have one of the most effective, long-term sages to remind us of the evils of socialism. Allow me to introduce my coauthor: Sergiy Saydometov, who was eleven.
>
> Books like this one didn't exist in the Ukraine in 1990. Now, he has coauthored one. We should listen to his message about

the value of God-granted freedom in producing a country that has an economy that allows human flourishing. Human freedom and human flourishing are thus not just associated with each other; they are intimately connected with doing good and avoiding evil.[129]

2. Work Is Good

As creator, God has made us with the awesome power and responsibility to *create*. Work itself is part of God's original blessing, not his curse after the fall. The way in which we work, then, should reflect the fact that we are a unity of matter and spirit, of heaven and earth, neither pack animals nor angels.[130] Work is not a product of the fall but is actually part of the creation order. While it is true that work was deformed by the fall, so that there is now toil and drudgery,[131] work is not a curse but a gift from God. By our work we employ useful skills to glorify God and love our neighbors.[132]

According to Anne Bradley, thirty-nine of the forty parables in the New Testament are about work. In Genesis, God works to create humans, then gives humans the command to work. In the creational garden, before the fall, humans had work to do, such as naming the animals, and tending the garden. Work was perfect and produced perfect results. After the fall, work became toil, and hard. But we're still commanded to do it. Work remains essential to human dignity and integral to man's nature.[133]

In the first century, creating wealth was difficult because the vast majority of the population was employed in subsistence farming. The most common way of accumulating riches was through oppressing the weak, leveling heavy taxation, and exploiting slaves. For this reason, it is not surprising that the New Testament contains many denunciations of rich people from that time, but still encourages honest work and diligent labor.[134]

When we analyze minimum wage in chapter 4, we will return to this work command, and find that work is good. If minimum wage discourages work, we will not favor it. One of ten ways to alleviate poverty: work hard.[135] People are precious, valuable resources—at *least* as precious as any other of God's creatures. Finding mere busywork for people is not an appropriate use of their creativity, talent, or ingenuity. Instead, society should be more concerned with channeling individuals into their most highly prized uses—just like any other valuable resource.[136]

Work is worship. The words are very similar. In *The Call*, Os Guinness tells the wonderful story of a woman considering suicide by drowning, when she gets distracted by the perfect plowing of a farmer with a mule. The distracted woman turns away from suicide to become the author's great-grandmother.[137] It's a unique and intense example of the power of work to distract us from the fallen world we live in.

For the Christian, life without work is meaningless; but work must never become the meaning of one's life.[138] So what comes before work? Our primary call is to *be* followers of Christ. Our secondary calling is to *do* something to build the kingdom.[139] John Calvin taught that every believer has a vocational calling to serve God in the world in every sphere of human existence, lending a new dignity and meaning to ordinary work.[140]

Work is precisely the point of the Old Testament Sabbath and Jubilee legislation. Debt cancellation and return of land to the family whose inheritance it was did not represent charity or distributing wealth, but was a restoration of *opportunity to create wealth*. This is clear from the stipulation that the value of the land to be bought and sold was not based on its intrinsic worth as real estate but on the number of harvests available from it until the year of Jubilee. Crops and harvests do not just happen; they require work and husbandry. Seed must be sown, weeds pulled, fields harvested and threshed, and grain milled.[141]

John Calvin's claim on Colossians 3:23, "Whatever you do, do it as unto the Lord," was called "The Protestant Work Ethic" by Max Weber in *The Protestant Work Ethic and the Spirit of Capitalism*.[142] While there are other work ethics—Shinto, etc.—the idea that work is good is what has produced the kind of wealth we enjoy today. But that's the outcome. We also consider the input. We believe God commands us to work, based on the Genesis 1:28 mandate: "Be fruitful and increase in number; fill the earth and subdue it. Rule over the fish in the sea and the birds in the sky and over every living creature that moves on the ground." The Theology of Work Project says it this way, "The book of Genesis is the foundation for the theology of work. The created universe that God brings into existence then provides the material of human work—space, time, matter and energy. Within the created universe, God is present in relationship with his creatures and especially with people. Laboring in God's image, we work *in* creation, *on* creation, *with* creation and—if we work as God intends—*for* creation."[143]

Our personal talents, and the natural resources we use in work, are God's provision for us. They are entrusted to us, and we will have to give account to God for the use we have made of them. We exercise our stewardship particularly in work. The fruits of our work are goods and services, which enable man to live in a way which respects his dignity.[144] So work is an extension of our Christian belief system.

Others don't see the connection. In *The Enlightenment*,[145] Steven Pinker essentially says that now that we are enlightened and no longer need "angels and fathers in the sky." We wonder if Pinker notices the names of the hospitals and schools en route to his office in Boston where he wrote the book. Tufts Medical Center was founded by a Congregational minister named Rufus Tobey. Beth Israel Deaconess needs no explanation. The two largest hospital systems in Dallas are Baylor (Baptist) and Methodist (Methodist). Barnes-Jewish is the largest hospital system in the state of Missouri. Christendom *invented* the hospital, notes Rev. Robert Sirico.[146] The examples go on and on. Pinker seems to overlook the immense economic contribution that people have made in the name of God. He assumes this work would have been done by atheists. We don't know of an atheist hospital nor university. We're not aware of an atheist version of The Salvation Army. The work being done in these institutions is because of their founders'—and current workers'— commitment to God.

It was thus no coincidence that the medieval period witnessed the church creating and building the world's first universities in cities ranging from Bologna to Oxford, Salerno, Paris, Prague, and St. Andrews.[147] The charitable institutions we take for granted all come out of the Judeo-Christian tradition's profound respect for the individual human person, who is invested with an innate dignity.[148]

Harvard University, where Pinker wrote his book, was named for a Presbyterian lay minister named John Harvard, where the purpose statement was "Let every student be plainly instructed, and earnestly pressed to consider well, the main end of his life and studies is, to know God and Jesus Christ." Note also the Harvard motto: *Veritas Christo et Ecclesiae*, meaning "Truth for Christ and the Church," which can be found in many locations on the Harvard campus where he wrote the book.

From the beginning, these institutions were based on a belief that God existed, that he made man in his image, and that people had to be free to seek the truth through logic, attention to evidence, careful scholarship, and free discussion. As it turns out, part of that search for truth—the truth about the nature of things, but also the truth about doing good and evil—involved the exploration of the new economic things of the time, including the emerging markets for capital by scholastic theologians.[149] But Pinker seems to think that God is out of fashion and not needed anymore. His university would not exist without his predecessors, who founded the institution on their belief in God.

We suppose he is thankful for the "Mission Drift"[150] that removed those original sentiments. And now he assumes that since humans have become enlightened, we don't need God anymore. Here's how he writes it more specifically: "The US was founded on the Enlightenment ideal that human ingenuity and benevolence could be channeled by institutions and result in progress." In *Who Really Cares*,[151] Arthur Brooks found that religious people are much more benevolent than non-religious folks. And we've just pointed out that the institution where Pinker wrote the book was founded on religious principles. When work is detached from God, it becomes an idol. Pinker apparently does not see that.

The Christian tradition of education and capitalism goes back much further than the founding of Harvard. It emerged not with the Reformation nor the Enlightenment, but in medieval monasteries. In *Money, Greed and God*, Jay Richards cites Rodney Stark: "Finance and banking emerged in northern Italy's city-states centuries before Luther nailed his ninety-five theses to the Wittenberg door. The British colonies were founded on production," Stark writes, "the Spanish colonies on extraction."[152] Thus, Christianity provided the prerequisites for the kind of vibrant capitalism that has made the United States the most powerful economic engine in human history.

Pinker again: "Our ancestors replaced dogma, tradition and authority with reason, debate and institutions of truth-seeking." Oh. There *is* truth? Only one? "And they shifted their values from the glory of the tribe, nation, race, class or faith toward universal human flourishing." Pinker has the "human flourishing" part right, but he's got the causality in the wrong direction. He says humans flourish when they turn away from faith. But humans flourish when people *practice* their faith.

We've tried nations without religion. Mao killed 60 million and Stalin killed 40 million. I doubt if Pinker would consider that "Enlightened." He asks, "Do people need to believe in magic, a father in the sky. . . ?" If you want them to flourish, yes, they do. The historical economic record is clear: The Christian worldview *causes* people to flourish. It founded the hospitals that care for Pinker's body and the university where he uses his mind.

"Nearly every leading university in the world was founded by Christians. The first nine colleges in the US were founded by Christians," writes John Dickerson.[153] He also found that each of the top ten universities in the world, according to the Center for World University Rankings, was begun by Christians.

It's through work that we "love our neighbor as we love ourselves." If you love your neighbor, you will provide products and services they demand. This love demands work. Hugh Whelchel writes in *How Now Shall We Work?*, "For the Christian, life without work is meaningless; but work must never become the meaning of one's life."[154] We are human *beings*, not human *doings*.

In *Joy at Work*[155] Dennis Bakke explains it this way, "God intended that the workplace be beautiful, exciting, and satisfying. Work was to be filled with joy. Work was a major reason for our creation. It was intended to be an important act of worship. It was one of the most significant ways in which we could honor our Creator." To quote Whelchel again, "Work is not a curse, but a gift from God. By our work, we employ useful skills to glorify God and love our neighbors."[156]

In the movie *Return to Me*, Minnie Driver plays the niece to Carroll O'Connor's character. As he is cleaning up the bar one night, she asks, "Uncle, can I help you clean up?" He responds in his character's Irish brogue: "Oh no, me darlin'. I'm blessed by me work." God invited us into his work. Amazing. He is sovereign. He could do it on his own. For some mystical reason, he invited us along on his great adventure: to help him redeem the world. What an invitation! James Davison Hunter, in *To Change the World*,[157] says we are "enjoined to participate . . . in the creative and renewing work of world-making and remaking." His word "remaking" we identified as "re-creation" in chapter 1.

Sigmund Freud said we need something to do and someone to love. If you're doing God's work, you have both. That's because you can love God and do his work. That's how we see work in the Christian worldview, and it explains why, in general, Christian societies are more productive than non-Christian nations.[158] One root cause of poverty is a lack of work, so the key to ending poverty is putting people to work. But too often, government social-welfare programs discourage work by making government benefits more attractive than work or by penalizing the rewards of work.[159] We will have more to say about this negative impulse in upcoming chapters.

Some students were late for Dave's 8:00 a.m. Economics class, so he locked the door and rewarded the on-time students by giving them a five-minute opportunity to earn a couple bonus points. The subject for the day was productivity, so he asked them to write three answers to the question,

"Why I work." It was fascinating. After the expected answers, "to pay for things" and "to make money," it got a little more philosophical. Two often-repeated answers were "to serve others" and "to please God."

The next week Dave was guest-lecturing for his consulting partner at a state university so he asked them the same question. The first few answers were about the same: "to buy things." Then it got interesting. Where the Christian university students had written answers about integrating their work as worship, the state university students saw work as a separate entity. They said they work to *do* good, but that work *itself* is not good. They work and take the money to do good things with it, like help their family. They saw work as a means to an end. The Christian university students, who had taken the university's Christian worldview course, saw their work as an end in itself. The other noticeable difference was that the Christian university students saw work as a way to serve others, which is consistent with the economic idea of consumer surplus. They assumed work was part of creation. The state university students saw work as a means to serve themselves, and as a part of the fall. Two often-repeated answers from the state students were "achievement," and "independence," which are directed at the self, not others.

The summary: Christian university students who have a greater understanding of the Christian worldview, see work as worship, as an end in itself that serves others, because they work as an extension of creation. The state university students saw work as a *means* to a *personal* end. They assume work is part of the fall, thus it is to be used as a means to do good.

In *Every Good Endeavor* Timothy Keller writes, "Think of the cliche that nobody ever gets to the end of their life and wishes they had spent more time at the office. It makes good sense, of course, up to a point. But here's a more interesting perspective: At the end of your life, will you wish that you had plunged more of your time, passion, and skills into work environments and work products that helped people?"[160]

In the classroom Dave follows this with a video clip from the end of the movie *Schindler's List*, where Liam Neeson cries over his failure to save more people. "I could have saved more," he anguishes. The point is: Schindler wished he had spent *more* time at the office. This is an example of the integration we find in the Christian worldview: Our work is our worship. Why would you hope to spend *less* time at your worship?

If you are poor—work.

If you are rich—continue to work.

If you are burdened with seemingly unfair responsibilities—work.

If you are happy—keep right on working. Idleness gives room for doubts and fears.

If disappointments come—work.

When faith falters and reason fails—work.

When dreams are shattered and hope seems dead—work.

Work as if your life were in peril. It really is.

No matter what ails you—work.

Work faithfully—work with faith.

Work is the greatest material remedy available.

Work will cure both mental and physical afflictions.

3. Don't Steal

"You shall not steal" (Exodus 20:15).

Our students don't want us to redistribute their grades. They say they have a private-property claim to their grades. Dave redistributed a grade once. In an online class, a student wrote an effective argument for redistribution of wealth. So, he awarded her the full ten points, then redistributed three points each—to students who did not participate in the discussion board. That's a 60 percent tax, which is actually pretty low in a socialist system. The student accused Dave of theft. She claimed that she had a right to the full-grade based on her convincing argument that redistribution was good. Think about it.

"Thou shalt not steal" presupposes the validity of private property. You cannot steal something, after all, if no one owns it.[161] Does Acts 2 call for common ownership of property? It is this ancient notion of voluntary action or freedom that we speak of when we say that the informal communism of the early Christian community was voluntary.[162] Thus, the disciples voluntarily "sold a piece of land" to give to the community. They sold the land in a free-market economy. How could they sell it if they didn't own it? We will revisit Acts 2 in later chapters.

In 1736 Benjamin Franklin established the Union Fire Company in Philadelphia. The United States did not have government-run fire departments until around the time of the Civil War. What happened between those two events provides a revealing look at free-market capitalism, as it relates to theft. When the country was expanding west in the early 1800s, it was common for a free-market capitalist fire company to locate in a growing city that was built almost exclusively of wood structures. They would sell memberships to businesses and homeowners. When a fire broke out, they would hitch up the horses to the water tank and race to the location of the fire. If there was an emblem indicating a paid membership, they put the fire out. If not, they went back to the firehouse and let the structure burn down. Most of us would agree that this situation has *too much* free-market capitalism. And people of that time agreed that a socialist fire department would serve society better. So they instituted a tax and built a socialist fire department that served everyone in the city. Economists call that a common good.

Interesting side note: In the terrible California fire season of 2019, there were private fire departments. Insurance companies offered discounts to high-value homeowners for the right to enter their property and fireproof it during a fire threat. These private fire preventers had a list of "subscribers," much like the nineteenth-century type. They would drive into a neighborhood that was in the path of a fire, and provide fire prevention services. They would cut brush, pump water from the swimming pool to douse the house, and rush to the next address on their list. That's freedom—freedom to use the common good provided by the socialist fire department, but also the freedom to hire a private service.

But there is a meaningful assumption in the story about a socialist fire department. There is an assumption that the tax being expropriated from the home and business owners is used to protect the taxpayer, not someone outside the taxpayer's jurisdiction. This is what Christian economists support: the forcible extraction of wealth from citizens to provide services for them. That's not stealing. But when a taxing authority forcibly extracts tax from its citizens to use on a project that cannot be traced to creating value for the taxpayer, that's theft. We will continue to keep this commandment of biblical economics in mind as we explore taxes in chapter 6.

In *Economics in One Lesson*, Henry Hazlitt writes, "When your money is taken by a thief, you get nothing in return. When your money is taken through taxes to support needless bureaucrats, precisely the same situation exists."[163] Notice, he didn't say *all* taxes are stealing, only those taxes that "support needless bureaucrats." This is consistent with our assumption that taxes are a payment for services rendered. When a reasonable argument can be made that the person being taxed is in some general way rendered a service, we consider that within the biblical guidelines, that's not stealing.

Notice two "wiggle words" in that sentence: "reasonable" and "general." We do not expect a *perfect* argument for a *specific* service. This is consistent with our Christian worldview of imperfection. We're after the same thing Hazlitt is: intention. If the government bureaucrats are enlarging their realm, just so they can have more bureaucrats employed, we find that a violation of the Old Testament sixth commandment and our third commandment of biblical economics: Don't steal. If they enlarge employment to provide more services, that's not stealing, and it's biblical. So, we're going to posit that the government is there to serve others. When they use money that is extracted by taxes to serve others, that's biblical. When they use extracted tax money to serve themselves, that's not biblical. In 1978 Hazlitt wrote, "More and more people are becoming aware that government has nothing to give them without first taking it away from somebody else—or from themselves. Increased handouts to selected groups mean merely increased taxes, or increased deficits and increased inflation."[164]

Dave attended a seminar on Chinese wisdom in Hong Kong a few years ago. With a PowerPoint slide behind him stating the noble eight-fold path of Buddhism, the seminar leader stated, "There are no rights nor wrongs in Chinese wisdom." Dave was tempted to challenge him, asking how he could state there were no rights and wrongs when his PowerPoint slide stated eight of them. But he reflected on the "Seven Habits" by Stephen Covey where he learned, "Seek to understand, then to be understood." So he patiently waited for a logical answer—but never got one. That's because Chinese wisdom draws on Eastern thinking, not Western logical reason.

In a relativistic society like China, you can't seek justice through logical reason, because there are no rights and wrongs. Thus, the only remaining form of governance is power. The guy with the biggest gun steals resources from weaker rivals, and there's no system of Western logical reason to produce justice. There are no rights in China because there is no right in China. So stealing is allowed.

4. Don't Covet

"You shall not covet your neighbor's house. You shall not covet your neighbor's wife, or his male or female servant, his ox or donkey, or anything that belongs to your neighbor" (Exodus 20:17).

Nearly every discussion about income inequality is a violation of the Old Testament tenth commandment (our fourth), as we will see in chapter 12. Desiring what others have is a violation of that commandment. As Christians, we are taught to care about the poor, not the rich. When you worry about the distance between the rich and the poor, you're being covetous. Here's what the Ligonier Ministries website says about covetousness:

> In many ways, covetousness can be seen as the one sin that gives birth to all the others. Adam and Eve coveted God's knowledge and ate the forbidden fruit in order to make themselves wise, an idolatrous grasp at the Lord's prerogatives (Gen. 3:1–7). An adulterer must first want someone other than whom he married before he breaks the commandment (see David's example in 2 Sam. 11:1–4). A thief is envious of his neighbor's estate before he steals his goods. Voters grow jealous of what other people in a nation have and use the ballot box to "redistribute" wealth.[165]

Thomas Sowell said, "Envy was once considered to be one of the seven deadly sins before it became one of the most admired virtues under its new name, 'social justice.'"[166] He's right. There is no end of "repackaging" old ideas under new banners that make them sound better, but they are still a violation of the rule against coveting. Karl Marx summed up socialist theory in the single phrase, "abolition of private property."[167] Marx wanted to abolish it because he knew he was striking a nerve among the working classes: Jealousy. It's not surprising that Marx, an atheist, would do this. We're surprised when respected Christian thought-leaders do it.

Redistribution of income is discussed in depth in chapter 12. For now, we will simply make the point that if we try to run the economy for the benefit of a single group or class, we shall injure or destroy all groups, including the members of the very class for whose benefit we have been trying to run it. We must run the economy for everybody, not just for covetous groups who want what others have.[168]

The most powerful religious man in the world said, "Inequality is the root of social evil." Think about it: Pope Francis is at the pinnacle of power of the most hierarchical religious organization in the world. What type of inequality was he talking about? He has unequal religious power, so he probably was not judging his own position. Although it seems rather hypocritical for the most unequally powerful religious person to condemn economic inequality.

"Fair" is a junior high concept that is not in the Bible. In creation, before the fall, the world was not "fair." Goods were not distributed equally. People are different, with different natural traits from their creation as individuals. When they use those different levels of creational ability, they will earn different levels of rewards. When we delve into this issue in chapter 12, we will search for a scripture that endorses equal outcomes, but we won't find one.

We will propose that everyone has an equal chance to accept Christ as their personal savior, but there will not be equal economic outcomes. We believe that special revelation allows some humans to be presented with the gospel in specific terms: from a copy of the Bible, a sermon, or a friend or missionary. General revelation via creation enables everyone the chance to accept. That's where "fair" ends. As Dave wrote in his book *Corporate Cults*, "Fair is an annual celebratory event."[169] Christ never promised fair outcomes. As a matter of fact, he promised the opposite, "In this world you will have trouble" (John 16:33). If life were fair, why would he promise trouble? He was preparing us for a world of economically unequal outcomes.

When a toddler grabs a toy from his playmate, it's covetousness. It's natural; it's the fallen nature of children. Think about it: if children were not born fallen, you would not have to teach them to share. Not sharing (covetousness) is part of the fallen nature. But some adults never learn this. They want what others have. Cain wanted what Abel had. Jacob wanted what Esau had. Covetousness is at the heart of many unbiblical economic practices.

"The earliest Christians held all things in common not claiming anything as their own," writes Roman Montero in *All Things in Common*[170]—a book to which he owns the copyright. It's not covetousness that caused Montero to defend the copyright to his book; nor is it covetousness that leads us to own the copyright to this one. It's our private property, and you can't steal it, any more than a student in our classes can steal grades from a fellow student.

Christians must guard against the effect of wealth on their spiritual lives. There is nothing wrong with owning possessions. The problem comes when the possessions own us.[171] Or when we want to own what others have. That's covetousness.

The hostility to the market and the prosperity it has produced is a mark of ingratitude, a refusal to give thanks to the Giver of his gifts. Ingratitude also fuels envy, one of the capital sins. Is it possible that our zeal for social justice encourages deadly sin? And is it not the church's task to counter deadly sin rather than contribute to it?[172] In his powerful five-minute video on the subject, Dennis Prager says there is one thing that separates happy people from unhappy ones: gratitude.[173] And he says this as a Jew—one who doesn't believe Jesus died for him! Christians should be the most grateful people on earth. But we're not when we notice income inequality, which we will discuss in chapter 12.

If I obsess about the disparity and lay awake at night thinking about how unfair this all is, then my problem is not the disparity but the illness of discontent and envy in *my* soul. I have become ungrateful. What is true for us as individual Christians is also true for us when we consider the disparities in our world. We should pause to note that "fairness" is often a code word used by those who want to manipulate feelings of envy and resentment into a political force.[174]

5. Use Honest Measures

"You shall not have in your bag differing weights, a large and a small. You shall not have in your house differing measures, a large and a small. You shall have a full and just weight; you shall have a full and just measure, that your days may be prolonged in the land which the LORD your God gives you" (Deuteronomy 25:13–15, NASB). There are eleven verses about honest measures in the Old Testament; this is just one of them.

It wasn't for idle reasons that Aquinas stressed that the very word for "money" was derived from *monere* (to warn), because it warns against fraud.[175] There is fraud in every industry. We've heard too many diatribes against fraud in the financial system from the media, who is just as corrupt. We're all fallen. There is no greater level of fraud in banking than in the media, education, or the ministry. To assume the opposite is to deny the fallen nature. Everyone is fallen, and everyone is tempted to use dishonest measures.

Economics has earned its reputation as the "dismal science." At the end of his eight-year term, President Barack Obama correctly stated, "I cut the budget deficit in half"—after he had doubled it. The data is there. When he came into office the budget deficit had been around $500 billion a year. He doubled it to one trillion dollars, then correctly reported that he cut it in half, back to $500 billion. That's not an honest measure. We write more about this in chapter 11.

Hillary Clinton famously stated, "Don't let anyone tell you it's corporations who create jobs." Huh? Then who does? That's not an honest measure. There is more about the biblical view of unemployment in chapter 8. Likewise, when President Trump claimed that reducing the trade deficit would make Americans richer, he was using faulty measures. We discuss the biblical view of balanced trade in chapter 3.

Justice is served when promises are kept, contracts are honored, goods and services are of high quality, and when workers provide an honest day's labor and are rewarded with a fair wage.[176] We discuss justice in many chapters of this book. For now, we shall maintain that this statement is accurate. *The market is where everyone votes.* "Fair" is determined by the most democratic process ever invented: the market. This will be covered in chapter 4 when we discuss minimum wage.

President Obama intimated that voting for unemployment insurance helps people and creates jobs, and voting against it does not. Paying people *not* to work encourages them to work? We don't think we'll try that with our students in the classroom, because the president was not using honest measures.

Kenneth Barnes, in *Redeeming Capitalism*,[177] cites a study stating there has never been shown a long-term relationship between increasing minimum wage and unemployment. Really? If you raise the price, people *don't* buy less? That can't be an honest measure. One requirement of commutative justice is equality in exchange. In the case of remuneration, this means that salaries and bonuses must match the service provided.[178] This definition gives a clue to a method for determining a fair wage, when it used the term "equality." Because the equilibrium point, where demand meets supply, is the point reached when everyone votes.

These are just a few examples of not using honest measures. As we explained in chapter 1, economics is a social science, which suffers from the same maladies that all social sciences do. But the examples cited in this section should cause a casual observer to ask, "Ignorance or malfeasance?" Did the politicians really not know that corporations cause jobs, or that the budget deficit had been doubled before it was halved? Yes, they knew. That makes it malfeasance.

What about different levels of taxation for the rich and poor? Those who favor progressive taxing systems (more on this in chapter 6) claim that treating rich people different from the poor is just. The assumption is the rich got that way by taking from the poor. Which brings to mind the famous Milton Friedman statement: "Most economic myths grow out of a misunderstanding of the zero-sum fallacy." Can greater income and social equality, including genuinely progressive taxation for the rich and greater income support for the poor, be achieved consistent with biblical justice, which requires impartial treatment of rich and poor? Deuteronomy 1:17 (ESV) says, "You shall not be partial in judgment. You shall hear the small and the great alike. You shall not be intimidated by anyone."

Absent in many poor countries are honest, efficient, and responsive governments at all levels.[179] Corruption and crony capitalism are not fair measures. Bribes are not fair measures. When economic goods and services are traded on an open, free market, the equilibrium price determines what should be made and what should not be made. That's an economic definition of fair measure.

Many currencies still bear the name "crown," but in different spellings. The Danish Krone, the Swedish Krona, the Czech Koruna, and the

Brazilian Real are just a few examples. These derive from the time when a sovereign's crown was imprinted on the currency. It was supposed to be a reliably honest measure. The king had great power. "Money, was called up or down, according as the king was creditor or debtor."[180] That's not an honest measure.

The lack of fair measures is particularly hard on the poor, who don't have the resources to fight against injustice. Mark Cuban made this case when he defeated a five-year insider-trading accusation from the Securities and Exchange Commission. Most insider-trading cases are settled out of court. Cuban pursued the case in court to try to show that the SEC was being unjust by using its power to force the accused to capitulate. His point was that he had the economic power to fight the SEC, but others did not.

In March of 2019, there was a great deal of media coverage of the Mueller report, which found that President Donald Trump did not collude with Russians to affect the 2016 election. The mainstream media's support for the Russian collusion story was brought into question. Was it ignorance or malfeasance? It was malfeasance. The media knew there was no factual evidence, and pushed the story anyway. The Russian collusion case was compared to the premise for the Iraq war about weapons of mass destruction. The US and her allies invaded Iraq but found no weapons of mass destruction. Ignorance or malfeasance? It was ignorance. The US and British intelligence agencies said Saddam Hussein had weapons of mass destruction. He had used them on the Kurds in Halabja, killing five thousand people in ten minutes.

Sidenote to that story: Dave gave a speech in Sulemania, Iraq, and was driving out of town when he saw two awkward-looking displays in the median of the road, each about the size of a Volkswagen beetle. His host, a US missionary, was busy on her cell phone, trying to get business done before heading out into the desert, far from cell towers. When her service cut off, Dave asked about the memorials. "One is an apple; the other is a pear. That's the scent of the poisonous gas that was dropped on the people of Halabja by Saddam Hussein's troops. Halabja is just forty kilometers on that road, but we can't go there because it's danger-ous. The Kurds who lived in Halabja were killed so that Saddam's people could move in and take over the city and the oil reserves in that area. Not all the citizens were killed. Saddam sent in his people to live in their houses, and now there is great strife about who owns what." So any-one who claims "Saddam did not have weapons of mass destruction" has not had a conversation with the family survivors of the five thou-sand who died in Halabja. How could he use weapons of mass destruc-tion but not have them? He did. But, he did not have them *after* the US military invaded the country. This is a clear example of ignorance, not malfeasance.

Ignorance is the reason we teach economics, and why we wrote this book. The immensity of economic ignorance, especially among our fel-low Christians, is just staggering. And it's not that hard to understand. A few hours in one of our classrooms increases our students' understand-ing about biblical economics by a huge margin. The purpose of this book is to do the same.

Economics is replete with dismal statements of malfeasance. When dissecting those statements, the Christian economist will ask, "Ignorance or malfeasance?" In a March 2019 interview by Dallas Federal Reserve Bank president Robert Kaplan, Harvard Economist Gregory Mankiw said, "Politicians ask us questions we can't answer, like, 'What's the econ-omy going to do?' They don't ask us questions where we can provide good answers, like rent control."[181]

In chapter 4 we ask the question, "When the legislature of Oregon instituted statewide rent control in March of 2019, were they practicing ignorance or malfeasance?" If it's ignorance, that's not a violation of the commandment about honest measures. We find it hard to believe that no one in the Oregon legislature knew what Nicole Gelinas of the Manhattan Institute said in a PragerU video, "One economist said rent control is the most effective way to destroy a city, other than bomb-ing."[182] One study indicated that 93 percent of economists agree that it results in a lower quality and quantity of housing. Another found 95 percent agreeing. It appears as though the legislature of Oregon was not using honest measures.

6. Trade Is Good

Jesus was involved in the production and distribution of scarce furniture. He worked with his dad in the furniture-making business from about the age of fifteen until he was thirty. His ministry lasted about three years. Thus, he spent five times more years in free-market trade than he did in ministry. What do you suppose was the nature of his work? Our graduate students have surmised that he probably produced high-level furniture of the best quality and workmanship. It's also a good assumption that he sold it and made a profit. If he didn't make a profit, how did he keep the command to give? Some of our students have guessed that he charged only enough to live a subsistence life. Then, where did he get the money to give?

It's quite clear that Jesus was involved in free-market capitalism for about fifteen years. So, we're quite startled by a headline in the March 20, 2019 *Wall Street Journal*: "Banishing Profit Is Bad for Your Health."[183] The first line tells about a Medicare-for-all bill that states, "A moral imperative . . . to eliminate profit from the provision of health care." Are they suggesting that what Jesus practiced for fifteen years is "immoral"?

In *Be Fruitful and Multiply*[184] Anne Bradley calls profit "left-overs." After paying the expense of operating a business, there are "left-overs." These must exist for us to follow the command to give. Trade enables these left-overs to exist. You only get richer when you trade what you have, for what you don't have. It's that simple.

The "trade is good" commandment is closely related to the first commandment about freedom. When people are free to trade, they serve others *and* themselves. We are continually encouraged in the classroom when students gain an appreciation for consumer surplus. We don't have to tell them that Walmart sells items for more than the acquisition price and makes producer surplus. That's easy to understand. The scales fall from their eyes when they realize that they get economically richer every time they *buy* something from Walmart;

those concepts are explained more fully in the next section. As for capitalism, it isn't based on greed; it isn't fueled and fired by greed. It is fueled by human creativity in a system that rewards people for serving the wants and needs of others.[185]

Here's a quote from the book *All Things in Common*: "In Josephus's telling of the story, the man who invented violence (Cain) also seems to have invented the profit motive and markets; violence, markets, and the profit motive are all related phenomena in this tradition."[186] Was that an act of violence perpetrated by the author? From the beginning of the first forms of capitalism in northern Italy, Flanders, and other parts of medieval Europe from the eleventh century onward, many of the merchants involved in increasingly sophisticated forms of finance wrote inscriptions such as *Deus enim et proficuum*, meaning "For God and profit."[187] We think that's a better description of free trade.

Trade makes everyone richer. Milton Friedman has noted, "Most economic fallacies derive from the tendency to assume that there is a fixed pie, that one party can gain only at the expense of another." In the "fixed pie" assumption, people get rich only while others get poor. Friedman is right, and the "fixed pie" group is wrong. We all grow richer as we trade what we have, for what we don't have.[188]

Markets elicit new ideas, create jobs, solve consumption problems and grow incomes that may be dedicated, in part, to helping others. The inherent freedom, creativity, and ability to coordinate collective action is made possible in market economies where people trade what they have for what they don't have.[189] Free trade makes both parties richer. We will explore the dangers of tariffs in chapter 3.

Trade satisfies the diversity crowd, because markets are perhaps the world's greatest example of diversity. People with diverse talents to provide products and services bring them to the market. Imagine what the world would be like if we were all identical replicas. There would be no trade, because we would all be equally talented and equally impoverished. Our differences bring us together to serve one another, largely through market trade.[190]

A market doesn't just distribute goods and services. It's a highly sensitive network for gathering and disseminating information that would otherwise elude us. It leads to specific prices for the goods and services of interest.[191] The old game show "The Price Is Right" is a great example of this. If there was not a "right price," the game would not exist. There *is* a right price. It's the equilibrium price, where everyone votes.

The movie *Black Panther* is set in the mythical African country of Wakanda, where they have carefully guarded their scarce supply of vibranium. It's a great movie, with stereotypically good guys and bad guys. And true to the Christian worldview, the good guys win. But the assumption that the Wakanda society developed and became rich without trading their valuable vibranium is not consistent with economic reality. It's like living on top of a gold mine, and assuming you're the richest guy in the world. What are you going to do with it, eat it? Build a house of it? Take a vacation on it? You're going to trade what you have (gold) for what you don't have—food, a house, a vacation. That's how people get rich. That's what we all do when we work. We trade our skills for money. The Wakandans could not have become rich by hoarding vibranium. To get rich, they would have to trade what they have—vibranium—for what they don't have.

The fact is that no foreign aid program has come anywhere near achieving the level of improved living standards earned and enjoyed by people who are increasingly connected to global markets.[192] This point is made clear in the "Poverty Cure" program by the Acton Institute. "Show me a country who got rich by aid," says a businessman from Ghana. He continues, "There isn't one. Countries get rich from trade, not aid."[193] Trade is good for poor people. It allows them to trade what they have—even if it is very little—for what they don't have.

Thus, we will assume that since Jesus did it, and that both parties to a free-market exchange get richer by doing it, so *we* should do it. The idea of "both getting richer" in economics is called consumer surplus and producer surplus. We explain it in more detail in the next section.

7. Love Your Neighbor as Yourself

If you love your neighbor as you love yourself (Matthew 22:39), you will care for both yourself and your neighbor. Capitalism is the best chance we have ever had to love our neighbor and to serve strangers.[194]

Consumer Surplus

This is an interesting concept that we show in class by asking students how much they would pay for an offer from an internet site called Groovebook, to have up to one hundred photos printed and mailed to the customer each month. The students typically make guesses ranging from ten dollars to $25. Then we show them the real price: $3.99. Admittedly, Groovebook is probably losing money on the deal, trying to build market share instead of making profit. But the point is still made. The students expect to pay $25, but the website offers the service for less than four dollars. That means their consumer surplus is $21. They are paying four dollars for what they are willing to pay $25. That's quite fascinating to students in our class—as it is for lots of people who don't understand free-market economics.

In a perfectly competitive market, when you buy something, you get richer. (Please don't tell our wives that.) But it's true. Why would you make any exchange that made you poorer? The answer is, you wouldn't. Private property implies the right of use to advance personal interests; the Christian concept sees responsibility as being exercised in service to others, as well as to one's self.[195] That's the beauty of free markets: producers use their private property to provide services for their neighbors.

Catholic University of America research fellow Father John McNerney explains why socialism does not work in *Wealth of Persons*. He writes that the "real wellspring" of human progress emanates from "the unique, irreplaceable and unrepeatable . . . reality of the individual acting in relation to his neighbor."[196] He's right, and it's consistent with consumer surplus and its traveling companion, producer surplus.

Richard Doster states, "God's people can, as agents of His redemptive plan, transform business, stripping it of selfish ambition and pursuing instead what's best for their neighbors."[197] We tend to disagree with this quote. Nothing needs to be "stripped" from free-market capitalism. Adam Smith said it correctly in *The Wealth of Nations*: "Each person, while seeking his own interest, provides for the interest of all."[198] Jay Richards also says it effectively in *Money, Greed, and God*: "The market is, as Hayek said, 'probably the most complex structure in the universe. It deserves our admiration.' And yet very few Christian critics . . . have fully understood it. Fewer still have thought of it as a stunning example of God's providence over a fallen world. . . . It is just what we might expect of a God who, even in a fallen world, can still work all things together for good."[199] What's best for your neighbors is also best for you, in a free market.

How does this affect the poor? They are made richer when they are allowed to make exchanges with their neighbors in a free market. The poor must be given opportunity *to create wealth*. Put that way, we can see what is so troublingly wrong about using coercive redistribution as the primary means of alleviating poverty. Redistribution assumes that wealth is a given and that it is only a matter of cutting up the existing pie. Poverty is caused by greedy people who take more than their fair share. But that is to turn things on their head; it fails to ask how the wealth pie was created in the first place and by whom. Wealth is created because of the *value* that God and human beings place on things.[200] Since God values humans, he values their freedom (expressed in the first commandment of biblical economics) to make exchanges with their neighbors. It's hard to imagine how a redistributionist would justify the taking of goods as moral.

Dave and his wife Ginger were on a tour of the wealthy neighborhoods of Fort Lauderdale. The tour guide continually pointed out the multimillion-dollar mansions of the rich and famous; one was the home of the actor Gene Hackman. Some on the boat may have felt bad about the repeated statements of wealth. But not a free-market economist.

That person would think, "Isn't it wonderful that the rich guy produced so much consumer surplus for his neighbors?" One of the primary ways we glorify God and love our neighbor is through our vocational calling to work.[201] If Gene Hackman owns a seven-million-dollar house in Fort Lauderdale, that means he produced more than seven million dollars in entertainment for his neighbors. He loved his neighbors by providing entertainment they anxiously paid for.

Producer Surplus

Everyone understands that Walmart buys a box of tissues for about $0.60 and sells it for about $1.25. That's called producer surplus, and you don't need an economics lesson to understand that. But if you interviewed customers leaving Walmart, most of them would say that, in the exchange they just made, Walmart got richer while they got poorer. That's not economically accurate. *Both* parties get richer when both parties make arms-length trades in a perfectly competitive environment. Now, all environments are *not* perfectly competitive, and that's called market power, which is a subject for another chapter.

Anyone who sells anything profitably in a market is in some sense making money off the "dis-ease"—the lack, or insufficiency—of others. The home builder is making money off the homelessness of home buyers, clothing manufacturers off the nakedness of clothing buyers, restaurants off the hunger of diners.[202] Students pay their university for information that leads to a college degree, which enriches them. You bought this book, hoping it would increase your understanding of biblical economics. Dave asks his students, "If tuition is too high at DBU, why are you here?" Apparently, the tuition price is not "too high," because the student agreed to pay it. Students are seeking a cure for their "dis-ease."

The implication is that for the covenant people, love for God and love for one's neighbor cannot be separated or divided. Both are appropriate to a holy life.[203] Colossians 3:23 provides the biblical sustenance for this idea: "Whatever you do, work at it with all your heart, as working for the Lord, not for human masters." When there are both consumer surplus and producer surplus, economic resources are used to help our neighbors in need.[204]

At this point, we make this very common-sense conclusion: if both parties get richer during trade, we should do more of it. Here's the Christian economic suggestion from the producer's (Walmart) point of view: if you love your neighbor as you love yourself, you will participate in economic exchanges where your neighbor gains consumer surplus, while you gain producer surplus. Both parties get richer. This works only in competitive environments—which leads us to our next concept.

8. Take Care of Widows and Orphans

> "Religion that God our Father accepts as pure and faultless is this: to look after orphans and widows in their distress and to keep oneself from being polluted by the world" (James 1:27).

In some versions of the Bible, this includes immigrants. The reason the church is commanded to take care of these three groups is because in the ancient world, these were the people who didn't own land. In an agrarian society, if you didn't own land, you could not create value for yourself, and someone needed to take care of you. In the first century, that was the job of the church.

Donald Hay summarizes his book *Economics Today* this way: "work, and the obligation on the rich to help the poor."[205] We are commanded to care for the poor. But how? And, by whom? Art Lindsley has a clear answer: "The government should punish evil, but not do good. The church should do good, but not punish evil."[206] We *wish* it was that clear. There are examples of the early church punishing evil. And there are multiple examples of the government doing good—or at least trying to do good. But Lindsley was talking about normative economics, not positive economics. He was stating how things *should* be, from the biblical perspective.

Paul gave specific instructions to Timothy to provide aid only to widows who were really in need. He included criteria for those worthy of receiving aid, such as being "well known for her good deeds, such as bringing up children, showing hospitality, washing the feet of the Lord's people, helping those in trouble and devoting herself to all kinds of good deeds."[207] The requirements are quite stringent. Some of those requirements were that the widows on the list were to have been long-term members of the community and that they themselves were known to have aided others in need in the past.[208] The judgment task for the providers of care for widows and orphans is much different than the entitlement that takes place in government programs.

Smaller government size and stabilization from inflation disproportionately benefit the poor, by raising the share of income accruing to the bottom quintile. Indeed, social spending is negatively related to the income share possessed by the poor, which reminds us that public social spending is not necessarily well targeted to the poor.[209] Our history confirms that change-oriented compassion has three dimensions: it needs to be personal, spiritual, and challenging. That is a central theme of Marvin Olasky's *The Tragedy of American Compassion.*[210] Government struggles with the personal and spiritual parts of Olasky's requirements.

It is our contention, from biblical study, that the government should not try to do good. We believe the church has either forfeited its role or the government has assumed it. In this section, we're not going to argue about causality; we're only going to conclude that the outcome has not been biblical. In *When Helping Hurts*, Steve Corbett and Brian Fikkert write, "While the rise of government programs may have exacerbated the church's retreat, they were not the primary cause. Theology matters, and the church needs to rediscover a Christ-centered, fully orbed perspective of the kingdom."[211] In the socialist's vision, widespread government redistribution replaces private charity by ensuring that the working classes and the poor do not have to depend on benevolence.[212] That robs Christians of our commandment to care for widows and orphans.

Jesus was not opposed to wealth in itself, but only insofar as it becomes an obstacle to response to God. An indication that it has become such an obstacle is an unwillingness to share the proceeds of wealth with those who are needy.[213] The strangest thing would not necessarily be that there was sharing, or a community of goods; but rather that it took place across class and across culture—and in a way that put the needs of the truly poor and disadvantaged (orphans and widows) first.[214]

Are we saved by joining God in his identification with the marginalized and oppressed? This would be, we should note, a salvation by works and not by grace alone.[215] Our statement is: *Most religions believe you behave to be saved. Christians believe we are saved to behave.* Thus, we care for widows and orphans not as means to be saved, but because we *are* saved. That produces our eighth commandment of biblical economics, "Take care of widows and orphans."

We hope you already have a heart for the poor. Lots of Christians do. But do you have a *mind* for the poor? Unfortunately, that's in rather short supply.[216] This famous quote from Jay Richards became the theme of the video series *Poverty Cure* by the Acton Institute.

We often see that caring for others produces a positive reward. But there's a punishment for not carrying out God's commands. God was furious over Israel's failure to care for the poor and the oppressed. He wanted his people to "loose the chains of injustice," and not just go to church on Sunday. He wanted His people to "clothe the Naked."[217] They have done this since the church was founded in Jerusalem and deacons were ordained to look after poor widows. Christians have the calling, the means, and the gifts to provide services ranging from education to care for persons with physical and mental limitations.[218]

In *Money, Greed, and God*, Jay Richards writes about the ineffectiveness of government-to-government aid in alleviating poverty, "While some (government) aid has helped a few things around the edges, it has utterly failed as a solution to third-world poverty."[219] That's because it is not in alignment with the biblical command for the church to take care of widows and orphans. Misalignment with God's creational intent does not produce sustainable reduction in poverty. When Jesus said, "The poor you will always have with you" (Matthew 26:11), He was giving the church a long-term assignment to care for widows and orphans.

"Always" is the operative word in the sentence. Richards again: "What does tax money sent from one government to another have to do with speeding up the creation of wealth? Nothing. No developing country ever got rich that way." Governments continue to try to care for widows and orphans, but their attempts almost always fail, due to a lack of alignment with God's creational intent.

Since it is made clear in the passage that what is given is up to the giver, and that what is distributed is systematic and quite widespread (the sick, strangers, orphans, widows, and all in need), we can surmise that there must have been both enthusiastic encouragement as well as great moral and cultural pressure to give.[220] That kind of enthusiasm for giving did not exist in 1780s Britain, when William Wilberforce began his political career. He set two goals for his life: the abolition of the slave trade and the reformation of manners. What he meant by "manners" was the content of our biblical command to care for widows and orphans. There was a general agreement at the time that the poor were meant to be poor, and intervening to help them would go against God's intent. Wilberforce did not agree. By the time he died in 1833, the slave trade was abolished, and "manners" were reformed. Because of his influence, it became fashionable to help the poor, and it remains so today.

On this point, we take a radical departure from current-day political events. Our study of this biblical command seems to indicate that the church is responsible for taking care of widows and orphans. We find no biblical command for the government to "do good." If the government is not supposed to "do good," who is? The Good Samaritan story provides a biblical answer.

9. Be a Good Samaritan

Notice the emphasized words in the following passage from Luke 10:25–37:

> On one occasion an expert in the law stood up to test Jesus. "Teacher," he asked, "what must I do to inherit eternal life?"

"What is written in the Law?" he replied. "How do you read it?"

He answered, "'Love the Lord your God with all your heart and with all your soul and with all your strength and with all your mind'; and, 'Love your neighbor as yourself.'"

"You have answered correctly," Jesus replied. "Do this and you will live." But he wanted to justify himself, so he asked Jesus, "And who is my neighbor?"

In reply Jesus said: "A man was going down from Jerusalem to Jericho, when he was attacked by robbers. They stripped him of his clothes, beat him and went away, leaving him half dead. A priest happened to be going down the same road, and when he saw the man, he passed by on the other side. So too, a Levite, when he came to the place and saw him, passed by on the other side. But a Samaritan, as he traveled, came where the man was; and when he saw him, he took pity on him. He went to him and *bandaged* his wounds, pouring on *oil* and *wine*. Then he put the man on his own *donkey*, brought him to an *inn* and took care of him. The next day he took out two *denarii* and gave them to the innkeeper. 'Look after him,' he said, 'and when I return, *I will reimburse you* for any extra expense you may have.'

"Which of these three do you think was a neighbor to the man who fell into the hands of robbers?"

The expert in the law replied, "The one who had mercy on him."

Jesus told him, "Go and do likewise."

If we attempt to "go and do likewise," we help people with our own money, as the Good Samaritan did. Jesus could have told the story in the following manner:

But a Samaritan, as he traveled, came where the man was; and when he saw him, he took pity on him. He roused some Roman soldiers and they went door-to-door extracting taxes from the citizens who had earned money in their business pursuits. They put the money into public coffers, and used it to buy public bandages, public oil, public wine, and public donkeys. They built public hospitals (inns) with public denarii and reimbursed the medical staff with public denarii.

That's *not* how Jesus told the story. Why didn't he? Certainly the Roman government was strong enough to institute such a tax. Those who argue that "it was a different context," support our argument. They certainly are not suggesting that the current US government has, or should have, more power over its citizens than the Roman government did. Much of the New Testament contains complaints about the power of the Roman government—that it's too much, not that there is not enough. So, in a context two thousand years ago, of a more powerful government than we have today, Jesus didn't say, "You know those Roman government officials you've been complaining about? This is how their power should be used, to help those in need." He didn't say that. As a matter of fact, he purposely avoided saying that. We have come to believe that the government bureaucrat is a Good Samaritan.[221] It's not.

In modern liberal capitalist societies, we differentiate between private philanthropy and economics; we also differentiate between completely free actions and mandated actions. These differentiations were not so clear in the ancient world.[222] The power of what we today would call "culture" induced people to follow. They were not free in the modern use of the term, but they were also not constrained by government. It was a conscious choice made by individuals in a covenant community.

Let's think more carefully about the Samaritan in this story. We're not told where he obtained his money, but there is a good assumption that if he was traveling from Jerusalem to Jericho, he was a merchant, salesman, or trader of some kind. He is clearly not identified as a government official, because that would have been worth mentioning in the story. So, we're left with a for-profit merchant using the money he made in a free-market endeavor, using his *own* money to care for those in need. Let's go and do likewise.

The Samaritan using his own money enables him to be more specific in caring for the person who needs help. It is a serious failure of understanding and imagination for ethicists, analysts, and policy makers not to make important distinctions among the poor and attempt a one-size-fits-all approach to poverty alleviation.[223] Within the covenant communities, God requires those who are rich to help those who are in need.[224]

One of the main tenets of economics is division of labor. This specialization is expressed when the Samaritan uses his own money to care individually for those he has the knowledge about. Furthermore, the Samaritan can do so while tailoring help to meet the immensely varied needs of poor people. One family may need budgeting assistance; another, help getting into a training program; another, information about care for a disabled father or sick child. When government tries to be all things to all people, programs are often bundled in ways that adversely affect independence, self-respect, and joining churches and other groups to promote mutual care and responsibility.[225]

If the government weren't occupying most of the charitable ecosystem, charities would be profoundly different. The ecosystem would be filled with thousands of well-funded responsive charities accountable to their donors and communities. As it is, government has invaded the ecosystem, and mostly made a mess of it. In the United States, it started with FDR's 1930s programs. They were meant to end the Great Depression but deepened and lengthened it instead. Then came the War on Poverty by LBJ in the 1960s, as part of his grandiose Great Society agenda. Judged by its results, however, the War on Poverty was more a War on the Poor. Statistically, the poverty rate was already on a steady decline before Johnson put his hand to the domestic plow. It had dropped from about 22 percent to fifteen percent between 1959 and 1965. After 1965, just after the War on Poverty began, the poverty rate settled in, and it has continued to fluctuate between twelve and fifteen percent up to the present day, even though American society is now much more prosperous overall.[226]

A significant advantage of programs administered through local churches compared to governmental programs is that relief is voluntarily provided and personally administered.[227] Based on what we know from the first commandment of biblical economics, this type of freedom is consistent with the Christian intent.

10. Honor Those in Power

> "Let everyone be subject to the governing authorities, for there is no authority except that which God has established. The authorities that exist have been established by God. Consequently, whoever rebels against the authority is rebelling against what God has instituted, and those who do so will bring judgment on themselves" (Romans 13:1–2).

These authorities are established by God, but they are staffed by fallen humans. The danger, Lord Acton insisted, is not that a particular class is unfit to govern; *every* class is unfit to govern.[228] Thus, it is the Christian's difficult task to know when to follow the governing authorities, and when to subvert them. In the fascinating book *Bonhoeffer,*[229] Eric Metaxas explains how Dietrich Bonhoeffer and his group of subservient spies struggled with this scriptural mandate during the evil reign of the Nazis. In general, we are going to assume that we should follow the rules made for us. Very few circumstances are as dire and extreme as the Hitler situation in Germany from 1932–45.

From the beginning of the Christian church, its view of government has *not* been negative. Despite the often brutal persecution of Christians by the Roman authorities, nowhere does one find in Scripture or the church fathers any claim that government is an essentially illegitimate institution, let alone the suggestion that any form of state coercion whatsoever is wrong.[230]

Romans 13:15 says we are to obey civil authorities in order to avoid anarchy and chaos, but there may be times when we may be forced to obey God rather than men (Acts 5:29).[231] Martin Luther King Jr.'s "Letter from a Birmingham Jail" provides a good middle point for this consideration. "There is nothing new about this kind of civil disobedience. It was evidenced sublimely in the refusal of Shadrach, Meshach, and Abednego to obey the laws of Nebuchadnezzar, on the ground that a higher moral law was at stake. It was practiced superbly by the early Christians, who were willing to face hungry lions and the excruciating pain of chopping blocks rather than submit to certain unjust laws of the Roman Empire. To a degree, academic freedom is a reality today because Socrates practiced civil disobedience."[232] MLK found this middle ground quite successfully. But he didn't say that civil disobedience should go unpunished. He was happy to spend his time in jail, and Bonhoeffer was willing to die for his disobedience.

Alexis de Tocqueville made many fascinating observations about the American experiment in his book *Democracy in America*,[233] published in 1835. Perhaps his biggest contribution is the idea of "mediating institutions" that occupied the space between individuals and government. He noticed a number of philanthropic organizations that cared for the poor and tried to redeem the worst of society's ills. Before he wrote the book, the term "individualism" was seen as a social dysfunction. He explained the American concept as a positive term. The Americans honored those in power, but built voluntary mediating institutions to operate alongside the coercive governmental system. What he called "individualistic" is in fact properly characterized as a form of "associationalism"[234] via these mediating institutions.

Univision anchor Jorge Ramos challenged President Obama for not keeping his promise to La Raza to pass immigration legislation during his first year in office, 2009. Ramos was correct; Obama had not kept his promise, which was especially painful since his Democratic Party had control of the White House, and both houses of Congress, for all of 2009 and 2010. The result is a subcategory of Americans called "illegal immigrants." Yet when interviewed, illegal immigrants say they want to be in the US because it's a law-abiding society. Let's run that through our rational thought machine: they want to break the law in order to live in a country that doesn't allow law-breaking. Think about it.

"There is no authority except from God, and those which exist are established by God. Therefore he who resists authority has opposed the ordinance of God." This is a strong endorsement of the intrinsic goodness of government, in its proper role,[235] which is to maintain competition and fairness in all dealings. As a consequence, governments can contribute to the health of an economy, in large part, by establishing fundamental rights and rules that promote both competition and fairness.[236]

Romans 13 seems to endorse changing laws, but not breaking them. We will try to consistently follow this first-century commandment while analyzing twenty-first-century economic policies like trade, taxation, unemployment, and many others.

With an acceptance and understanding of the Ten Commandments of Biblical Economics, we are ready to analyze the current economic questions that face us. The tools are designed and ready to make prescriptive determinations in chapters 3–13.

Chapter 3

International Trade

Free Trade or Managed Trade?

Trade is an important part of life. We trade money for the desired goods and services, we trade our time at work for wages, and we trade current consumption for the anticipated increase in future consumption. We already established in chapter 2 that trade is good and that loving your neighbor as yourself can result from trade by maximizing producer and consumer surplus. One outcome of living in a global economy is that trade can easily happen with a neighbor down the street or someone living a thousand miles away. In this chapter, we are interested in trade, which expands beyond national borders and the role of the government in this process.

The government can either allow the flow of goods and services freely in and out of its national borders or it can actively restrict the inflow of such goods and services by imposing tariffs, quotas, and other trade barriers. We acknowledge that the arguments for free trade or managed trade comprise a centuries-old debate, with each side offering some convincing arguments. Our objective is to apply some of the ten economic commandments from chapter 2 to evaluate this issue.

International trade played an important role throughout history. From the times of ancient Greece through the fall of the Roman Empire, trade of valuable spices flourished in Europe, which were brought from the Far East, including India and China. Trade helped the Roman Empire to prosper and endure as long as it did. During the Middle Ages, Central Asia was the economic center of the world because of its east-to-west trade route known as the Silk Road.

During the times of absolute monarchs in Europe roughly between 1500s and 1800s, a national economic policy known as mercantilism was directed to maximizing the exports of a nation. The monarchs treated precious metals as the major components of national wealth and maximizing exports would ensure a continuing inflow of gold and silver, thus increasing the national wealth. Mercantilists argued for imposing various restrictions on imports. High tariffs, especially on manufactured goods, was a prevalent feature of mercantilist policy.[237]

Similarly, the United States in the 1800s went through the period of protectionism, which was an economic policy of erecting tariffs and other trade barriers. A protectionist sentiment reemerges every now and then, and many attribute the victory of Donald Trump in 2016 presidential elections to his appeal of bringing manufacturing jobs back to the US—jobs which were once lost due to international trade and competition.[238] The protectionist sentiment can be seen in one of the tweets by President Trump in December of 2018, which read, "remember . . . I am a Tariff Man. When people or countries come in to raid the great wealth of our Nation, I want them to pay for the privilege of doing so. It will always be the best way to max out our economic power."[239]

Some of the current arguments in support of free or managed trade can be summarized from one of the sessions the authors of this book visited at the 2016 Free Market Forum in Atlanta. The session featured Don Boudreaux and Ian Fletcher, who exchanged ideas on the topic of "Free Trade or Fair Trade?" Boudreaux outlined ten arguments in support of free trade, while Fletcher offered some arguments against free trade and in support of fair (managed) trade. Fletcher mentioned his support for trade, but trade with government-imposed regulations. His concern was that other nations take advantage of the American people by selling goods at low prices, thus driving some labor-intensive jobs out of the United States to lower labor-cost countries. The people who lose higher-paying manufacturing jobs often settle for lower-paying jobs. Another concern was that the US experiences trade deficits because some trading partners implement a number of mechanisms to prevent US exports entering or competing with the products within their countries.

Boudreaux made several strong points in defense of free trade and exposed some of the fallacies of the opposing view; we summarize some of his points. First, the benefits from trade are not diminished just because one trading partner happens to live across political borders. One of the benefits of trade is that it helps us maximize our consumption which is the end goal, while production is the means.

Second, specialization increases output since it uses resources more efficiently and taps into comparative advantage. Trade is required to allow individuals to specialize and trade expands with the size of the market. We benefit by having doctors who specialize in different areas of medical care and research since it allows them to save more lives and reduce more pain. Larger cities enjoy a greater variety of restaurants with more diverse cuisines due to the expanded market. As the size of the market expands, it allows doctors and restaurant owners to specialize and benefit from their comparative advantage.

Third, economic competition encourages entrepreneurial creativity and directs workers and other resources to those production activities in which they can be most efficient.

Finally, people are the ultimate resource, as the economist and book writer Julian Simon often affirmed. He taught that this "ultimate resource"—which also happens to be the title of the book he wrote in 1981—is not any physical or natural resource but the capacity of humans to invent and innovate. Indeed, it's only because of human creativity and ingenuity that we learned to convert raw materials into valuable products.

One of our favorite economists, Thomas Sowell reminds us:

> When the British first confronted the Iroquois on the east coast
> of North America, the mental and material resources at the dis-
> posal of these two races were by no means confined to what they
> had each developed themselves. The British had been able to
> navigate across the Atlantic, in the first place, by using the com-
> pass invented in China, doing mathematical calculations with a
> numbering system from India, steering with rudders invented in
> China, writing on paper invented in China using letters created
> by the Romans, and ultimately prevailing in combat using gun-
> powder, also invented in China.[240]

In other words, the British were able to trade with the Native Americans because they had first traded with the most advanced societies of
the world.

As we examine the issue of free versus managed trade, we explore
the implications of several economic commandments we established in
the previous chapter. We will use the commandments of freedom (1),
trade is good (6), and love your neighbor as yourself (7) as the guide-
posts in navigating through this issue.

Freedom. There are two sides to freedom—we have a freedom "to"
and we have a freedom "from." The first freedom ensures we can engage
in any activity as long as it does not infringe on someone else's freedom.
The second freedom ensures we are not coerced into an act or choice
without our consent. At creation, God gave Adam and Eve the freedom to eat the fruit from any tree they liked except one. They had the
freedom to obey or disobey God's command. God also endowed Adam
and Eve with the freedom from the power of sin. Adam and Eve had
the freedom to object to the serpent's tempting words and refrain from
eating the fruit from the forbidden tree. If Adam and Eve fully realized
the consequences of their bad decision, they would likely erect the fence
around the forbidden tree, lock the gate, and throw away the key. If we

were in charge, we would be very uneasy in giving so much freedom to Adam and Eve, knowing that their misjudgment could negatively impact all future inhabitants of the earth and the earth itself.

If you had a time machine, as in *Avengers: Endgame*, and could travel all the way back to the garden of Eden prior to the fall, what would you do? Would you try to reason with Adam and Eve or would you try to set the off-limits zone around the tree? In either case, God happened to give more freedom to Adam and Eve than we would, given our knowledge of the consequences resulting from the original sin.

Applying the concept of freedom to trade, we posit that trade should not be limited or managed by the government. Political and economic freedom implies individuals should be free to trade with a neighbor across the street or a foreigner living across the globe. Government-instituted tariffs, quotas, and other trade restrictions limit the amount of trade and reduce the potential gain which individuals are able to enjoy. Managed trade is designed to benefit a certain interest group at the expense of other groups. For example, implementing a 25 percent tariff on leather handbags is equivalent to adding a tax of 25 percent, which reduces the quantity of handbags traded since both buyers and sellers of these leather handbags share the burden of a higher cost. The interest group that benefits from such a tax are local manufacturers of leather handbags, since they can now sell more of their leather hand-bags at relatively lower prices or enjoy higher profit margins by charging higher prices. The individuals who are hurt by such a tax are local buy-ers and foreign sellers of leather handbags. The benefit of trade which is lost exceeds the gain which is acquired. The higher effective price of leather handbags causes some consumers to refrain from buying the product and thus reduces the potential gain from trade, which is known as consumer surplus. The benefit is concentrated while the cost is dis-persed. An arbitrary choice of the government of which interest groups to shield from competition limits the freedom of other individuals in at least two ways. First, the consumers are refrained from enjoying the full benefit from trade, which they could enjoy by paying lower prices;

second, they are effectively coerced to subsidize the local manufacturers of leather handbags.

Trade is good. The benefits from trade are realized by both—the buyer and the seller. The decision to enter into a trade willingly reveals that a buyer perceives more value from owning a product than the price paid for it, while the seller perceives more value from the accepted price than holding on to the product.

Trade is good since each party is better off after the transaction, even though the terms of trade may benefit one party more than the other. Someone who is better in trade negotiations may end up with better terms of trade, just like someone who has a greater market power. Competition is important to ensure that the benefits are not skewed toward one party only. The two extremes of concentrated market power are known as monopoly, which empowers the seller to set the price; and monopsony, which empowers the buyer to influence the price. Managed trade imposes trade barriers and reduces competition, which leads to higher prices.

Jesus worked as a carpenter prior to his public ministry and benefited from trade. If trade is managed and reduces the amount of benefit derived by buyers and sellers, then managed trade reduces the welfare of individuals and reduces the amount they could give toward improving the welfare of the local community. The *Poverty Cure* documentary series establishes that trade is the most thoughtful way of helping the poor—not aid, which keeps poor nations in a state of perpetual dependency.

If trade is mutually beneficial to both parties then reducing trade via various trade barriers is not a desired outcome. Based on the economic commandment "trade is good," free trade preferable to managed trade.

Love your neighbor as yourself. This is the command which shifts our focus from ourselves and toward our neighbor. Trade helps us maximize the welfare of our neighbor, since trade makes both parties better off. If we don't trade directly with our neighbor, supporting free trade helps improve his or her wellbeing by allowing our neighbor to take full advantage of the benefits from trade. Managed trade limits the amount of trade, and thus works to reduce the amount of good we are able to do toward those around us.

Competition helps to maximize social welfare by means of producer and consumer surplus. While competition helps to dilute the concentration of market power and increase social welfare, the trade barriers are used to limit competition or achieve an upper hand in trade negotiations. In light of recent trade negotiations, there is an abundance of news articles highlighting the usage of trade barriers in promoting national interests. One of the articles from *The Washington Post* stated, "President Trump is moving to impose escalating tariffs on Mexican imports to force that government to take a harder line to stem the flow of Central American migrants into the United States."[241] One *Wall Street Journal* article stated, "President Donald Trump said . . . he has offered President Xi Jinping more favorable trade terms . . . in exchange for help on confronting the threat of North Korea."[242]

If trade barriers are not used to promote a desired foreign policy but to improve the terms of trade, it is important to understand the benefits and the costs of trade. Let's assume that an impartial third party was tasked to set the terms of trade, so that the benefits were spread equally between buyers and sellers. Such a task would be hard to impossible to complete since the value placed on the product varies from buyer to buyer and the costs vary from seller to seller.

In economics, the value placed on the product can be measured by the maximum price someone is willing to pay; it is called willingness to pay, or WTP for short. As WTP reveals the perceived value placed on the product by the buyer, the opportunity cost reveals the true cost to the seller. The opportunity cost includes the implicit and explicit costs. The explicit costs result in cash outflows and are tracked by accountants. These are the costs which include payments to suppliers, workers, creditors, landlords, etc. The implicit costs are much harder to measure since they vary from seller to seller and include the value derived from the best alternative use of a given resource. For example, if the entrepreneur starts a business of selling pancakes and has to forgo a job as a financial analyst, then an income derived from a job as a financial analyst would be considered as an implicit cost in starting a business of selling pancakes. Another example would be the use of entrepreneur's own savings in starting a new business. If savings earned an interest, then the interest income, which now would be forgone, should be considered an implicit cost in starting a new business. In economics, the implicit costs are important since they play a role in a decision-making process and thus help us better understand the various decisions businesses make.

The task of estimating WTP of each buyer and true costs of each seller would be an equivalent to estimating consumer and producer surplus. Consumer and producer surplus depend on relative elasticities of demand and supply curves. In general, the greater the elasticity, the greater the sensitivity to price changes. If demand curve is price-elastic, then slight increases to price will cause many buyers to switch to other products. If supply curve is price-elastic, then slight decrease in price will cause many sellers to stop supplying the good. If demand curve is more price-elastic than supply curve, then sellers share more of a burden in adverse price moves such as an added tax due to tariffs. A tariff will impose a greater burden on foreign sellers if the supply curve is inelastic while the demand curve is elastic. In such a case, tariffs reduce the amount of trade and hurt local consumers too, who are resorted to paying higher prices.

Our support goes in favor of free trade—which is consistent with the economic commandments of "freedom," "trade is good," and "love your neighbor as yourself."

Should the Government Institute Tariffs?

A tariff is defined as a government charge on goods entering or leaving a country. Countries usually impose import tariffs to protect local businesses from foreign competition and export tariffs to slow down the exit of domestically manufactured goods overseas. A tariff is one of the tools of managing trade, so the discussion in our previous section applies here as well.

Opening up a country to international trade creates some winners and losers. If a world price, which is the price of the good that prevails in the world market, is higher than a domestic price, then a country becomes an exporter of that good. Being an exporter country will benefit producers but hurt consumers, because prices for goods being exported would go up. However, the benefit to producers is greater than the loss to consumers and overall economic well-being of a nation increases.

If the world price is lower than the domestic price, then a nation becomes an importer of that good. The domestic prices would go down and consumers are better off, while the producers are worse off. The benefit to consumers exceeds the loss to producers and the overall economic well-being of a nation goes up. The use of import tariffs is more common, since the costs are concentrated within a specific industry, which can be more vocal and gather political clout. The benefits to consumers are widespread, but consumers are not as organized as producers and are not as vocal about their improved economic state. Free trade not only lowers the prices to consumers but increases the variety of products, makes markets more competitive, and facilitates the spread of technology.

At first glance, protecting local jobs from foreign competition sounds like a noble objective. After all, foreign governments might subsidize their exporting industries to engage in predatory pricing, domestic labor costs might be much higher than foreign labor costs due to higher standards of living, growing trade deficit might negatively impact employment and economic growth, and foreign governments might manipulate the value of their currency in order to increase their exports. All of these concerns might lead the government to respond by implementing tariffs or other trade barriers to promote national interests.

However, good intentions to help local businesses often result in unintended consequences which create negative ripple effects throughout the economy. A tariff does not only penalize the importers but the consumers of the imported goods as well.

Earlier this year, *The Wall Street Journal* reported that the president's claim on Twitter that his tariffs were one reason for the strong US economy was the opposite of reality. The economy is growing despite the tariffs, and US manufacturing jobs have declined this year in part because of China's slowdown.[243] Henry Hazlitt, in *Economics in One Lesson*, writes that tariffs are the result of looking only at the immediate effects of a single tariff rate on one group of producers, and forgetting the long-run effects both on consumers as a whole and on all other producers—that they end up paying higher prices and realize smaller consumer surplus. Producers that are sheltered from foreign competition become less efficient than their foreign counterparts and all other producers realize smaller producer surplus. *The Wall Street Journal* reported in another article that a 25 percent tariff on all automotive imports would increase the average price of a vehicle sold in the US by $4,400, and the price of an imported vehicle could rise by $6,875.[244]

The Holy Scriptures stay silent on the topic of tariffs, but we can infer God's intent from other passages. The same economic commandments applicable to the question of managed versus free trade—freedom, trade is good, and love your neighbor as yourself—would apply to the issue of tariffs. A new economic commandment we could add here is to take care of widows and orphans.

Trade is good. Tariffs lower the size of trade and limit the benefits, which otherwise would be possible to achieve and improve the well-being of individuals within a nation. Tariffs are equivalent to a tax, which create a wedge between the price sellers receive and the price buyers pay. Using the graph of supply and demand, the burden of such a tax is shared by both parties, regardless of which party is required to pay the tax. This can be clearly seen from the demand and supply curves, whereas a portion of a one-dollar tariff placed on all sunglasses that are imported into the US will be shared by the buyers, who end up paying a higher price; and by the sellers, who end up receiving a lower price. From the law of demand, a higher price reduces the quantity demanded, which translates into less trade. In addition, the loss to consumers and producers is greater than the amount of tariff that the government collects. In economics such a loss is known as the deadweight loss. The deadweight loss results from unrealized trades, which would take place in the absence of a tax.

Love your neighbor as yourself. Don Boudreaux, economist and professor at George Mason University, makes a claim that nothing can justify treating trades that cross national borders differently than those that do not.[245] Benefits from trade occur regardless of whether we trade with someone who lives across the street, or the state, or the national border. Jesus expanded the definition of a neighbor to mean not just someone who lives down the street but someone we show grace to and a helping hand. Loving your neighbor as yourself would imply reducing trade barriers, which reduce the level of trade and thus benefit to our neighbor.

Take care of widows and orphans. Tariffs are paid mostly by the widows and orphans who buy products from low-labor-cost countries that are sold at discount stores. Tariffs are a regressive tax on widows and orphans.

Tariffs tend to favor local manufacturers at the expense of consumers. Consumers end up paying higher prices for imported goods, which reduces the incentives for local companies to remain competitive and achieve greater efficiency. Tariffs imposed on food and other basic necessities have a disproportionately negative effect on the working poor, who spend a large portion of their budgets on basic necessities. Eliminating trade barriers would decrease the prices of imported goods and encourage local producers to find new ways of lowering the costs to stay competitive.

The Bible and Balance of Trade

The balance of trade is defined as the difference between the value of exports and the value of imports. If the value of exports exceeds the value of imports, then a country runs a positive balance of trade or a trade surplus. On the other hand, if the value of imports exceeds the value of exports then a country runs a negative balance of trade or a trade deficit. In the United States over the last two decades the trade deficit has grown from 39 billion in 1992 to 628 billion in 2018.[246]

U.S. INTERNATIONAL TRADE BALANCE FROM 1992 TO 2018 (IN BILLIONS)

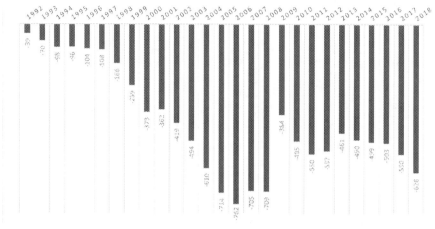

Figure 3

Trade deficit implies that a country purchases more goods and services from foreigners than it sells to them, and as a result, more US dollars are being supplied in the foreign exchange market. The demand for US dollars is driven by foreigners who purchase goods and services from the US and need to convert their currency to US dollars. Likewise, the supply of US dollars is driven by the US nationals, who are making purchases of foreign goods and services. Persistent trade deficit creates a scenario where the supply of dollars exceeds the demand and puts pressure on the US dollar to depreciate against other currencies, all else equal. However, over the same time period as the US trade deficit has grown, the US dollar index has grown as well from 77 to 123. Figure 4 depicts the dollar index, which tracks the relative value of the US dollar against a basket of currencies of major US trading partners.[247]

One of the reasons to explain this counterintuitive result is that all things did not stay the same—or as economists like to term it, *ceteris paribus*. Inflow of dollars to the world markets due to persistent trade deficit was absorbed by increased demand for US dollars by foreign individuals

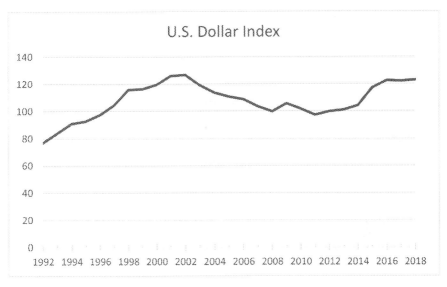

Figure 4

and governments. One example of such a trend can be observed in the growth of sovereign wealth funds. A sovereign wealth fund is an investment pool of foreign currency reserves owned by a government.[248] The growth in value of such funds went from 272 billion in 1992 to 7.5 trillion in 2018.[249] China's reserves alone went from 43 billion in 1992 to 3.1 trillion by the end of 2018[250] and based on the International Monetary Fund (IMF) data, over 62 percent of all foreign exchange reserves are held in US dollars.[251] The dominance of the US dollar as the preferred currency for foreign reserves goes back to the Bretton Woods agreement, which outlined the design of the postwar international monetary system and was ratified by the majority of countries in 1945. Under the Bretton Woods system, each country tried to maintain a certain exchange rate in relation to the US dollar, which was the only currency fully convertible to gold at a fixed rate of $35 per ounce. In order to maintain a certain exchange rate, foreign governments had to keep a certain amount of foreign reserves in US dollars. The US dollar has become a dominant currency used in international trade. For example, the prices for most commodities are expressed in dollars. The strength of the US economy and a perceived safety of investing in the US Treasury securities are some other contributing factors of the increased demand for the US dollar.

The strength of the US dollar helps consumers purchase foreign goods at relatively lower prices but penalizes producers who sell their products overseas. From the perspective of national balance-of-payments accounting, the outflow of money due to imports exceeding exports is offset by the inflow of money in the form of investments into the country. The investment might be in the form of foreign direct investment (FDI), when a foreign company acquires a company in the US; or a portfolio investment, when financial assets are purchased such as stocks or bonds. In either case, the trade deficit must be financed either by borrowing from foreigners or selling some portion of previously accumulated foreign wealth. The increased demand for the US dollar helps the US government to borrow money at reduced rates via the sale of Treasury bonds. Consumers benefit as well, since the lower interest rates on Treasury bonds translate into lower interest rates used for consumer lending. Households are able to get more favorable rates on mortgages, student loans, auto loans, credit cards, etc.

Not all debt is good debt, but debt that is used as an investment and generates greater return than its cost is a good way to build capital. Foreign governments and individuals find it favorable to invest in the United States, and this extra capital inflow helps entrepreneurs as well as small and large businesses to develop viable business ideas and improve the world around us. However, if debt is used as a way to finance consumption, then growing debt is a bad debt.

Someone may wonder: Is it a bad thing that the trade deficit grows over time? Not necessarily, if the trade deficit grows at the same time as the economy grows, then the trade deficit nearly keeps pace with it. If we examine the growth in real GDP, which is used as a measure of the economy's size, we notice that it grew from 9.5 trillion in 1992 to almost 19 trillion by the end of 2018.[252] Another important consideration is the importance of international trade as it relates to GDP. In the US,

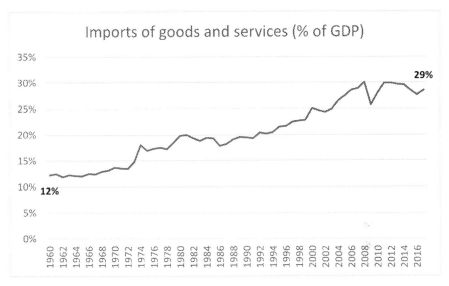

Figure 5

the imports as a percentage of GDP have increased from about ten to fifteen percent between 1992 and 2017. The importance of trade for the world as a whole is even more striking. We are more interdependent than ever before and the ratio of imports to GDP has gone up for the world from twelve percent in 1960 to 28.5 percent in 2017.[253] The graph above shows this trend.

Based on the Organization for Economic Cooperation and Development (OECD) data, the terms of trade have improved as well over the last twenty years. The OECD defines the terms of trade as the ratio between the index of export prices and the index of import prices.[254] For the United States this ratio has improved by about seven percent since 1992, which means that the export prices increased more than the import prices and a country can enjoy more imports for the same amount of exports. The United States has been a winner because of the international trade, but so have the other trading partners. Trade deficit, when broken down by trading partner, shows that the US is running a trade deficit with China, Germany, and Japan, but a trade surplus with

Brazil, Belgium, and Ukraine. It shows again that each nation has something to offer to benefit the other, and trade inspired by the comparative advantage mutually enriches each country involved in trade.

Trade based on comparative advantage often results in trade deficit or surplus between two parties, but it is more of a rule rather than an exception. The following illustration may help to convey this point. Let's say Milton works as an economics professor at a local university. He trades his labor in exchange for a monthly paycheck, and thus runs a consistent trade surplus with the university. At the same time, Milton likes to dine at his favorite Chinese restaurant once a week and thus runs a persistent trade deficit with the restaurant. If we tried to minimize trade deficit in this situation, asked the university to find a more equitable trading partner, and requested Milton to limit his visits to the Chinese restaurant, we would do more harm than good.

Trade is good, as one of our ten economic commandments states, and limiting trade limits the benefit free individuals can enjoy. People should be free, as another economic commandment states, conveys the idea that individuals can decide on their own whom to trade with and how much to trade with each trading partner. Free markets help to allocate the resources to their best possible use, but the assumed goal of balanced trade takes away the resources from its efficient use and uses them inefficiently.

The Bible has several examples of trade between nations.[255] In Genesis 42, Jacob, the grandson of Abraham, sent his sons during the extended drought to trade with the Egyptian pharaoh. Both David and Solomon had a commercial agreement with Hiram, the ruler of the Phoenician city of Tyre. In 2 Samuel 5, with the help of Phoenician carpenters and stonemasons, David acquired cedar logs to build a palace for himself; and in 1 Kings 5, Solomon got the cedar and cypress wood along with the help of skilled foreign workers to build a temple for the Lord.

In Matthew 19:21 (ESV), Jesus addresses a rich young ruler by saying: "go, sell all that you have and give to the poor, and you will have treasure in heaven; and come, follow me." Dr. R. Mark Isaac brings up an interesting point that Jesus inadvertently advocated the markets since selling possessions implied trade and the purpose of trade was to benefit the poor:

Imagine the rich young man showing up at a poor person's home with a gold-threaded camel blanket. What would he or she do with it? Jesus recognizes that the rich young man can better help the poor by selling his goods, presumably in an organized market. This way, he can take advantage of the mutual benefit advantages of the marketplace, maximizing the value of the sales and thus having more money to give to the poor.[256]

Jesus was concerned with the attitude of a young rich ruler toward his possessions and not the market system in general, which possibly contributed to the growth of his possessions.

In sum, trade deficit or surplus is an inevitable part of trade and neither one or the other is indicative of better or worse terms of trade. Since 1980s, the United States has run a consistent trade deficit, which in part was caused by increased government spending, strengthening of the US dollar, and growth of the US economy. International trade has lowered the prices of many goods and services in the United States and improved the well-being of widows and orphans.

Should the Government Allow Outsourcing to Low-Wage Nations?

Outsourcing is the business practice of hiring a foreign supplier to perform services and obtain goods that previously were supplied by the firm's own employees.[257] The primary benefit to the firm is that it can lower its costs; the main critique of this practice is that local jobs are being lost to foreign countries. The practice of outsourcing expanded rapidly in the 1990s, and Michael Corbett estimates that by the early 2000s the average manufacturer outsourced 70–80 percent of its finished product.[258] Manufacturing is not the only industry that has been affected; it also includes IT services, research and development, distribution, call centers, etc.[259] Corbett also finds that outsourcing can increase productivity and competitiveness at least tenfold and in some cases one-hundredfold. He suggests that governments should not view outsourcing as a mere business tactic, but as an essential tool in remaining competitive on the world's stage.

Thomas Friedman, the author of *The World Is Flat: A Brief History of the Twenty-first Century,* writes: "No matter what your profession—doctor, lawyer, architect, accountant—if you are an American, you better be good at the touchy-feely service stuff, because anything that can be digitized can be outsourced to either the smartest or the cheapest producer. . . . When I was growing up, my parents told me, 'Finish your dinner. People in China and India are starving.' I tell my daughters, 'Finish your homework. People in India and China are starving for your job.'"[260]

The phenomenon of outsourcing exists because of the benefits of trade, which are possible when each party utilizes its comparative advantage. Our question of interest involves a low-wage nation, which absorbs a lot of jobs which were previously conducted in a high-wage nation, such as the United States. The benefit these low-wage nations gain is paramount. Even the skilled workers who are paid much less than comparable workers in the United States are still better off than they would be otherwise. For example, Corbett reports that a Java programmer in the United States typically earns $60,000 a year, but the outsourced programmer in India would earn only $5,000 a year, twelve times less.

It seems unfair that a company would pay so much less to a worker just because he or she happens to reside in a foreign country. To understand the reason for the apparent difference in pay, it helps to compare the average income per person in each country. In 2004, GDP per capita in India was $621, but in the United States it was close to $42,000. The average income in India was sixty-eight times less than that in the United States in 2004. This gap has shrunk by more than half over the last fifteen years and based on 2019 data, this gap is now twenty-seven times. A Java programmer in India is definitely better off than the average person in India, even though his wage is well below his American counterpart.

The benefit to unskilled workers in low-wage nations due to outsourcing is similar if not greater. China, as the major trading partner with the United States, has experienced unprecedented growth in its living standards over the last four decades. The graph below illustrates how GDP and GDP per capita grew since the 1980s for both countries.[261]

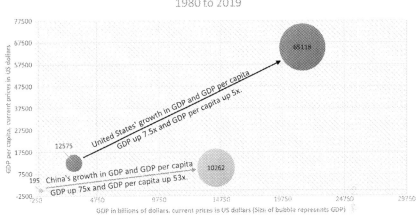

United States versus China: GDP and GDP per Capita Growth over 1980 to 2019

United States' growth in GDP and GDP per capita
GDP up 7.5x and GDP per capita up 5x.

China's growth in GDP and GDP per capita
GDP up 75x and GDP per capita up 53x.

GDP in billions of dollars, current prices in US dollars (Size of bubble represents GDP)

Figure 6

GDP per capita in China increased fifty-fold since 1980, and in the US it increased fivefold over the same period. The size of the economy in China is now comparable to that of the United States, amounting to 14 trillion versus 21 trillion, respectively. Wages of the lowest-paid workers have increased as well, helping to alleviate millions from extreme poverty.

The benefit to a low-wage nation that is engaged in trade can be clearly seen from data, but the question we posed concerns a well-developed economy, such as that of the United States, and whether it benefits from local jobs being outsourced to other countries. We would argue that the United States benefits tremendously from outsourcing, but we also recognize that some jobs are lost and may never come back. Some people lose their jobs for a number of reasons, whether it is due to outsourcing, automation, demand shifts, or innovations in technology. Firms in free-market economies are well aware of competition and its demands on being innovative, responsive to new trends, and expecting change to happen. The pressure is not only on firms but on individuals as well, whose skills may no longer be needed when old positions are eliminated and new ones created. Individuals need to be ready to learn new skills, get more education, or even switch careers. Outsourcing is just one example when the resources are shifted to their best economic use and some jobs are lost while others are created.

Those who lose typically represent a small, concentrated group, but those who gain are widely disbursed. For example, as the manufacturing of furniture has shifted to China, many craftsmen ended up looking for new jobs. The beneficiaries are the consumers who pay lower prices to buy furniture and who may not even realize the reason behind it. However, local manufacturers of furniture are well aware that their jobs are in jeopardy, and they can unite to lobby to be sheltered from foreign competition.

Outsourcing allows firms to lower their costs and focus more on their core business activities. The economic commandments which support our stance are: trade is good, love your neighbor as yourself, and be a Good Samaritan. When we love our neighbors who happen to live in poor countries, we benefit them when trading with them by buying their goods or hiring out their labor. In fact, we are seeding love when we help to improve the welfare of a stranger. Jesus extended love to foreigners and did not discriminate against those who were not part of a Jewish nation. He seeded love to a Samaritan woman by the well. In a vision, Peter was instructed not to call anything impure that God has made clean. That vision became one of the catalysts of the gospel spreading out to Gentiles, described in Acts 10. The Good Samaritan story encourages us to help those in need, regardless of whether they live in our neighborhood or not. By creating jobs overseas, we extend grace and help those in need. By training for new jobs at home, we help those who may lose their jobs due to outsourcing or other changes within a robust economy.

Are Free-Trade Agreements and Trading Blocs Biblical?

Any agreement that promotes free trade between two or more parties is beneficial because of our previously established economic commandment that trade is good. Thus, any agreement that reduces trade barriers and allows for free flow of goods and services across economic and political borders is good.

At a conceptual level, trade agreements can be made at one of three levels based on the number of parties involved. When one country agrees with another country to reduce trade barriers, a bilateral agreement is made. When several countries make an agreement to reduce trade barriers, then a trading bloc is formed, such as NAFTA or the European Union. These countries are typically part of the same geographic region and share some commonalities. NAFTA was ratified by the United States, Canada, and Mexico's national legislatures in 1993 and went into effect on January 1, 1994. Since then, the value of exports from Mexico went from fourteen billion in 1994 to 117 billion in 2019.[262] Canada and Mexico are the second and third largest trading partners for the US, and the relative importance in the share of trade among all three counties has increased since 1994. Canada and Mexico are the top two markets for US exports, with Canada absorbing eighteen percent and Mexico sixteen percent of all US exports.[263] Each country has benefited from increased trade with each other by utilizing its comparative advantages.

The final level of integration includes nations becoming part of the World Trade Organization (WTO) in order to abide by the global rules of trade. The main function of the WTO is to ensure that trade flows as smoothly, predictably, and freely as possible.[264] The WTO came into being in 1995 and is the successor to the General Agreement on Tariffs and Trade (GATT), established shortly after World War II in 1947. GATT was designed to reduce tariffs and facilitate global trade. One approach they implemented is known as the most favored nation (MFN) clause, which was aimed to ensure that no single country would hold a trading advantage over the other. If one country had a more privileged status over the other, the MFN clause required the same concessions, privileges, or immunities to be granted to all other WTO member countries.[265]

In 2019, WTO included 164 members and accounted for 98 percent of world trade. The world map below highlights member states in dark grey.

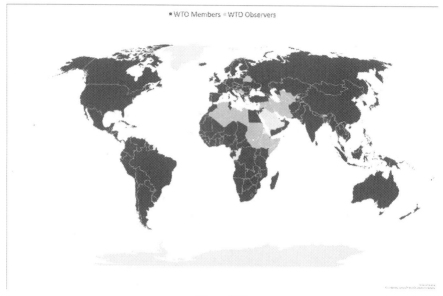

WTO Members WTO Observers

Figure 7[266]

The WTO is headquartered in Geneva, Switzerland and has an annual budget of about $200 million and employs about 630 staff members. They make agreements, which are ratified in all members' parliaments, which means that WTO rules become part of each country's legal system.

The WTO promotes and makes a strong case in support of open trade. On their website, they write: "The data show a definite statistical link between freer trade and economic growth. Economic theory points to strong reasons for the link. All countries, including the poorest, have assets—human, industrial, natural, financial—which they can employ to produce goods and services for their domestic markets or to compete overseas."[267] We agree with this statement. They also highlight the importance of comparative advantage in trade and explain how it is oftentimes a misunderstood concept, since people confuse it with absolute advantage.

As such, the WTO has encountered a lot of criticism and public discontent from those groups who are in favor of more protectionist trade policies. In 1999, a WTO meeting was taking place in Seattle. Street clashes prompted the city's mayor to declare a civil emergency and impose an overnight curfew. About 30,000 labor-union members marched in a display of anti-WTO fervor. Graffiti was spray-painted on buildings, with messages such as "No Sweatshops" and "No WTO." Hard choices were faced by the US government at that time. The conflicts put the Clinton administration into a negotiating box. To placate underdeveloped countries, the US would have to open its market to textile imports, ease up on its strict enforcement of antidumping rules, and back off from its demands that the WTO start looking at labor rights. But to placate the protesters, including thousands of labor-union members, the US needed to do just the opposite: limit textile imports, crack down on dumping, and pursue a labor-rights agenda.

The conflict faced at the WTO meeting more than twenty years ago is still relevant today. Over the last twenty years the US has opted for more open trade with other nations, including developing and least-developed countries (LDCs). WTO agreements contain preferential treatment of developing nations by allowing them more time in implementing their trade agreements and commitments and providing more trading opportunities.[268] Many developed nations took even further steps on reducing tariffs and quotas on imports from LDCs.[269]

However, the US has been reevaluating its position on free trade since Trump took office as president in 2016. In one of the recent *Wall Street Journal* articles, Trump is quoted to have sent the following tweet: "The WTO is BROKEN when the world's RICHEST countries claim to be developing countries to avoid WTO rules and get special treatment. NO more!!!"[270] His criticism is that China—along with other countries such as Turkey, Mexico, the United Arab Emirates, and Qatar—represent leading economies and should not be treated as developing countries, reaping the benefits of the preferential status assigned by the WTO.

The progress in lowering trade barriers and then raising them back is a sign that the world is fallen and in constant need of redemption. The principles which brought the times of relevant prosperity and peace may be forgotten and need to be relearned by each successive generation. In light of our economic commandments, we treat free-trade agreements favorably since they increase the levels of trade and provide for more work opportunities in the respective economies. Free-trade agreements are also consistent with the biblical commandment of loving your neighbor as yourself. By removing trade restrictions, we "benefit" our neighbors in trade by increasing their economic welfare; at the same time, our economic welfare goes up as well.

Chapter 4

Government Policies

The Benevolent Social Planner

The effective benevolent social planner would need to have perfect vision through two "eyes": information and intent. She has neither. It is not a perfect world, and hoping to find a benevolent social planner assumes it is. Thus, social planning denies the fallen nature, which is critical to a Christian worldview of economics. A market is where everyone votes. A benevolent social planner is similar to kings and monarchs and other elites deciding what is best for everyone else. If they're fallen, they make decisions based on what's best for them. That's why social planners are very seldom benevolent: most economic myths stem from a denial of the fallen nature. Social planners are not benevolent, because they are fallen. Christian opposition to these policies flows from the principle that the just price is normally the *market* price.[271]

Social planning is about maximizing power, not maximizing profits. Government doesn't make profits, has no incentive to show profits, and wouldn't know a profit if it hit it in the head. Inside government there are no markets or price mechanisms to act as a divining rod finding hidden productivity. Socialism handcuffs Adam Smith's invisible hand.[272]

Social planning can only exist until the voters exercise their fallen nature and discover that they can vote themselves largess from the public treasury. From that time on the majority always votes for the candidates promising the most benefits from the public treasury, with the results that a democracy always collapses over loose fiscal policy, always followed by a dictatorship.[273]

The first commandment of Christian economics—freedom—is violated in social planning. The social planner takes freedom from individuals and moves decision-making to elite bureaucrats. That loss of freedom is concerning to Christians, who above all other freedoms believe we are free to accept or reject the invitation of Christ.

Social planning also violates the second commandment of Christian economics: work is good. Social planning punishes work by reducing the rewards of work. And it encourages sloth, because people are rewarded for not working.

You can *feel good* about the outcome of social planning, but you can't *think good* about the input. There is no free lunch. The social planner must take from a productive person before it gives to an unproductive one. There are many biblical commands to give, but there is not a biblical command to take. Social planning must take before it can give. We cannot distribute more wealth than is created.[274] Taking is a violation of the third commandment of economics: don't steal. It's also hard to imagine how "loving your neighbor" (the seventh commandment) could be exercised accurately by taking goods from them.

Social planning encourages covetousness, which is a violation of the fourth commandment of Christian economics. Social planners intend to lower the gap between rich and poor, by exercising a "Robin Hood" program of taking from the rich and giving to the poor. This encourages covetousness. In one of their signature comedy routines, Laurel and Hardy quipped, "Why don't we just tell the poor to rob from the rich, and take Robin Hood out of the middle?" In the 1950s, that drew a laugh. Today, there is an assumption that the government should be in the middle, increasing covetous ideas of the poor.

In the first two pages of *The Wisdom of Crowds*,[275] James Surowiecki tells about eighty-five-year-old Francis Galton attending the West of

England Fat Stock and Poultry Exhibition, where he hoped to find support for his ideas of eugenics. "If it works in animals, it should work in people," was Galton's assumption. He missed the point that humans are made in God's image and animals are not. After a contest where people guessed the weight of an ox, he collected the tickets and ran some statistical tests. He expected the guesses to be way off the mark, but he was astounded to find that the average guess missed the true weight of the ox by only one pound. Galton wrote later, "The result seems more creditable to the trustworthiness of a democratic judgment than might have been expected." He had discovered "the wisdom of crowds," according to Surowiecki. Economists call that a market.

Social planners destroy the market by taking away the "vote" of those whose goods are being taken from them, and those to whom the goods are being redistributed. Sixty percent of people under the age of twenty-four voted for a socialist in the last election, but in twenty-five years of teaching, none of Dave's more than five thousand students have asked to redistribute their grade to a student who skipped class. If they don't trust their professor to be a benevolent social planner, why would they trust a nameless, faceless bureaucrat in Washington, DC? Lord Acton famously said, "Power corrupts and absolute power corrupts absolutely." So if we're concerned about power, why on earth would we want to hand more power over to the most powerful entity in human history—the US government? That doesn't make any sense.[276]

Even back in 1960, Wilhelm Röpke wrote the following :

> If it is liberal to entrust economic order, not to planning, coercion, and penalties, but to the spontaneous and free co-operation of people through the market, price, and competition, and at the same time to regard property as the pillar of this free order, then I speak as a liberal when I reject social planning. The technique of socialism-that is, economic planning, nationalization, the erosion of property, and the cradle-to-the-grave welfare state—has done great harm in our times; on the other hand, we have the

irrefutable testimony of the last fifteen years, particularly in Germany, that the opposite-the liberal-technique of the market economy opens the way to wellbeing, freedom, the rule of law, the distribution of power, and international co-operation. These are the facts, and they demand the adoption of a firm position *against* the socialist and *for* the liberal kind of economic order.[277]

If there is any support for social planning in the Ten Commandments of Christian Economics, it's found in number 8: take care of widows and orphans, and in number 10: honor those in power. First, the widows and orphans. It's quite easily understood that most Christians believe the church should take care of widows and orphans. There is a segment of believers who read the Scriptures and then tell us that the government should take care of them. Government has replaced the church's mission in caring for the poor. While the rise of government programs may have exacerbated the church's retreat, they were not the primary cause. Theology matters, and the church needs to rediscover a Christ-centered, fully orbed perspective of the kingdom.[278] Totalitarian governments tend to act in their own interest, so they distinguish the benevolence system of charity, through which people help themselves. Then individuals are dependent on the government for their sustenance.

Honoring those in power requires Christians to go along with what their government requires. But it certainly does not mean that Christians find support for government social planning in the Scriptures. As Jesus taught, Christians were prepared to "render unto Caesar the things that are Caesar's"—they were not rebels in that sense—but they refused to render to Caesar the things that were God's. This amounts to a *de facto* insistence on limited government,[279] which most Christian economists would suggest. The political system is more ably manipulated by the influential than by the poor, so there is no reason to presume that the result of government redistribution would be to aid the least among us. Rather, such political schemes all too often result in legal theft by the influential.[280]

In 1978, Henry Hazlitt wrote, "Coincident with the extraordinary growth of these welfare expenditures has been the development of a 'national welfare industry.'"[281] It was a cottage industry in 1978. In 2020, it's become a thriving industry that relies on reducing freedom, distributing pork, stealing, and covetousness to further its goal.

Jay Richards says it well, "Socialism only works in heaven, where they don't need it, and in hell where they already have it."[282]

Should the Government Set a Minimum Wage?

Minimum wage causes the two evils of macroeconomics: inflation and unemployment.

Inflation hurts the poor more than the rich, because the poor are forced to make daily purchases of necessities like diapers and milk from the daily market at inflated prices. The rich can delay purchases, and they have the ability to protect themselves from inflation by investing in stocks, gold, and land that rise with inflation.

The unemployment argument is easy: when the price goes up, demand goes down. Minimum wages cause unemployment. The only question is "How much?"

Minimum wage removes freedom—the first commandment of biblical economics—from both employers and prospective employees. The government steps in between the buyer and seller of labor and demands a minimum wage. If the minimum wage is fifteen dollars, prospective workers who can only produce $14.99 an hour are discriminated out of the workplace. Minimum wage laws replace cooperation with coercion, since they make it a crime for individual employers and employees to enter freely into agreements for work and wages.[283]

That also makes minimum wage a violation of our second commandment: work is good. Minimum wage arbitrarily commands that only work creating value in excess of fifteen dollars an hour is good; other work is not good. Despite the devout and painstaking intellectual work of some of the best minds of all time, including Thomas Aquinas, no one has ever given a satisfactory answer regarding what determines a just level for wages.[284]

In a PragerU video titled "The Correct Minimum Wage," David Henderson states, "'The right minimum wage: $0.00.' That was a headline in *The New York Times* on January 14, 1987. The story went on, 'There's a virtual consensus among economists that the minimum wage is an idea whose time has passed.'"[285] But self-serving politicians continue to dredge up the old idea that labor should be controlled by government fiat. *Policies that promote production is all that separates rich from poor nations.* Minimum wage does not promote production. It stifles production, because it discriminates against workers who can't produce value above the minimum wage. These are the poor whom we Christians care about. Raising the minimum wage benefits those lucky individuals who keep their minimum-wage jobs, but it decreases the number of such jobs in the future. And it may end up keeping minimum-wage workers at their current wage level for longer periods of time without salary raises. Furthermore, since the holders of minimum-wage jobs may not be from low-income families—they may be the children or spouses of primary earners who make higher incomes—the minimum wage may not be effective at helping poor families.[286]

As we're writing this book, Congress is considering the Raise the Wage Act, which would set a fifteen-dollar minimum wage by 2024. The trade-offs from this legislation are even worse than what David Henderson cited in 2014. The Congressional Budget Office finds a fifteen-dollar minimum wage would pull 1.3 million workers out of poverty—at the cost of 1.3 million jobs in the median scenario, and 3.7 million jobs in the worst-case scenario. Put differently, as many as three people would lose their jobs for each person no longer in poverty. The CBO's conclusions, based on a review of dozens of empirical studies, even suggest that the title of the Democrats' bill is a misnomer. The Raise the Wage Act would reduce real family income by nine billion dollars once phased in, as reductions in employment (among other impacts) offset the increase in some workers' pay.[287]

Minimum wage deprives society of the value of a man's services. We have deprived people of the independence and self-respect that come from self-support, even at a low level, and from performing wanted work. At the same time as we have lowered what the man could have received by his own efforts.[288]

So, do Christians favor allowing people to work at slave wages? That's a rather illegitimate question, because slaves don't earn wages. And, if the question is about whether labor should be controlled, minimum wage controls labor, so it is a step toward slave labor. Free labor can work at any wage. Unfree labor is controlled by a price mechanism called the minimum wage. Thus, state-enforced minimum wages violate the first commandment of biblical economics: people should be free.

We cannot in the long run pay labor as a whole more than it produces.[289] Thus, minimum wage is also a violation of the fifth biblical commandment of economics: use honest measures. It's not honest to pay fifteen dollars when the worker is creating fourteen dollars in value.

Think about it this way: You can load an airplane with fuel and it can work against the laws of gravity for a few hours. When it runs out of fuel, it must return to the physical laws of equilibrium and return to the earth, where the gravity on the top of the plane is equal to the weight of the wheels on the tarmac. Businesses have the same types of rules in economics. You can load a coffee shop with dollars and it can work against minimum wage for some prescribed amount of time. But it is "burning dollars" each hour, just as the plane is burning fuel. Eventually, the coffee shop will be forced to return to economic equilibrium, which we call the equilibrium wage. That's where buyers will buy and sellers will sell labor. Economists understand this, and they are almost uniformly opposed to any law that would artificially determine wage rates apart from market forces.[290] That's because they understand that real wages come out of production, not out of government decrees.[291]

Raising the wage above its equilibrium level will result in a surplus of labor. An equilibrium wage is where everyone, all suppliers and demanders, "vote" on the proper wage. Each day, thousands of businesses demand labor at a wage they freely set. Each day, thousands of widows and orphans supply labor at the wage they freely demand. The result of all these votes each day is the equilibrium wage.

The equilibrium wage works to allocate the economy's resources most efficiently without government's intervention or coercion from any single private party. This equilibrium wage varies for different job markets and adjusts in response to changing market conditions, as demanders and suppliers of work cast their "votes." Any deviation from this equilibrium causes unemployment or shortages of labor and carries an additional social cost that economists define as a deadweight loss. A deadweight loss equals the value of lost transactions due to price controls or taxes. With respect to the minimum wage, the deadweight loss equals the social value of all the jobs, in which the laborers would be willing to work for wages below the fixed minimum. In this case, setting the minimum wage infringes on the right of the workers by limiting their choices.

Without minimum wage, honest measures—the fifth commandment of biblical economics—prevail. The equilibrium wage rate acts as a very powerful signal that labor is "needed" more in some sectors and less in others, and that demand for some skills has risen while demand for other skills has fallen. Without such signals it would be extremely difficult, costly, and time-consuming for anyone (including government) to acquire enough information to guide workers from one industry or region to another, or students from one career into another.[292] Thus, minimum wage is a dishonest measure.

First Timothy 5:18 (NASB) reads: "The laborer is worthy of his wages." Other translations use "deserves" or "should be given." This and other similar passages are consistent with portraying God as being just and who cares that the worker is rewarded for his labor. It is less clear from Scripture regarding fair wages or whether there should be minimum wages for someone's work. In the parable of the workers in the vineyard from Matthew 20:1–16, Jesus describes a landowner who agrees on a certain pay with some workers, while other workers are just reassured that the payment will be right. At the end of the day every worker gets paid the same, regardless of the time that each laborer worked. The workers who labored more grumble about this apparent injustice, and the landowner has to remind the workers that he paid what he promised and it's not their business if he decides to be generous with the others. One underlying principle addressed in this story is that the landowner and the workers enter into their agreement freely and have clear expectations about the scope of work and the appropriate pay. The landowner also has the right to pay more than what would be considered fair.

Biblical commandment of economics number six reads: trade is good. Minimum wage constrains trade. It disallows low-level workers from trading their labor for goods. Labor unions like higher minimum wages, since they make it more costly for employers to hire less-skilled workers who have to be trained.[293] But unionized workers benefit indirectly from higher minimum-range rates because the higher rate makes it more expensive for employers to replace one union worker with two minimum-wage employees.[294] This locks out the poor and the underskilled and keeps them out of the dignity of producing value that would enable them to take care of themselves. The terrible irony of all minimum-wage laws is that they hurt the very people who are most disadvantaged, such as teens and minority workers. Those are the people least able to defend themselves against well-meaning legislators who support such laws at their expense.

Minimum wage does not take care of widows and orphans—the eighth commandment of biblical economics; it discriminates against them. They are the less visible losers. They include workers who are let go, communities who lose businesses to other areas without such laws and taxpayers (who must now pay more for services contracted by the city or other government body). The majority of losers, though, are invisible to the public, because they are people who will not be able to get a job or the job of their choice.[295] They are the widows and orphans that Christians are commanded to show discretion toward.

Thus, a good intention to help the poor creates an unintended consequence of making it harder for widows and orphans to find work. The laborer is worthy of his wages, and the equilibrium wage is arguably the most equitable way to compensate the laborer for his work. Raising the minimum wage forces employers to fire widows and orphans who have the least skill level, training, or experience.

Distress is bad. Eustress is good. We would like to suggest there are three levels of stress among our college students. At the lowest level, a student feels so little stress that he doesn't get out of bed to come to class. That's not a healthy level of stress. At the extreme other end is distress, where a student can't enter the economics classroom. That's also unhealthy. Between these extremes is something called "eustress." That's good stress. The student comes to class just a little nervous about the content of that day's quiz. We want our students to have eustress, because we have it each time we enter a classroom. We are concerned about how the class will go. That's good. We're concerned that many people have eustress, but they consider it distress.

The Wall Street Journal, August 27, 2017, told the story of a woman working at a McDonald's in St. Louis. The municipal minimum wage of ten dollars had been overruled by a state-level wage of $7.70, causing her wages to decline. The weekly income of Bettie Douglas was reduced about $63 a week—money she said had allowed her to get her water turned back on and buy school supplies for her son.[296] Some would consider that loss of $63 distress. It would be more properly considered eustress. We want our students to have eustress about each week's quiz, whether they will pass our economics courses, about graduating and getting a job. It's eustress that encourages them to attend class, successfully pass classes, and makes them graduates of the university. We want Bettie Douglas and every other minimum-wage worker to have the same eustress. We want her to be concerned about how she will pay for her son's school supplies. That encourages her to seek promotions at the McDonald's where she works. She might become line manager, then assistant manager, and maybe someday, manager. That's what we call "policies that promote production." If Ms. Douglas has no stress, she won't move up. Moving up is good. As a society, we want minimum-wage workers to have eustress.

Does Rent Control Lower the Housing Cost for the Poor?

In chapter 2, we wrote about what Nicole Gelinas of the Manhattan Institute said in a PragerU video, "One economist said rent control is the most effective way to destroy a city, other than bombing."[297] The *Journal of Economics* reported that 93 percent of economists agree that it results in a lower quality and quantity of housing. Then why do cities continue to use it? It's a classic case of seeing the intended positive outcome for renters, while denying the negative incentive for the owners. In 1978 Hazlitt wrote, "They continue rent control in the face of the obvious devastation it has caused."[298]

As we will see in many economic policies, it limits the first commandment of biblical economics: people should be free. The landlord loses her freedom to charge the market price for rental property. Instead, a governmental entity intrudes between the buyer and seller, distorting the equilibrium price, where both want to make an exchange. The natural consequence of price controls is a petrified totalitarian economy, with every business firm and every worker at the mercy of the government, and with a final abandonment of all the traditional liberties we have known.[299]

The outcome of rent control serves as a warning to us to be suspicious of political and economic programs that claim they can bring solutions to problems of human need. It is also a warning concerning the dangers of concentrations of political and economic power.[300] If the bureaucratic committee who determined rent control levels was free of self-interest, it would work just fine. They're not, and the scheme is a political mess of fallen people serving their own self-interest at the expense of landlords and widows and orphans seeking low-level rents.

The fourth commandment of biblical economics—don't covet—is violated by rent control. Renters covet the housing of others, and want to have what they can't afford. If they can get the governmental entity to engage on their behalf, they get to exercise their covetousness at the expense of the landlord.

Rent control violates the fifth commandment of biblical economics: use honest measures. Under rent control, the rent that is paid is not honest. It is determined by a bureaucratic committee and does not reflect the market price. That's not an honest price.

What's often missed is who else "pays" for rent control: potential renters (widows and orphans) who want to rent at market prices but can't. That's because rent control freezes the level of rent of existing housing. That acts as a disincentive to maintain and modernize the units, so the quality suffers. It also disincentivizes the building of low-cost rentals, because they can't compete with the rent-controlled units. Thus, new housing is built only to meet the higher end of the market, leaving widows and orphans with no available rental space. Price-fixing begins a discriminatory price-fixing which gives most to those groups that are politically powerful and least to other groups.[301]

After rent control fails, the politicians denounce the capitalist system as having failed again, stating, "Private enterprise cannot do the job"; therefore, the state must step in and build low-rent housing.[302] That low-rent housing is not ruled by the market, so it falls into disrepair, and the politicians step in again to create another program. If they would just leave the market alone, rental housing would be in ample supply at reasonable prices, just like about every other item we buy on a daily basis.

Should Saving Be Encouraged?

John Wesley said, "Earn all you can, give all you can, save all you can." Noticeably absent from his advice is the encouragement to "spend all you can." This is at the heart of the demand-side hypothesis: That demanders should spend more to keep the economy growing. Even well-known supply-siders like President George W. Bush, after 9/11 encouraged Americans, "Get down to Disney World in Florida. Take your families and enjoy life, the way we want it to be enjoyed." While part of his message was to restore faith in air travel, he also clearly was encouraging Americans to spend money, assuming it was their responsibility to sustain a growing economy.

The fourth commandment of biblical economics is "don't covet." Covetousness, or "keeping up with the Joneses," is an exercise in spending more than you make, which causes negative saving. That's why many marketing campaigns are designed to appeal to the consumers' covetousness. They continue to remind us that the car we drive, the clothes we wear, and the beverages we drink contribute to our standing in society. They encourage us to covet the lifestyles of others, which requires spending more than we make. That's negative saving, or borrowing.

In the past, economists have shown that the saving policy that was in the best interests of the individual was also in the best interests of the nation. They showed that the rational saver, in making provision for his future, was not hurting, but helping, the whole community. But today the ancient virtue of thrift is under attack, while the opposite doctrine of spending is in fashion.[303] That was true when Hazlitt first wrote it in 1946, and even more true today.

If we love our neighbor, as commanded in the seventh commandment of biblical economics, we want her to have lower interest rates to borrow and build her business. We do so by increasing the savings rate. It's simple economics that an increase in savings lowers the interest rate for borrowers. That enables businesses to add new products, new locations, and to hire new employees. That grows the economy.

If you're going to be a Good Samaritan, as called for in the ninth commandment of biblical economics, you will have to save. That's because you can only help others out of your savings. If you intend to help others from the savings of others, that's not biblical, and it is not economically sustainable.

Conclusion

God wants us to have as much freedom as possible, in a fallen world. The government policies analyzed in this chapter limit that freedom, so Christians should not support those policies. This is summarized in chapter 1: In a fallen world, we assume that everyone is fallen: business-men and women, as well as government bureaucrats. But in the competitive environment of business, the fallen nature is controlled. In the monopolistic environment of government control, the fallen nature is encouraged.

Chapter 5

Markets Work

In a Fallen World, Should Regulations Be Increased or Decreased?

Christian ethics is opposed to regulatory regimes that either by design or in practice nullify economic freedom. Between these polarities of no regulation and endless regulation, however, there is considerable room for Christians to debate among themselves and with non-Christians the scope, character, and fairness of varying forms of economic regulation and other forms of government intervention.[304]

The Obama administration added more than six hundred "big regulations," measured by the Congressional Budget Office as costing over $100 million each. President George W. Bush added about 350. Regulations don't create value, they consume value—and, they favor big companies who help write the regulations and have the scale capacity to abide by them. They hurt widows and orphans who have to pay for the regulations and get blocked from jobs because of them. " The only people who benefit are the progressive elite, who by controlling government gain more control over society."[305]

The Federal Register is the daily repository of all proposed and final federal rules and regulations. It is not a perfect measure of regulation's scope but does provide a perspective on the regulatory activity. At the end of 2016, the number of Federal Register pages stood at 95,894, an increase of 19.4 percent from the previous year. The earliest record on the number of pages goes back to 1936, which stood at 2,620 pages. The growth in the number of new or proposed rules is alarming. Economist Clyde Wade Crews estimates the cost of enforcement and compliance to these regulations to be about $1.8 trillion. That is just below the value of all annualized corporate profits in the United States reported in the first quarter of 2017.

> The morass of big government regulation chokes economic growth. Approximately 350,000 more federal regulations existed in 2016 than in 1989. The cost of this regulatory web amounted to more than two trillion dollars each year. The Obama administration added some 20,642 new regulations in 2015 alone, at a cost of more than $22 billion annually. The Mercatus Center estimated that government regulation had caused a 25 percent reduction in the US economy from 1980 to 2012. This amounted to a loss in real income of approximately $13,000 for every American. The Mercatus Center also found that federal regulations are about six to eight times more costly for low-income households than for high-income ones.[306]

What does the Bible say about regulations? For one, the Holy Scriptures are filled with various rules and regulations. The most prominent set of rules is outlined in the Ten Commandments. In general, each commandment or rule is consistent with protection of human life, private property, or widows and orphans.

> The foundational argument underlying big government is a myth. Big government does not help the poor, the working class, and the middle class, even though those groups provide the justification for big government. In fact, big government

often hurts the supposed beneficiaries of government largesse. Those who gain the most from big government are the elite and the powerful.[307]

One issue with the growing number of government regulations is the cost of compliance. It is of particular concern to small businesses, which cannot absorb the rising costs of compliance as easily as the larger firms can. Many smaller businesses are started by immigrants who came to the US in hopes of increasing their standard of living by "loving their neighbor" when they provide goods and services for their local community.

The existence of too many rules has led one Bible scholar to observe that "the primary cause of poverty in the Old Testament is oppression and injustice, with natural disasters and sloth (particularly in Proverbs) much less significant."[308] Humans are fallen. They want control over their business environment and their fellow man. Economic regulations allow that type of control.

Regulations favor special interest groups who write them. A branch of economics called public choice applies the theories and methods of economics to the analysis of political behavior. It suggests that politicians are not benevolent "public servants" who strive to promote the common good, but fallen individuals who are guided by their own self-interest.

We can learn a lesson from the ancient Israelites, who went to their prophet Samuel and requested a king like the other nations that lived around them. Samuel issued a dire warning, summarized 1 Samuel 8:14–18. Samuel tried to dissuade the people from electing a regulatory king by emphasizing that the new authority would oppress the people and take away their personal property. In hindsight, we should heed the same warning since as the power and authority of an ancient king was often used against its own people, so can it be abused today by a growing government.

While some level of regulations is certainly necessary in a fallen world, our view is that a lower level of regulation is more biblical than a higher level. Now, we consult the Ten Commandments of Economics for advice.

Freedom

Lower levels of regulation produce more freedom for individuals in a society, and that's what the Bible favors. But in a fallen world, too much freedom turns into chaos. Among the polar extremes of not enough freedom versus too much freedom, generally, free-market capitalism is favored. That's because it is "a system in which bad people can do the least harm, and good people have the freedom to do good works."[309]

Lightly regulated free markets are, as Victor Claar and Robin Lunn have argued, "one way in which God's providence works to sustain and bless humankind."[310] We believe God's providence guards and guides a society that honors biblical principles. When that happens, God's providence provides for the growth of the economy, love of neighbors, and allows the church to take care of widows and orphans, and allows individuals to be Good Samaritans. In *Christians and Economics*, Kerby Anderson states the case concisely, "The primary function of government is to set the rules and provide a means of redress."[311]

Lower levels of regulation are epitomized in the charter school movement. "The charter school movement has many supporters in minority communities due to built-in incentives: they must attract students by offering better education than traditional public schools."[312] Thus, the market works. Sweden and Denmark are often seen as socialist states, but in Sweden the family of every child is allowed to use their voucher system to send their children to a private school. Twenty percent of Danish students attend private school, even though a very high tax rate produces quality schools. These low levels of regulation explain why Denmark is #14 on the Heritage Index of Economic Freedom and Sweden is #19, just below the US at #12.

> There is a profound ethical reason why an economy governed by free prices, markets, and free competition implies health and plenty, while the socialist economy means sickness, disorder, and lower productivity. The liberal economic system releases and utilizes the extraordinary forces inherent

in individual self-assertion, whereas the socialist system sup-
presses them and wears itself out in opposing them.[313]

Work Is Good

"Hernando de Soto had students try to open a small garment shop with
one worker in Lima, Peru. The team worked six hours a day, and it took
289 days to get the permit. The cost was about three years' salary."[314]
This level of regulation discourages work. When a high level of regulation discourages work, people stop doing it. It's very simple: People seek
their own self-interest. If the rules of society encourage work, they will
do it, but in the Peruvian case, work was discouraged by the high level
of regulation.

Regulation discourages work in many of its other forms as well. Minimum wage, taxation, tariffs, and labor unions are just a few examples
that are more carefully explained in other chapters of this book.

Don't Covet

Firms covet the goods and market power of other firms, so they participate in concentrating their industry. In *The False Promise of Big Government:
How Washington Helps the Rich and Hurts the Poor*, Patrick Garry explains the
self-reinforcing cycle of government and big business. When Republicans
are in power, they adopt a laissez-faire attitude, and business chooses to
concentrate power via acquisitions. Then, when Democrats are in power,
they want to control business. It's easier to control an industry dominated
by five big giants than an industry fractured among hundreds of small
competitors. The Obama administration found this easy to do, when they
invited the heads of five large insurance companies into the White House
and made a deal that the entire industry had to follow. Garry adds:

> Another prevailing myth holds that big business opposes big
> government. But just the reverse is true. Big corporations sup-
> port big government. They are comfortable with increased regu-
> lation precisely because it hinders their competitors, making it

harder for new businesses to form and for smaller firms to compete against bigger ones. Huge corporations can afford the costs of complying with regulations. Furthermore, the biggest businesses can afford expensive lobbyists to manipulate government bureaucracies to act in their interests. And the more corporate welfare that big government doles out to big business, the more allegiance and complicity that big government acquires from big business.[315]

As an industry becomes concentrated, it moves from perfect competition to an oligopoly to a monopoly. Monopolies develop for two reasons: too little government and too much government.[316]

> With the spread of deregulation in advanced economies over the 1980s and 1990s, we would expect differences between the pay of men and women to have diminished. This is because regulation tends to insulate firms from competition, allowing them to charge higher-than-competitive consumer prices in industries like transportation, utilities, and banking. In an iterating study of the banking industry, Black confirms this expectation by showing that shrinkage of the pay gap between women and men in banking began in the mid-1970s, when deregulation shook up the industry.[317]

Trade Is Good

Among the many regulations that limit trade are tariffs and import taxes, as explained in chapter 3. When there is free trade, both parties get richer. When trade is regulated, one party gets richer, while the other has smaller gains. Where free markets exist, producer and consumer surplus enriches both markets. But where markets are controlled, regulators have used the power granted to them to enrich themselves at the expense of the other party. "It is not the free market that is the problem but the sinful behavior of individuals" who rig the market to their advantage.[318]

Love Your Neighbor

Adam Smith wrote that the free-market economy is driven not by greed, but by love of self. This brings to mind the two great commands from Mark 12:30–31, "'Love the Lord your God with all your heart and with all your soul and with all your mind and with all your strength.' The second is this: 'Love your neighbor as yourself'" (Mark 12:30–31). We make no apology for repeating this scripture many times in this book, because we agree with Adam Smith: That is the animating motivation of free markets.

If you love your neighbor as yourself, you will want both parties to be subject to regulations that make the exchange fair. As Claar and Klay point out that markets "are not primary vehicles for rampant materialism. In fact, they support the highest forms of cultural and spiritual expression."[319] That expression is the love for both parties.

Despite fears that markets undermine communities and convert human relations into opportunities for individuals to profit at the expense of others, the research shows that "participants in the market system interact with and enjoy a wider circle of interactions than did their ancestors in pre-market societies."[320] This is perfectly consistent with the functioning of free markets as providing love for others and self.

Lowering the Cost of Food: Government Dictate or Free-Market Competition?

Disposable income spent on food in the US has gone from fourteen percent in 1960 to under six percent today. That's remarkable. I often remind my students, "Food comes first." It's a necessity. But if 90 percent of the population is involved in producing food, like it was in the US in 1800, there would be only ten percent of the population free to make other goods. The percentage went to 60 percent in 1900 and today, 2.5 percent of the US population produces more food than we can eat, so much of it is exported.

The government's contribution to the great increase in the efficiency of farming is almost zero. It's all due to competitive market forces driving up the efficiency of farming and driving down the prices of food commodities. There is a limited amount of land, and God isn't making any more. But he *is* making creative humans who find ways to use it more efficiently. So we need to encourage "the making of more humans," not the writing of more regulations.

In the important book *For God and Profit*, Samuel Gregg writes, "There is something fundamentally wrong with allowing people to be capitalists in good times and socialists in bad times."[321] Gregg's quote could be applied to socialists cheering on the War on Poverty in the 1960s, then buying and consuming cheap food sixty years later that has been produced not by governmental intervention but by the power of free markets.

Food comes first. But in the twenty-first century, food is so plentiful and so cheap that availability of food is assumed. That's because the market has increased the supply. In the small number of cases where there is hunger in the world, "Attempts to 'correct' the results of the market in the direction of 'social justice' have probably produced more injustice in the form of new privileges, obstacles to mobility and frustration of efforts than they have contributed to the alleviation of the lot of the poor."[322]

Utopians are continually reminding us about social justice and "a living wage." As explained in chapter 1, Christians don't believe in perfection. So as these amateur writers on economics are always asking for "just" prices and "just" wages, we should be reminded that these nebulous conceptions of economic justice come down to us from medieval times. "How are we to know precisely when labor does not have enough to buy back the product? Or when it has more than enough? How are we to determine just what the right sum is?"[323] Hazlitt had it right in 1946: the "best" price is where everyone votes. That's the competitive free market. Price-setting has never worked, and it never will work because a well-meaning price-setter would have to have perfect vision through two "I"s: perfect information and perfect intent. No one has this perfect vision. That's why the best prices are set by popular vote, which economics recognize in the market.

Equilibrium wages and prices are the wages and prices that equalize supply and demand. The best prices are not the highest prices but the prices that encourage the largest volume of production and the largest volume of sales. "The best wage rates for labor are not the highest wage rates, but the wage rates that permit full production, full employment, and the largest sustained payrolls."[324]

> The best way of alleviating long-term poverty is not giv-
> ing people money (and welfare) but providing opportunities
> through markets for them to provide for themselves. In the
> last twenty years, twenty-five countries have virtually elimi-
> nated poverty within their borders in this fashion.[325]

The Index of Economic Freedom makes it very clear: where free markets exist, people get richer. The lack of biblical support for price controls is confirmed by Anne Bradley and Art Lindsley, "Nowhere in Scripture . . . do we find the state engaged in welfare programs."[326]

"In politics, the pie is fought over to determine who gets what portion of the pie: in the market, the pie can grow."[327] Father Sirico is right. From automobile emissions to aircraft safety to food price setting, the government fails miserably, because all the government can do is divide the pie. It has no means for growing the pie. This is an interesting thought experiment: In true socialism, the government would own all of the means of production and distribution. Since the producers would be charged with producing goods and services at the lowest price, where would profits come from? There wouldn't be any.

In *Economic Shalom*, John Bolt points to "the rise and fall of [three] retail giants"—A&P, Montgomery Ward, and Kmart: "Their failure proves that markets and open competition work, and that is to say nothing yet about the enormous benefits to consumers from retailers such as Walmart."[328] Walmart is surviving quite well, indeed. But why did the other three firms fail? Because they didn't align themselves with the market environment. In a free market, everyone votes, and consumers voted against those three. In the process, they were voting for their competitors: Walmart, Amazon, and Target.

"Producers compete with each other, yes, but it is a competition in serving others in an ever more excellent way. This is not a dog-eat-dog situation, but rather a system that incentivized service to others."[329] The supplier who serves her customers best wins the customer," without government interference. "Thanks to its corporate purchasing power, Walmart has been an enormous blessing for the consumer," producing $2,300 worth of consumer surplus for each family in the United States.[330] They don't do this because an ever-present government regulator forces them to do so. It's the opposite: they do it because they are relatively unregulated.

We might be told that the Bible does not support markets, but it does. Sometimes it's in obvious ways, other times it's more subtle, as in

> Matthew 19:21 (ESV): "go, sell all that you have and give to the poor and you will have treasure in heaven; and come follow me." Jesus specifically directs the young man to use the market to unload his possessions. Most strikingly, Jesus could have said, but did not say, "Go give all of your possessions to the poor." What is the difference? To an economist there is all the difference in the world.[331]

Also in the Acts 2:44–45 "all things in common" scripture, it says that believers sold land. "This clearly shows that the selling of property and laying the proceeds at the feet of the apostles was not a systematically enforced program; rather, it was more something which people did of their own accord to support the community."[332] And they did it in the market.

> In order to show that Acts teaches socialism, you would have to show that the passage teaches state control of communal money, abolishment of private property rights, voluntary

giving replaced by state coercion, and government ownership of production and distribution—and that they are endorsed in the rest of Scripture.[333]

Goods are going to get distributed. Adam Smith called it "the desire to truck and barter." We only have two choices: to distribute goods via free markets, or controlled markets. Paul Heyne points out the value of markets to the poor: "The rise of market systems has arguably conferred its largest benefits on the poor, making the poverty of those who are least well-off under a market system the envy of people in societies where markets have not flourished."[334]

Free markets or controlled markets: the choice is ours. The Bible clearly tells us to allow producers and consumers to have freedom. It's the same kind of freedom we exercise when we knock on the door. Don't miss the two themes of freedom and eating in this scripture: "Behold, I stand at the door and knock. If anyone hears My voice and opens the door, I will come in to him and eat with him, and he with Me" (Revelation 3:20, NKJV).

Chapter 6

Taxes

What Is the Purpose of Taxes?

We established in chapter 2 that the purpose of taxes was to provide services that the voters demanded of their government. In that light, we hold up the Ten Commandments of Biblical Economics as a lens for determining their relationship to biblical theology. Matthew 22:19–21 reads:

> "Show me the coin used for paying the tax." They brought him a denarius, and he asked them, "Whose image is this? And whose inscription?"
>
> "Caesar's," they replied.
>
> Then he said to them, "So give back to Caesar what is Caesar's, and to God what is God's."

This familiar scripture about paying taxes seems to indicate that we should pay them. "Taxes are the fee for living in a free society," said Oliver Wendell Holmes Jr. But as they become higher, taxes deny individuals the ability to perform our biblical command to give. And often, taxing authorities then use the taxes to care for the widows and orphans that *we* are commanded to take care of.

Economists are tempted to put the emphasis on the wrong portion of this passage. We like to use it as a justification for taxing, and perhaps that is correct. But the most interesting part of this passage is the conversation about "image." Meaning: The denarius was made in man's image, so it should be given over to Caesar. Humans are made in God's image, so humans should be given to God. This is consistent with the Christian worldview we explained in chapter 1: humans are creative because we're made in the image of the Creator.

But let's return to the discussion of taxes. "Nowhere in the New Testament does Jesus advocate for the government to punish the rich or even to use tax money to help the poor."[335] So the purpose of taxes is to operate the governmental mechanism. It's not to redistribute wealth. It's worth repeating Reed's statement: "Nowhere in the New Testament does Jesus advocate using tax money to help the poor." This should shake your world in 2020, where it is so often assumed that the purpose of government is to help the poor. Eighty-three percent of economists agree with the statement, "The redistribution of income in the United States is a legitimate role for the government."[336] This is perhaps one of the most critical ways in which Christians are called to be countercultural. Our New Testament does not teach us to use the government to help the poor. It teaches *us* to do it: individually, and through the church.

Before our students take economics, they think that taxes are simply a transfer of money from individuals and corporations to the government. That's not the whole story. Each dollar that gets transferred has a deadweight loss effect. It is more than a simple transfer. When the price is artificially inflated by taxes, consumers buy fewer products, and suppliers bring a small quantity to the market. We all get poorer, not just by the money transferred to the government, but also by the loss in the quantity of goods demanded and supplied.

Deadweight loss impacts both suppliers and buyers. Suppliers bring fewer products to the market, because they make less on each item. The price is artificially increased for consumers, so they buy fewer goods. That's deadweight loss. Consumers pay higher prices and get fewer goods. The higher the taxes, the more deadweight loss there is. Thus, a Christian economist would want to limit taxes to providing just the basic services required to maintain a free society, and would allow individuals to maintain ownership of as much income as possible, because it is only in the hands of individuals that value is created for our neighbors. Government cannot do it. Government cannot grow the pie; it can only divide the pie that's already been created by free-market capitalists.

Government has no money of its own. It cannot create value, it can only take it from one person and give it to another. There is no biblical command to take. There are many commands for individuals to give; more on that later. The free market is the only thing that can create value, and it is the only thing that has pulled people out of poverty.

Freedom

Taxes reduce freedom, but they are taxes that are agreed to by the group. Thus, we tend to view taxes as a necessary evil. And they're not evil if they are consistent with the demand of voters, as we will explain in the next section.

In the Christian worldview, we seek a midpoint between two extremes. On the "statist collectivism" end of the spectrum there is no freedom at all, because the state owns all of the means of production and distribution. That's a governmental tyranny that occurs in very few countries in our age; North Korea and Cuba come as close as we can find. At the "radical autonomy" end of the spectrum, there is a tyranny of individual freedom, because individuals have too much freedom.[337] It's in that midpoint where we find Christian economics. We believe that taxes do restrain freedom, but the services they buy: Military, police, and fire protection, among the most noticeable, protect freedom. Thus, Christians favor taxing that increases freedom.

Work Is Good

If work is good, it should not be discouraged by government policies. Many times in this book, we return to the phrase "policies that promote production," as a determinant of rich and poor nations. Income tax discourages work, so it's not the favorite tax from our Christian point of view. Consumption taxes, like the Value Added Tax and sales tax, are more attractive to our worldview because they penalize consumption, not production. Taxes that lower production, like income tax, discourage work.

It's a rather simple equation: we must have some form of supporting governmental activity. Something has to be subject to economic punishment. We choose between punishing labor or consumption. A brief reading of Scripture tells us that labor is more important to God than consumption, so we should protect labor from punishment and punish consumption.

In *Atlas Shrugged*,[338] Ayn Rand paints the picture of a future where collectivist statism controls much of American life. She even uses the phrase "fair shares" that was used extensively by President Barack Obama. Her book forces us to ask the question, "When will Atlas shrug?" Her point is that taxes discourage work. If we as Christians believe work is good, we don't want it discouraged.

Don't Steal

Christians argue about the extent, prudence, and justice of different forms of taxation; we will discuss those different levels and forms of taxation later in this chapter. But Christian ethics has never viewed taxation per se as theft.[339] Theft is taking something without returning anything of value. When taxes return something of value, it's not theft. When taxes do not provide something of value to the person being taxed, it could be considered theft.

Honest Measures

Taxes should have two maxims: efficiency and equity. Efficiency minimizes the cost of complying with the rules of taxation. When taxing systems are complex, like the IRS tax code, it causes distortions in the economy as taxpayers try to avoid the taxes. Much of the complexity of the IRS code, at 74,608 pages (that's only an estimate) create preferential treatment for special interest groups. That's not an honest measure. Tax loopholes are accessible only to the wealthy who can afford to find and exploit them; the same benefits are not available to widows and orphans. As we pointed out in the "work is good" section, income taxes discourage work, by increasing the cost of labor for demanders of labor and decreasing the reward of work for suppliers of labor.

In *Simple Rules for a Complex World*,[340] Richard Lewis calls for simple laws, like the 2013 Federal Reserve Act that was forty pages. He rails against policies like the Affordable Care Act at 2,700 pages, but the regulations that support it were more than 20,000. And the fact that the number is not known even makes Lewis's point more impactful.

Equity means taxes should be fair. The ability-to-pay principle often takes two forms: vertical equity and horizontal equity. Vertical equity supports progressive taxing systems, like income tax in the US. The more people make, the higher their tax rate. Horizontal equity means that people of the same ability to pay, should pay the same rate of taxes.

Love Your Neighbor

If you love your neighbor, you want her to be safe from harm. When taxes provide that safety, they are good taxes. Of course, there are other means of loving your neighbor, like protecting the neighbor yourself, but there is certainly room in the Christian worldview for a tax-supported state police system that provides professional policing for your neighbor.

Honor Those in Power

This is what Jesus was talking about in the "give unto Caesar" passage. If the government demands taxes from us, we should pay them. While there certainly is a level at which taxes become confiscatory, a reasonable level of taxation is considered within the realm of Christian acceptability.

What Is the Proper Level of Taxes?

In current political economic arguments, we hear about taxes as a redistribution scheme. We'll cover that in chapter 12, "Income Inequality." If we assume the purpose of taxes is to maintain the government, taxes should be relatively low. Taxes that deliver services on a reasonable level are within the realm of Christian acceptability.

The Laffer curve shows that an income tax above 33 percent actually decreases the total income to the government. The most reliable study was done by Cynthia and David Romer. Ms. Romer was Barack Obama's chief economic advisor, who found the 33 percent threshold. So even those who want an aggressive system of high taxes want to stop at 33 percent, if the purpose is to maintain the government; a tax rate above that number would decrease the revenue needed to maintain the government. When then-Senator Obama was asked about this by Charlie Rose, he admitted that high tax rates decrease the total revenue for government. His defense of high taxes was, "It's more fair"—not to maintain government. That is not a Christian role for taxes; it's stealing.

In *Was Jesus a Socialist?* Lawrence Reed states, "Jesus said, 'Render unto Caesar, the things that are Caesar's, and render unto God the things that are God's.' But that has absolutely nothing to do with high taxes nor wealth redistribution. It certainly wasn't the same as saying that whatever Caesar says is his, must then be so, no matter how much he demands or what he intends to use it for."[341] Taxes that increase freedom are supported by Scripture. Taxes that reduce freedom—because they are too high—are not scripturally supported.

Don't Steal

From Genesis to Revelation, the Bible is full of examples and warnings of abusive government.[342] High taxes are a form of abuse. In the Bible, the right to have private property is nowhere stated but everywhere assumed.[343] When government uses its power to take private property in the form of abusive taxation, it's a violation of our commandment about stealing.

Take Care of Widows and Orphans

Equitable means the person is able to pay the tax. In the US, our progressive taxing system attempts to deliver a level of equitable taxing. The US Government reports taxes in quintiles. In our classroom, we like to ask groups of students to guess what percentage of tax is paid by each quintile. On average, the students guess that the richest quintile pays about 40% of income taxes, and the bottom quintile pays about 10%. The facts: The richest quintile pays 84 percent and the poorest pay -2%—negative, because of the earned income tax credit. In truth, the poorest 47% of Americans pay no income tax at all. When people claim "This is a tax cut for the rich," it's axiomatic. You can't cut income taxes for the poor because they don't pay any. If you want to improve the economic environment for them, you would cut taxes to decrease the deadweight loss. Suppliers would get richer, and consumers would get richer. Taxes create deadweight loss that makes all of us poorer.

The negative numbers are produced by the earned income tax credit, whereby the IRS estimates what those folks could have earned, then grants them a tax return based on that estimate. The US income tax system has become so progressive that the poorest 47 percent pay no income tax. The United States has the *most* progressive taxing systems in the world.

Former President Obama often said, "The rich should pay their fair share." It's interesting that "fair shares" is used in Ayn Rand's *Atlas Shrugged*. But President Obama didn't state a number. If 84 percent is not "fair," what is? He should realize that people respond to avoid punishment, and tax is a punishment. The rich can live anywhere they want. Why would they remain in the US and pay confiscatory taxes when they could choose to live in a lower-tax country? When Dave worked in pro tennis, it was widely known that Bjorn Borg, one of the highest-ranked players of his generation, was from Sweden but lived in Monaco, where the tax rate was zero.

You're probably aware of the Swedish furniture company IKEA. It was founded by a Swede who didn't live there. Here's how Wikipedia summarizes it: "Ingvar Kamprad was a Swedish business magnate best known for founding IKEA, a multinational retail company specializing in furniture. He lived in Switzerland from 1976 to 2014."[344]

Arthur Laffer's book, *An Inquiry into the Nature and Causes of the Wealth of States*,[345] explains why eliminating or lowering tax burdens at the state level leads to economic growth and wealth creation. The book shows that even states with small populations can benefit enormously with the right policies. The book points out that people move from high-tax states like New York, New Jersey, and California, to low-tax states like Texas and Florida. Again, economists raise an eyebrow and ask, "You didn't know this?"

Does this system take care of the poor, as we're biblically commanded to do? Absolutely, yes. Widows and orphans are more protected from taxation in America than in almost any country. Phil Gramm and John Early, writing in *The Wall Street Journal*, make it clear: "The US has the most progressive income tax system in the world."[346]

Be a Good Samaritan

Taxing away a person's income is not a very good way to be a Good Samaritan. We believe that Good Samaritan activities should be performed by churches and individuals. We will continue to point out that the Good Samaritan did not rush into town and enact a tax. He used his own resources that he had gained in a free-market economy to help the man who had been robbed en route to Jericho. So taxing, even for Good Samaritan purposes, does not seem to be justified in this economic commandment.

Is It Better to Tax Corporations or Individuals?

Corporations don't pay taxes; they pass them along to widows and orphans who consume their products. Higher corporate taxes chase companies out of the US. Many were leaving at the end of the Obama administration via inversion, where they would arrange for their company to be bought by a competitor in a low-tax country, like Ireland, and pay taxes there instead of the US. The classic example was the sale of Burger King to Tim Horton's in Canada. Corporate taxes were higher in the US than in Canada, which we usually think of as a higher tax environment than the US. That makes the US poorer, and hurts the widows and orphans who must make up for the loss in taxes that were paid by those corporations who left.

When the US corporate tax rate was 35 percent, it was among the highest in the world. That has encouraged US firms to leave profits overseas, where they currently have stashed $2.5 trillion. To put this in context, the new fracking industry has revenue of $3.5 trillion and has created 4.6 million jobs. Based on that data, repatriation of $2.5 trillion would create about 3.2 million jobs. There are only 13.5 million unemployed in the US, as of this writing.

Taxes are a form of punishment. As we're writing this, *The Wall Street Journal* is publishing a story explaining how companies are rerouting goods to avoid US tariffs. That produces a great big sigh from economists. A *WSJ* headline is necessary to explain that people avoid taxes? Of course they do. We explained how a tariff is a tax in chapter 3. It's a form of punishment. You tax what you don't want. When lodged against tobacco and alcohol, they are called "sin taxes." The assumption is that the society wants less "sin," so it taxes it. What you tax, you get less of, which is deadweight loss.

So, if you want fewer corporations, you tax them, simple as that. If you want corporations to thrive, you do not tax them. Taxes are a punishment.

It's double punishment when taxes are taken from productive businesses to support failing businesses. History is littered with examples of dysfunctional companies bailed out by government—a double blow to the consuming public, which is deprived of both the benefits that an improved company would bring to the market as well as a large amount of tax money spent to shore up the dysfunctional company's finances.[347]

This is the message of *Economics in One Lesson* by Henry Hazlitt in 1946.[348] He says that we often only look at the first level of effect: A business was shored up and saved from failure. But if we look at the second level effect, we find that 1) money was taxed away from a productive enterprise which lowers the value that firm created for its customers; and 2) the tax money was given to a failing firm that was not able to create value for their neighbors. This is a double punishment.

Politicians often point at large, successful companies like Walmart and Amazon and claim they should pay more tax, so they increase the tax on those companies. When it's done at the industry level, all competitors in the industry simply pass those taxes onto their consumers.

We're continually surprised by consumers who favor companies that support charities. It's only after you understand consumer surplus and producer surplus that you begin to understand that a corporation that gives to a charity must first earn that money by reducing consumer surplus. Believing strongly as we do in a free market, we wonder why the consumer does not favor the supplier increasing consumer surplus and allowing the consumer to "vote with their dollars" by giving to whatever charity they choose. Instead, the consumer seems to assume that the company can give away money more effectively than the consumer can.

That's a violation of Adam Smith's idea of specialization. Walmart has proven they have a specialized capacity to sell consumer goods at low cost. How does that make them a good entity for choosing charities? When he started to give away money, Microsoft founder Bill Gates found it was a difficult job. He remade himself into an educated philanthropist by traveling, studying, and trying out many methods and organizations. Giving away money effectively is not easy. Yet, consumers assume that companies like Walmart should do it without any proven specialization in the industry. Economists think it would be much more effective for the Walmarts of the world to increase consumer surplus, and enable the consumers to donate where they choose. That creates a market for philanthropy that benefits everyone.

Again, markets are where everyone votes. A better decision is made when more input is considered. When everyone votes, charity is more effective. When only the elites vote—CEOs and CFOs—less input is contributed and worse philanthropic decisions are made. Companies like Walmart should simply lower prices to increase consumer surplus, then when charities come calling they should say, "We gave at the office. Our consumers are much better at selecting charities than we are." Think about the opposite: What consumer would be enchanted by a company that says, "We raised the price to reduce consumer surplus and increase producer surplus so we could give to a charity you might disagree with"? That makes no sense.

Chapter 7

Production

Policies That Promote Production

One thing separates rich from poor countries: *policies that promote production*. That's it. If people are encouraged to produce, they will. If they are discouraged from production, they will not. People respond to incentives. We can clarify our thinking if we put our chief emphasis where it belongs—on policies that will maximize production.[349]

One of the seminal books in economics is titled *Human Action*, by Ludwig Von Mises. The title says it all: economics studies how people respond to incentives. In this chapter, we analyze macroeconomic policies in terms of whether they promote production, based on the Ten Commandments of Biblical Economics.

Almost all variation in living standards is attributable to differences in countries' productivity—that is, the amount of goods and services produced by each unit of labor input. The relationship between productivity and living standards has profound implications for public policy. When thinking about how any policy will affect living standards, the key question is how it will affect our ability to produce goods and services.[350] Economies grow or contract because of good or bad economic policies.[351]

Although natural resources can be important, they are not necessary for an economy to be highly productive.[352] Japan and Hong Kong have almost no natural resources, yet they are among the richest regions in the world. Venezuela has more oil and gas reserves than any nation in the world, yet there is not enough food on the shelves, and people die on a daily basis because of the scarcity of simple medical devices and drugs.

Much discussion of policies toward third-world countries proceeds as if the fundamental problem in such countries is poverty and a lack of the skills and knowledge required to raise their standard of living. Supplying money, physical equipment, and technocrats with skills might seem to be the answer, as policies to help third-world countries advance. But many, if not most, poor countries already have within their own borders people with the human capital to advance the nation's economy. Yet there are formidable political obstacles to using that human capital, and many political incentives to avoid letting minorities with skills lacking in the majority of the population have free reign to put their skills to work, with resulting disparities in performances and rewards.[353]

Economic policy favors one of two diametrically opposed goals: growth vs. equality. The Obama administration favored equality, but strangely enough, inequality increased during the Obama years. The Trump administration favored growth. The country's economy did grow, at a much faster rate than during the Obama years, but strangely, inequality shrank.[354]

You can grow the pie or divide the pie. The Trump administration for the most part focused on growth. Its policy mix of deregulation and tax reform has unleashed more private investment and job creation that lifted productivity and wages for the non-affluent. The result was faster growth and less inequality.[355] Jesus cared about helping the least fortunate, so we should care about them also. He never would have approved anything that undermines wealth creation. And the only thing that has ever created wealth, and lifted masses of people out of poverty, is free-market capitalism.[356]

Dividing the pie assumes that the rich have obtained their wealth either via luck or malfeasance. We often hear the rich referred to as "fortunate." Think about it: Are they? If they are simply lucky, then their wealth should be redistributed. But if they earned it by enriching others, they should be allowed to keep it. The assumption about "fortune" is a bad assumption. It violates property rights and our third commandment of economics: don't steal. The best thing that politicians can do in regard to property is to enact and enforce just laws in accordance with natural law—to protect people from having their belongings unjustly confiscated. Divide-the-pie policies violate this protection of property rights because they steal goods that were not only legally obtained but were gained via the production of consumer surplus.[357]

Paying people for not working distorts incentives and denies the fallen nature of humans. As does the "Universal Basic Income" suggested by Mark Zuckerberg at the 2018 Harvard graduation. You have to wonder if the graduates who applauded him would have chosen to attend Harvard if they had been awarded "Universal Basic Grades." If Harvard had been granting "Universal Basic Grades," attendance in class would have been less. Students would have learned less. They would have been seen as being not very productive in their work. Students seeking a university would pass on Harvard because of its terrible reputation of turning out dull students—and those students who applauded Mark Zuckerberg would not be there to applaud him.

In the workplace, people respond just as students do: If they are rewarded for coming to work and doing well, they will do so. If they are commonly rewarded for common behavior (the universal grades example) they will not come to work and will not perform well. Citing the fallen nature of humans, you have to assume that a universal basic wage would make people less productive, not more. Mr. Zuckerberg claimed that it would give people freedom to do work that is "meaningful to them." Meaningful to the individual, not his neighbor. That's not consistent with the Christian command to "Love your neighbor as yourself." Zuckerberg wants people to "love themselves" by their own subjective measure. The free-market capitalist formula requires workers to satisfy the needs of others (their neighbors), before they are satisfied. So who comes first: me or my neighbor? We see the Bible encouraging servant leadership: serving others by supplying products and services they demand. Zuckerberg puts "loving yourself" before "loving others." That's a dangerous situation that will certainly lower productivity.

Satisfying your own "passions" by "doing what your heart tells you to do" is the biggest mistake we can tell people in society. That assumes they are not part of a community that serves one another. Only the individual is served by seeking their passion. What about their neighbors? If we could find a means by which to measure how much an individual is contributing to his society, that would seem to be a good measure of success. But satisfying individual passions has no such measure. Economists like to draw demand and supply lines and produce an equilibrium: where the demander will pay and the supplier will sell. In terms of making a contribution to society, that's a very good measure.

When graduates from our university have a $50,000 job offer in Dallas and a $75,000 job offer in Kansas City, we tell them they will make a greater contribution to their neighbor by moving to Kansas City. That's where the equilibrium point is higher for their skills and talents. To remain in Dallas for $50,000 is denying society its input measure on the value of their contributions to their community. Abraham left Ur of the Chaldeans for a land of milk and honey in the Promised Land. Our students should go where they produce the greatest good for their neighbors, whether those neighbors be in Dallas, Kansas City, Atlanta, or Denver.

We tell our students the following story, "If we could visit the home where you grew up, it's likely we would see a picture of you playing little league soccer." Less than one percent of our current students play competitive soccer. That means that somewhere in the lives of the remaining 99 percent, a wise advisor encouraged them to stop playing soccer, because they were passing up an opportunity cost that would create more value for their community: Playing another sport, or playing a musical instrument in the band. The students have passed through many of those opportunity cost ventures, and end up in the College of Business at Dallas Baptist University, supposedly because a degree in business will increase their contribution to their neighbors. Why should they stop paying attention to these types of guidance they have received all their lives? They should continue to seek the highest equilibrium paid for their services. So we assume someone told them, "You are better suited to business than teaching." Or, "You would make a good pastor, so study religion instead of kinesiology."

It's a simple question: What should determine what work we do: our individual passion, or the "vote" of others? Remember, the market is where everyone votes. We think it would be the height of narcissism to deny the voting of everyone around you and seek your own passion. That assumes you're smarter than those around you who "voted" for you to seek another profession.

It's pretty simple: The wealth of a nation flows directly from the productivity of its people. The more they produce, the more value they create: first for their neighbor, who is buying the product or service, and second for the worker, who earns wages. The objective, economic measure of value to society is the wage level. People are the ultimate resource. People normally create more than they consume.[358]

The standard living of a nation depends more on its output per capita than on the money received as income for producing that output. Otherwise, the government could make us all rich, simply by printing more money. By focusing on what is called "income distribution," many people proceed as if the government can rearrange these flows of money, so as to have incomes become more "fair"—however defined—disregarding what the repercussions of such a policy might be on the more fundamental process of producing goods and services, on which country's standard of living depends.[359]

Labor is too often seen as mouths and not as makers, as a locus of material needs rather than as creative beings packed with energy and capacity. Once you see poor people as bringing resources and not just needs to the table, your whole view of how to help them changes.[360]

We grow a little tired of people complaining that schoolteachers make less than pro athletes. They both make the equilibrium wage, which is determined when all of us "vote," with the expenditures of our dollars. If you want athletes to make less, you should convince your neighbors to stop watching them. Go ahead, you have the freedom to do so. Obviously, there are some activities that are out of the Christian belief system that are still rewarded by the market: pornography, prostitution, etc. No one believes in a total free market. Everyone agrees that products and services that harm society should not be allowed by the market. But in this chapter, we're seeking general answers to determine what makes some societies more productive than others. And policies that promote production is the only thing that makes a society richer.

People Should Be Free

When people have the freedom to keep the rewards of their labor, they will contribute their labor to the economic pool. When that freedom is restricted by taxes, minimum wage, labor unions, unemployment insurance, and other nonproductive schemes, they will not contribute their labor.

We need the liberty to make responsible use of the world's resources in the most productive and efficient manner possible to benefit everyone. We cannot help the poor escape material poverty *without using creation's riches.*[361]

Claar and Klay[362] list three reasons for poverty. Two of them apply here

1. First, *accidents of geography*
2. Second, *bad government* and *bad public policies*
3. Third, *excessive government regulations*

If government would improve their performance by reducing bad policies and regulations, people would be more free and more productive.

Excessive regulation caused President Barack Obama to earn three honors:

1. He never hit a three.
2. He was slow.
3. He was expensive.

That sounds to us more like a player in the National Basketball Association than a president, but all three awards were measurably earned. Let us explain.

1. *He never hit a three.* That's not a three-point shot in basketball; it's three percent GDP growth. He was the first president since Herbert Hoover in 1928 to not record three percent GDP growth in any year of his presidency. Even John F. Kennedy, who only served a thousand days, hit a three, mostly because he lowered taxes.

   "The tax cuts and the lifting of regulatory burden have produced an economic takeoff that had failed to occur under the policies of the previous administration, despite a doubling of the national debt and the greatest monetary easing in the history of the Federal Reserve. Many respected economists in those years concluded that America suffered from 'secular stagnation' and was incapable of strong growth. But today, greater than 3 percent GDP growth for the first time in thirteen years makes it clear that bad policies rather than fate were the cause of the failed recovery."[363] Proof for the ways in which deregulation and tax cuts favor the poor were produced when GDP growth exceeded three percent for 2018, and was 3.1 percent for the first quarter of 2019.

   The economy was so sluggish during the Obama years that economists were creating theories to explain it. "Secular stagnation" was coined by Larry Summers. It assumes that all sectors of the economy are stagnating because developed countries just can't grow at three percent anymore. This is like patent commissioner Charles Duell closing the patent office in 1899, proclaiming, "Everything that can be invented has been invented." It's a staggering denial of the *imago dei* of humans. It assumes we have lost our creative nature. It was not true of patents, it's not true of our creative nature, and it's certainly not true of three percent GDP growth.

2. *He was slow.* There have been eleven recessions since World War II. President Obama led the United States through the slowest recovery of the eleven. The economy always recovers. To assume it was not going to recover is to deny history. When you look at the economic cycle through the years, you see clearly that the economy cycles through growth and recession stages. That the economy recovered under President Obama is an easy observation to make. Did someone assume it would not have recovered if Mitt Romney were elected in 2008? That's an absurd assumption not supported by history. The economy has gone down eleven times and bounced back eleven times. So economists don't measure whether the economy recovers or not; we measure the *speed* at which it recovers, and President Obama set a record for the modern era by having the slowest recovery since World War II.

3. *He was expensive.* Gramm and Solon mention a "doubling of the national debt." We write more about this in chapter 11. For now, the debt doubled from ten to twenty trillion dollars, the greatest eight-year increase in history.

President Obama provides us with a perfect example of how not to run an economy for the poor. If you care about the poor, you want to grow GDP via policies that promote production. He supported many policies that did not, and the economic record is very clear.

When the economy allows people to have freedom, the economy grows, and the poor benefit, which is consistent with our Ten Commandments of Biblical Economics. The value of work is another of the ten commandments.

Work Is Good

If work is good, then policies that discourage work are not consistent with our Ten Commandments of Biblical Economics. As 2 Thessalonians 3:6–10 reads:

> In the name of the Lord Jesus Christ, we command you, brothers and sisters, to keep away from every believer who is idle and disruptive and does not live according to the teaching you received from us. For you yourselves know how you ought to follow our example. We were not idle when we were with you, nor did we eat anyone's food without paying for it. On the contrary, we worked night and day, laboring and toiling so that we would not be a burden to any of you. We did this, not because we do not have the right to such help, but in order to offer ourselves as a model for you to imitate. For even when we were with you, we gave you this rule: "The one who is unwilling to work shall not eat."

Minimum wage is covered more in-depth in chapter 4, but we need to mention it here as well. Minimum wage discriminates against the work of people who produce value at a level lower than the mandated wage, thus robbing them of their ability to enrich themselves and their neighbor. Some may ask, "Can't you just pay them more?" Paying people more does not increase their productivity; it only increases inflation. In chapter 10, we show how minimum wage causes the two evils of macroeconomics: unemployment and inflation. And we make the point that poor people are more impacted by both of these evils than the rich are.

Unemployment insurance discourages work. Should people be paid for not working? Yes . . . by the church. But it's likely the church will find something for them to do that sustains their dignity and makes a contribution to enriching their neighbors while they are being paid.

Labor unions discourage work. We have written a more in-depth analysis of this in chapter 8. For now, let's make the point that labor unions discourage work by setting rules and regulations that favor their members, and disfavor the poor who can't produce value at the minimum-wage level.

Economic history is littered with examples of policies that did not promote production. The Works Progress Administration was considered a mark of genius for the administrators to think of projects that employed the largest number of men in relation to the value of the work performed—in other words, in which labor was least efficient.[364]

An environment that encourages productivity is vital to the productivity of its people. Thomas Sowell writes about an important example: "Cuban refugees (to America) who found themselves at the bottom, when their exodus began in 1959, had children who, by 1990, earned more than $50,000 a year twice as frequently as white Americans. Forty years after these Cuban refugees arrived in the United States, the total revenue of Cuban American business was greater than the total revenue of the entire nation of Cuba. Similarly, as late as 1994, the 57 million overseas Chinese produced as much wealth as the one billion people in China."[365]

Work is worship. Thus, we must be committed to the idea that we express our Christian discipleship through our employment, which is an important part of our life in Christ.[366] It's not the only part of our life in Christ, but it is an important part.

Don't Steal

Many policies that prevent production are a form of stealing. Minimum wage steals work from those it disemploys. Unemployment insurance steals production from the people it pays to stay out of the workforce. Unions steal labor from non-union members.

Property, you see, is not this or that physical object. Property is a relationship between a person and a thing or idea. To own property is to be in a particular kind of relationship with something in the world—a relationship, moreover, that is recognized by others in the community.[367]

Don't Covet

Redistribution schemes are based on the assumption of covetousness. They take from the rich and give to the poor. This is an exercise that grows out of the poor coveting what the rich have. Winston Churchill said, "You don't make the poor richer by making the rich poorer." We would add, "Making the rich poorer, makes the poor poorer." Because it's the rich who employ the poor.

Honest Measures

Inasmuch as per capita GDP is the primary measure of a nation's economic growth, there is a moral imperative of economic growth for Christians. Economic growth is not some greedy, materialistic aim, although many Christians think so when they consider the often breathless financial reporting on quarter-to-quarter GDP results. Instead, long-term growth is the fundamental driver of sustained material well-being, and is fundamentally linked to job growth and to growth in the incomes of the poor.[368]

Thus, GDP is a pretty good measure of policies that promote production. It's not a perfect measure, as stated by Robert F. Kennedy, "Gross Domestic Product does not allow for the health of our children, the quality of their education, or the joy of their play. It does not include the beauty of our poetry or the strength of our marriages, the intelligence of our public debate or the integrity of our public officials. It measures neither our courage, nor our wisdom, nor our devotion to our country. It measures everything, in short, except that which makes life worthwhile, and it can tell us everything about America except why we are proud that we are Americans."[369]

RFK was right: there is more to life than GDP. But other measures put us on a slippery slope. The World Happiness Report includes such subjective measures as generosity and social support. The Gallup World Report attempts to measure happiness by asking respondents about their emotional experiences the previous day—were they angry or stressed or did they smile frequently? Another measure incorporates the amount of birdsong a person hears. If we're going to be subjective about it, we have one simple measure: the number of people who have accepted Jesus Christ as their personal Savior. That measures happiness not only in this life, but in the next as well. However, we don't expect that to be widely accepted by the non-Christian world, so we will keep that measure out of consideration for now and revert to the more objective measure of GDP. It's not perfect, but to refer back to our iceberg metaphor from chapter 1, all the measures are above the water.

Take Care of Widows and Orphans

We want a nation to be productive. That's the only way to pull people out of poverty. Free-market capitalism supports the growth and development of society. Socialists are the opposite. They are modern-day Luddites, destroyers of technology to preserve jobs. An economic system is about raising the standard of living of its participants. The best way to do that is to lower costs of goods and services so that profits and capital are freed up to be reinvested in future life-enhancing products.[370]

Widows and orphans are drawn out of poverty only by increases in GDP. Wealth does not fall from the trees; it is produced by human effort and grows when work is productive and profitable. Our heart for the poor must lead our heads to be positive about growth.[371] Economists have tried to find other determinants of wealth, without much success. It always comes back to policies that promote production. MIT economist Daron Acemoglu knocks down some of the simple straw-men theories about geography, climate, and ethnicity as predictors of wealth: "Rule of law and security and a governing system that offers opportunities to achieve and innovate. That's what determines the haves from the have-nots. Put simply: Fix incentive and you will fix poverty."[372]

The only way to truly lift the poor is to provide them with the opportunity to join other fellow image-bearers in being responsive, responsible, productive members of society. We need to pursue policies that encourage the poor to become active image bearers of God.[373]

Scarcity vs. Abundance

Scarcity thinking grows out of the fallen nature. If you watch small children during a balloon drop, their first (fallen) response is to grab as many balloons as they can. That's usually about two. Then they look around at other people with an abundance (creation) attitude. They are batting the balloons around and smiling and laughing. The kid tightly grasping two balloons figures it out pretty quick: if I share the balloons by tapping them to others, they will tap them back to me and we can have a lot of fun together.

Christians should have more of an abundance attitude than a scarcity attitude, because we believe there is enough salvation for everyone. It's not limited. This is what makes Christian economics "dismal," as we explained in chapter 1. Christians believe there is only one thing that is not scarce: God's love that leads to our salvation. The study of economics is based on the assumption of scarcity. What's a Christian to do? We believe we are to act counterculturally—like there is enough.

Thomas Robert Malthus is the champion scarcity thinker. He was an English minister and early economic thinker, who wrote "An Essay on the Principle of Population as it Affects the Future Improvement of Society"[374] in 1798. In that essay, he made one of history's most foreboding forecasts: increasing population would continually limit society's ability to provide for itself. As a result, humans would always live in poverty. His logic was simple: "Food is necessary to the existence of man" and "the passion between the sexes will remain," thus, "the power of population is infinitely greater than the power in the earth to produce subsistence for man." He predicted famines and starvation. Malthus was wrong. Why?

Much like Charles Duell who proposed closing the patent office in 1899, Malthus could not predict two future events: birth control, and technological improvements in agriculture. In 1800, 90 percent of Americans worked on farms. In 1900, the number was 60 percent. Today it's less than three percent, and they produce more food than all 327 million Americans can eat, so much of it is exported. Worldwide, the population has increased from 800 million in Malthus' time to 7.7 billion today; yet currently, there is an abundance of food in today's world. In the modern world, famines occur mostly because of distribution problems stemming from political corruption. And, about the "passion of the sexes" increasing population? The passion is still there, but developed countries are suffering from too few births, not too many. There is a campaign in a Scandinavian country to have more children, titled appropriately "Do it for Denmark." Malthus's scarcity prediction was way off the mark.

Even though he was a minister, Malthus overlooked the power of the creative nature of the human *imago dei* explained in chapter 1. We believe that human beings are made in God's image—the *imago dei*. Our creative freedom reflects that divine image. This is one of the least appreciated truths of economics.[375] Creative humans will continue to find new ways to produce and distribute food. They will continue to find new energy sources, and cures for disease. It's called "creativity," because it comes from our Creator.

Scarcity predictions are still popular. In 1972, the Club of Rome published *The Limits of Growth*, which sold 30 million copies, making it the largest-selling environmental book in history. The book was essentially updates of Malthusian dire predictions of famine, based on the limited carrying capacity of the earth. There seems to be increasing demand for predictions of decreasing supply. In 1976 US Presidential candidate Jimmy Carter called for "a realization that we have about 35 years of oil left in the whole world. We're going to run out of oil." That means we ran out of oil in 2011 . . . but we didn't. Economics rules mandate that when supply decreases, price increases. Carter might be surprised today to hear that our university freshmen pay less for gas than Dave Arnott paid as a college freshman in 1973. Dave paid 45 cents a gallon; with inflation, it should cost $2.78 today. It doesn't. And our students today drive cars that are about twice as efficient, so they're getting double the value from a gallon of gas, at a lower cost.

For decades, we've been harangued by supposed experts who nicely play the part of Chicken Little, shouting, "We're going to run out of oil." And yet, early in 2019 *The Wall Street Journal* published an article citing experts in the oil industry who predict we're five years away from peak oil demand.[376] Read that sentence again—not peak oil *supply*, peak oil *demand*. We may run out of *demand* before we run out of *supply* of oil.

What does the future hold? In a world of *imago dei* humans, no one knows. Here's what we know from economics: if you put incentives in the right place, creative humans will find ways to conserve and develop new sources of energy. Here's where the Christian economist struggles: the Christian says, "Creative humans will figure this out," and the economist retorts, "There is scarcity!" Which one is correct? Even if we could calculate the world's supply of food or oil, or water, we cannot predict what *imago dei* humans will do with the limited resources of the earth.

Norman Borlaug is a champion abundance thinker. He is called "the man who saved a billion lives." He earned a PhD in plant pathology from the University of Minnesota in 1942. He first went to Mexico and developed a semi-dwarf wheat that matured faster, meaning there could be two crops a year instead of one. By 1965 Mexico was a wheat exporter. Between 1965 and 1970, wheat yields nearly doubled in Pakistan and India because of Borland's work, and he performed similar food production increases in Africa. He is one of only seven people to receive the Nobel Peace Prize, the Presidential Medal of Freedom, *and* the Congressional Gold Medal. One of the two statues placed in the US Capitol by the state of Iowa is of Norman Borlaug.

When Borlaug died in Dallas on September 12, 2009, a long story about him was published in the *Dallas Morning News*. A few days later, Dave was attending a speech by the Indian consulate representative from Houston. As he approached the microphone, the crowd expected a common greeting like, "It's good to be with you in Dallas," or "I appreciate the invitation to visit with you today." But the first words the Indian consulate official spoke were, "Please join me in a few moments of silence in honor of Norman Borlaug." There was no explanation of who he was. The Indian consulate official assumed we all knew about him. He is a hero in India, and he should be a hero to all of us who care about the poor. He is "the man who saved a billion lives."

So, scarcity or abundance? Present scarcity is measurable. Future abundance is unknown. But we know that creative humans will find ways to turn present scarcity into future abundance. We've seen this play many times before. The Malthus crowd has never been right. Ask a small group to complete this sentence, "Life was better on earth before we ran out of . . ." There is no answer. We've never run out of anything. But the Malthus crowd continues to tell us we will.

"Life is better now than almost any time in history," is the first line of *The Great Escape*,[377] by 2015 Nobel Prize-winning economist Angus Deaton. The book explains how humans escaped centuries of destitution-level poverty. "Why 2018 Was the Best Year in Human History!" was a lead headline in the January 6, 2019 *New York Times*.[378] The article, by Nicholas Kristoff, was subtitled "Once again, the world's population was living longer and living better than ever before." Deaton and Kristoff are correct: by any reasonable economic measure, life is better on earth today than it's ever been. And, if *imago dei* humans have the right incentives, it's going to get better.

How is the world better? Here are a few data points:[379]

1. Absolute poverty is defined as living on less than $1.25/day. Over the last thirty years, the share of the global population living in absolute poverty has declined from 53 percent to under seventeen percent.

2. Child labor has decreased from 246 million in the year 2000 to an estimated 107 million in 2020. People in hazardous work has declined from 171 million in 2000 to an estimated 50 million in 2020.

3. In the US, the cost of eating at home has declined from fourteen percent of disposable income to six percent from 1960 to 2012.

4. In the 25 years ending in 2013, the world's infant mortality rate has been halved. If you looked at the last one hundred years, the decrease is even more dramatic.

5. Even something less impactful, but still important, births among teens in the US has dropped from eighty-nine out of a thousand in 1960 to under twenty-nine in 2010.

6. In the last two hundred years, the average number of years of education has skyrocketed from two to twenty-one.

7. World global literacy rates averaged about ten percent in 1500. Now it's close to 100 percent.

And here's another list, from information Dave compiled from various sources:

1. Extreme poverty fell from 18.2 percent of the world's population to 8.6 percent in the decade that ended in 2019. In the 1980s, it was 44 percent.

2. Globally, the gap in basic living standards is narrowing.

3. Literacy has skyrocketed. In 1820 just five percent of the world's population could read and write. Today 80 percent of the world's population is literate.

4. More people get to elect their leaders. In 1820, just 1.5 percent of the world's population lived in a democracy. Today, it's more than half.

5. Clean water is less of a luxury. Since 1990, 2.6 billion people have gained access to safe drinking water. Ninety-one percent of the world's population now have safe drinking water.

6. Famine has virtually gone extinct.

7. Mortality rates for women and children have been halved since 1990.

8. Primary education has become near-universal in nearly all of the world.

9. In the US, 73 percent of people will spend at least one year in the top quintile of income earners. Fifty-six percent will spend at least a year in the top ten percent.

10. In the US in 1800, 90 percent of the population worked in food production. In 1900, it was 60 percent. Today, it's 2.5 percent and they produce more food than the country can eat, so much of it is exported.

11. Malaria deaths have been cut in half just since 2000.

12. In the US, CO_2 from electrical production peaked in 2007.

13. Polio has been 99 percent eradicated since 1988.

14. Global life expectancy has gone from 29 in 1770 to 71 today.

15. The number of children in child labor has been reduced from 246 million to 107 million, just since 2000.

16. In the US, disposable income spent on food has gone from fourteen percent in 1960 to six percent today.

17. People living in poverty in the US have more average square feet of living space than the average European.

18. Globally, 86 percent of all one-year-olds have been vaccinated against diphtheria, tetanus, and pertussis.

And the future looks even brighter. Rich countries use less aluminum, nickel, copper, steel, stone, cement, sand, wood, paper, fertilizer, water, crop acreage, and fossil fuel every year. Consumption of sixty-six out of seventy-two resources tracked by the US Geological Survey is now declining.[380]

Here's how Stephen Covey explains the scarcity mindset in his popular book *The Seven Habits of Highly Successful People*:[381] "Most people are deeply scripted in what I call the Scarcity Mentality. They see life as having only so much, as though there were only one pie out there. And if someone were to get a big piece of the pie, it would mean less for everybody else."

In economics terms, the scarcity mentality is the zero-sum idea. These people don't share well. In our previous illustration, they hold onto their two balloons. Their view of life is, "If there isn't enough to go around, I better get mine first, and hold onto it with a tight grip." This focuses on the individual in the short term, instead of the group in the long term.

John Maynard Keynes was a part of this group when he uttered his famous line, "In the long run, we're all dead." Who is dead? "We." So we'd better get our resources before others take them from us. This has led to multiple economic stimulus fiscal plans, the latest just in 2008 and 2009. They attempt to stimulate the short-term economy, at long-term cost. To restate Keynes, "We are going to profit from a short term stimulation of the economy at the expense of long term debt for the next generation." That's a violation of our third commandment of biblical economics: don't steal. There is even evidence that stimulative fiscal policies don't work. We explain that in chapter 11.

Back to Stephen Covey, about the abundance mindset: "The Abundance Mentality, on the other hand, flows out of a deep inner sense of personal worth and security. It is the paradigm that there is plenty out there and enough to spare for everybody. It results in sharing of prestige, of recognition, of profits, of decision making. It opens possibilities, options, alternatives, and creativity." It focuses on the long term and what's good for all, not just the individual.

In an article titled "Happy Earth Day," one-time Federal Reserve bank nominee Steven Moore writes, "Since the first Earth Day back in the 1970s, the environmentalists—those who worship the creation rather than the Creator—have issued one false prediction of Armageddon after another and yet despite the fact that their batting average is zero, the media and our schools keep parroting their declinism as if they were oracles not shysters." Moore points out a few "inconvenient" facts:

1. Natural resources are more abundant and affordable today than ever before in history.
2. Energy—the master resource—is superabundant.
3. Our air and water are cleaner.
4. There is no Malthusian nightmare of overpopulation.
5. Global per capita food production is 40 percent higher than it was in 1950.
6. The rate of death and destruction from natural disasters has plummeted over the last 50 to 100 years.[382]

Why does all this conservation take place? The rules of economics never go away. As resources become scarcer, the price rises and people use less of them. Economics works. *As long as the fallen nature produces unlimited wants and the creative nature has unlimited creativity, there will be unlimited employment.*

We are told over and over again that we are "using up" the world's resources, that we will "run out of oil," or that we are "approaching the carrying capacity" of the earth. All these Chicken Little statements are based on the assumption that there is a fixed amount of resources. But we continue to exceed these seemingly factual limits, time after time. Scarcity thinkers don't realize that oil from the ground saved the whales. Not so long ago, people conserved tin because it was the only way to package food—then refrigeration came along. Economist Matt Ridley, a writer for *The Economist*, explains, "I used to espouse the carrying-capacity viewpoint—that there were limits to growth. I nowadays lean to the view that there are no limits because we can invent new ways of doing more with less."[383] There are no limits when humans tap into the *imago dei*.

Water seems to be a scarce resource with physical limits. But we're using less than expected, not more. Estimates made in the 1960s and 1970s about water demand by the year 2000 were grossly overestimated. When we got to 2000, we were using half as much water as the "experts" predicted thirty years earlier.[384] Scarcity causes prices to increase, which decreases the demand. Computer connectors today use one hundred times thinner coatings of gold than they used to. Less steel is used in cars. The examples go on and on.

The scarcity mindset causes all kinds of problems in economics. The French government was concerned with unemployment, so they declared a thirty-five-hour workweek in the year 2000. Their scarcity thinking was based on the improper assumption that everyone contributes the same value of labor at work. If you think that's the case, you might try to bump your pastor off the podium this Sunday and take over, or you could put on the uniform of LeBron James and take his place for a few minutes. What you'll find out is what the French found out: the best performers should work more, not less. They were denying the idea of division of labor and specialization that was explained by a guy just across the channel in 1776: Adam Smith. (Sidenote: Smith only made one trip out of the country in his entire life. It was to France, as the tutor to the son of the Duke of Buccleuch. He didn't enjoy the French philosophy very much.)

Spread-the-work schemes are based on the false assumption that there is just a fixed amount of work to be done. But those assumptions are wrong. There is no limit to the amount of work to be done as long as any human need or wish remains unsatisfied. In a modern economy, the most work will be done when prices, costs, and wages are in the best relations with each other.[385] Also, when work is done by specialists, they produce more value than nonspecialists. More value makes products and services cheaper to consumers and contributes to the overall growth of the economy, which makes a great contribution to thriving for the poor.

God works, and he intends us to work. We are commanded to use scarce resources to produce value for our neighbors, and for ourselves. We live in an environment of physical scarcity, but we should walk through that world with an abundance mentality. God's providence provides enough for us. So we should work, knowing we are contributing to God's redemption of the world through our hands. People are not mouths to be fed—they are hands and minds that work.

Chapter 8

Unemployment

Should the Government Encourage Work?

God ordained for people to be fruitful and multiply and fill the earth and subdue it (Genesis 1:28). A part of subduing the earth involved work and one of the first tasks Adam received was to name the animals and every living creature (Genesis 2:19). Moving through the books of the Old Testament, the theme of work reemerges multiple times. The book of Proverbs affirms the value of hard work and often contrasts it to laziness. Proverbs 10:4 (NKJV) says, "He who has a slack hand becomes poor, but the hand of the diligent makes rich." Another reference is just as pointed: "All hard work brings a profit, but mere talk leads only to poverty" (Proverbs 14:23). Proverbs 22:29 (MSG) highlights yet another benefit of someone's skillful work: "Observe people who are good at their work—skilled workers are always in demand and admired; they don't take a backseat to anyone." The wisdom literature found in the Bible seems to convince the reader to work hard, be diligent, and improve on their skills.

Several individuals throughout the Old Testament were given certain tasks that often required hard work, courage, skills, and organizational abilities. Some prominent examples are Noah who built the ark, Solomon who built the temple, and Nehemiah who restored the walls around

Jerusalem. All of these tasks were part of God's plan. Individuals realized that they had to play a crucial role in bringing God's plan to fruition.

The New Testament is just as supportive of hard work as the Old Testament. Jesus set an example by following in the trade of his earthly father Joseph, working as a carpenter until reaching the age of thirty when his public ministry began. The apostle Paul states in 2 Thessalonians 3:7–8: "For you yourselves know how you ought to follow our example. We were not idle when we were with you, nor did we eat anyone's food without paying for it. On the contrary, we worked night and day, laboring and toiling so that we would not be a burden to any of you." Paul encouraged all Christians to have the same attitude toward life as the runner has toward running in a race and to run with perseverance (Hebrews 12:1), having the goal of winning the race and receiving the prize (1 Corinthians 9:24).

Dallas Willard offered a good way to distinguish between someone's work and someone's job. He thought of each of the next four terms as a circle, with the first term being the smallest circle and each later term incorporating the previous one. The four terms are:

1. Job: What I am paid to do, how I earn my living
2. Ministry: That part of God's special work in my time that he has specifically allotted me
3. Work: The total amount of lasting goods that I will produce in my lifetime
4. Life: Me. My experience and who I am[386]

In light of Paul's analogy of life as being a race, it is helpful to think of work as a term inclusive of someone's ministry and a job. If we use Dallas Willard's definition of work as the total amount of lasting goods someone can produce in their lifetime, then work is intrinsically connected to human capital, which is the knowledge and skills that workers acquire through education, training, and experience.[387] The greater the human capital, the more impactful someone's work could be. For example, a pharmaceutical scientist can create a life-saving drug, an app developer can come up with a new app to enhance someone's productivity, or a family counselor can help to save a marriage. We are not diminishing the value of someone's work that does not require education or specialized skills, since any job done well is valuable in God's sight. Colossians 3:23 speaks to that truth by encouraging us to put in our very best effort in all we do, as working for the Lord and not for men.

The government should encourage the accumulation of investments in people, since it allows for individuals to be effective and competent within their chosen career paths. Building human capital will help to increase the total amount of goods and services individuals are able to produce during their lifetime. The purpose of maximizing labor productivity is to increase the standard of living, which also enhances the quality of life. In economics, standard of living is measured by real (i.e., inflation-adjusted) income per person, which is also known as real GDP per capita. Theory and history both confirm that there is a direct link between labor productivity and real wages.[388] As labor productivity goes up so does real income. Someone may argue that improvements in human capital should not be motivated by accumulation of money. We agree with that argument, since accumulation of money is not the end goal but just a tool in achieving other worthwhile goals. A country that enjoys a high standard of living allows its citizens to pursue their passions whether it be volunteering, traveling, learning arts and music, etc.

Senator Robert Kennedy gave a moving critique of GDP as a measure of well-being when he ran for president in 1968:

> Yet the gross national product does not allow for the health of our children, the quality of their education or the joy of their play. It does not include the beauty of our poetry or the strength of our marriages, the intelligence of our public debate or the integrity of our public officials. It measures neither our wit nor

our courage, neither our wisdom nor our learning, neither our compassion nor our devotion to our country, it measures everything in short, except that which makes life worthwhile. And it can tell us everything about America except why we are proud that we are Americans.[389]

Greg Mankiw, professor of economics at Harvard, acknowledges that Kennedy was correct in his assessment of GDP, but also notes:

Nations with larger GDP can afford better educational systems. GDP does not measure the beauty of our poetry, but nations with larger GDP can afford to teach more of their citizens to read and enjoy poetry. GDP does not take account of our intelligence, integrity, courage, wisdom, or devotion to country, but all of these laudable attributes are easier to foster when people are less concerned about being able to afford the material necessities of life. In short, GDP does not directly measure those things that make life worthwhile, but it does measure our ability to obtain many of the inputs for a worthwhile life.[390]

If God ordained work, and work allows us to obtain the inputs for a worthwhile life, then government should encourage people to work—or at the minimum, not discourage people from working. Government should encourage people to build their human capital, whether it be through the institutions of higher learning, vocational schools, or other educational opportunities.

When the government provides generous welfare programs to individuals, it works to distort incentives and discourage people from working. In 2013, the federal government spent nearly $680 billion on anti-poverty programs.[391] A study by Michael Tanner and Charles Hughes from the Cato Institute concludes that America's welfare system pays many people better than the jobs they would otherwise have.[392] Using the data from 2013, they find that the value of benefits varies widely across states, with a low of $16,984 in Mississippi and a high of $49,175 in Hawaii. They recommend that Congress and state legislatures ought to consider strengthening work requirements in public-assistance programs, removing exemptions and narrowing the definition of work. Casey Mulligan of the University of Chicago testified before Congress:

> Earning income requires sacrifices, and people evaluate whether the net income earned is enough to justify the sacrifices. When [welfare programs] pay more, the sacrifices that jobs require do not disappear. The commuting hassle is still there, the possibility for injury on the job is still there, and jobs still take time away from family, schooling, hobbies, and sleep. But the reward to working declines, because some of the money earned on the job is now available even when not working.[393]

Some of the recipients of various welfare programs make a calculated decision not to work, since working can reduce the level of benefits they receive and at times make them worse off than before. We can hardly blame someone for not seeking a job if finding a job reduces his overall welfare. It is not proper to describe someone in that position as a lazy person if he pursues his best interests, albeit being guided by distorted incentives. It is sad that a sure pathway of getting out of poverty is deemed as something undesirable.

The most recent US Census Bureau report at the time of this writing states that only 2.9 percent of full-time workers fall below the poverty line, as opposed to 30.7 percent for those who do not work.[394] Work is a good antidote to poverty and also improves the overall level of wellbeing. Using the data from the Gallup World Poll, De Neve and Ward conclude that the perceived quality of life is much higher for the employed as compared to the unemployed.[395,396] In the same survey they find that unemployed experience greater negative emotions in their daily lives, which signifies that the benefit of having a job is greater than just the salary that goes with it. Some of the nonmonetary aspects of employment, which have a strong influence on people's perception of happiness include social status, social relations, daily structure, and goals.

The government should encourage work in light of several economic commandments. Let's look at two of them: work is good, and don't steal.

Work Is Good. God created Adam and Eve and ordained them to tend the garden, name the animals, and subdue the earth. The commandment to work existed before the fall, so work is not the result of sin entering the world. If work is good and ordained by God, it should be encouraged by any government that is instituted on earth. The work increases the level of happiness and is the proven way out of poverty.

Don't Steal. Generous welfare programs totaling nearly one trillion dollars a year get their financing through tax revenue or government borrowing.[397] On the one hand, welfare programs discourage people from working, and thus reduction in benefits and stricter requirements are needed to encourage people to work. On the other hand, welfare programs necessitate the government to take the money from one group of people and give it to the other. Theft can be defined as taking other people's property without their consent. Michael Huemer builds a case around taxation as a form of theft:

> Imagine that I have founded a charity organization that helps the poor. But not enough people are voluntarily contributing to my charity, so many of the poor remain hungry. I decide to solve the problem by approaching well-off people on the street, pointing a gun at them, and demanding their money. I funnel the money into my charity, and the poor are fed and clothed at last.[398]

Huemer goes on to say that he would be called a thief in that scenario, and likewise so should the government using the threat of force to tax its citizens. He concludes: "Some thefts might be justified. If you have to steal a loaf of bread to survive, then you are justified in doing so. Similarly, the government might be justified in taxing, if this is necessary to prevent some terrible outcome, such as a breakdown of social order.

Why, then, does it matter whether taxation is theft? Because although theft can be justified, it is usually unjustified. It is wrong to steal without having a very good reason."

In sum, the government should encourage work by reducing some of the welfare programs and thus reducing the impact of unjustified theft.

What Causes Unemployment?

> For the kingdom of heaven is like a landowner who went out early in the morning to hire workers for his vineyard. He agreed to pay them a denarius for the day and sent them into his vineyard. . . .
>
> About five in the afternoon he went out and found still others standing around. He asked them, 'Why have you been standing here all day long doing nothing?'
>
> "Because no one has hired us," they answered.
>
> He said to them, "You also go and work in my vineyard." (Matthew 20:1–2, 6–7)

The passage above, as told by Jesus, is referred to as the parable of the workers in the vineyard. There are several important lessons found in this parable, but our focus is on the fact that unemployment exists today as it did at Jesus' time. First, some workers from the parable looked for work all day long, but could not find any until late in the afternoon when the landowner approached them with an offer of work. Second, there was a common understanding that the day's wage for a common laborer was a denarius. Two economic principles come into play here: first, when the quantity of labor exceeds the demand for labor, it causes unemployment; and second, the workers were paid the going market rate.

Before describing the possible reasons for unemployment, it is important to look into the way unemployment is measured. The Bureau of Labor Statistics (BLS), which is part of the Department of Labor, is tasked with measuring unemployment. The BLS estimates unemployment based on data from the monthly survey of about 60,000 households, called the Current Population Survey. The survey places each adult starting with age sixteen and above into one of three categories:

Employed: This category includes those who worked as paid employees, worked in the business they owned, or worked without pay in a family member's business. This category includes both full-time and part-time workers.

Unemployed: This category includes those who are not employed but are available for work, and who looked for a job in the last four weeks.

Not in the labor force: This category includes those who are not part of the first two categories and typically includes full-time students, homemakers, and retirees.

The Employed plus Unemployed categories add up to the number of individuals in the labor force. Unemployment, when reported as a percentage, takes a number of unemployed individuals and divides it by the number of employed plus unemployed individuals. For example, if our survey sample only included one hundred individuals over the age of fifteen, with fifty-four of them employed, six unemployed, and forty not in the labor force, then the unemployment rate would be:

$$6 / (54 + 6) = 0.1 \text{ or } 10\%$$

All surveys are prone to inaccuracies, and the Current Population Survey is no exception. For example, some unemployed might pretend to be looking for work only to qualify for some form of government assistance, while others might work but not report it if they get paid in cash or receive some other form of under-the-table payments. Both of these occurrences would push the unemployment statistic upward.

On the other hand, individuals who quit looking for work would not be part of the labor force, thus pushing the unemployment statistic downward. Unemployed individuals who quit looking for work are termed as discouraged workers. An increase in their numbers is a result of deteriorating conditions in the labor market, while at the same time the unemployment rate may wrongly show an improvement in labor markets. This is especially important during economic recessions when the unemployment rate is used as a gauge of changes in economic conditions.

How serious is the problem of unemployment? To answer that question, it is important to know whether unemployment is typically a long-term or short-term occurrence. If it is a short-term condition, someone may conclude that it is not a serious problem. However, if it is a long-term condition, someone may conclude that it is a serious problem, which creates not only economic hardship but also an emotional and psychological strain on the unemployed individuals.

Based on the US Bureau of Labor Statistics, the average duration of unemployment, as of June 2019, is 22.2 weeks.[399] That is an average of about five months without work, which might seem a long-term problem. However, when the data on the duration of unemployment spells is closely examined, it leads to a different conclusion. *Most individuals experience short-term spells of unemployment, but most unemployed at any given point in time experience a long-term spell of unemployment.* An example can help explain this seemingly contradictory statement. Suppose that we visited the government's unemployment office once a week for a whole year and noticed there are forty unemployed individuals who visit the office from week to week. Further, we notice that ten of those unemployed change from week to week but thirty remain unemployed throughout the year. Examining the stats for the whole year (i.e., 52 weeks), 520 individuals had short spells of unemployment, whereas only thirty had a long-term spell of unemployment. Summarizing the stats from this example, 95 percent (520 out of 550) of all unemployed individuals experienced a short spell of unemployment (one week or less), but on any given week 75 percent (thirty out of forty) of all unemployed individuals experienced a long-term spell of unemployment (one year or more). This subtle truth reveals that most people who become unemployed find jobs quickly, and that relatively few workers who are unemployed for long periods of time are at the heart of the economy's unemployment problem.

A simple answer to the question of what causes unemployment is that the supply of jobs is less than the demand for jobs. Price adjusts to balance supply and demand and so does the wage to balance the demand for jobs with the supply of jobs. In the perfect labor market, the wage would adjust so that there would be no unemployment. Economists offer several reasons for the labor market to fall short of the ideal labor market.[400] These reasons are job search, minimum-wage laws, unions, and efficiency wages.

Donald A. Hay, in *Economics Today*, writes: "Unemployment is a serious evil. This is largely due to technical failures of the market system, arising from intervention by governments or trade unions." A similar sentiment is shared by Henry Hazlitt in the third edition of *Economics in One Lesson*, which first appeared in 1946: "One of the worst results of the retention of the Keynesian myths is that it not only promotes greater and greater inflation, but that it systematically diverts attention from the real causes of our unemployment, such as excessive union wage-rates, minimum wage laws, excessive and prolonged unemployment insurance, and overgenerous relief payments."[401] The ideas introduced by Hazlitt have a lot of merit today, much as they did more than seventy years ago. In 1974, Nobel Prize winner in economics F. A. von Hayek said about Hazlitt's book: "It is a brilliant performance. It says precisely the things which need most saying and says them with rare courage and integrity. I know of no other modern book from which the intelligent layman can learn so much about the basic truths of economics in so short a time."[402]

We will elaborate on some of these causes for unemployment, but first it is important to note that it is inevitable to experience some level of unemployment regardless of the economy's strength. Economists refer to the natural rate of unemployment as the normal rate of unemployment around which the unemployment rate fluctuates.[403] In a dynamic economy, people change jobs in search of better opportunities, some industries experience the loss of jobs while others gain new jobs, and it takes some time for new entrants into the labor force to find a job. All these factors cause some level of unemployment because it takes time to find a job that best suits a worker's preferences and skills. This type of unemployment is called *frictional* unemployment and it is used to explain *short* periods of unemployment. The other type is *structural* unemployment, which arises in some labor markets because there are not enough jobs for everyone who wants one. Structural unemployment explains *longer* spells of unemployment and arises because the wage is set above the equilibrium wage, which is the wage which equates the demand for jobs with the supply of jobs.

Minimum-Wage Laws

It is helpful to turn to the graph of supply and demand to understand the reason for unemployment in the presence of minimum-wage laws. Minimum-wage laws impact those jobs, which have the equilibrium wage below the legal minimum level.

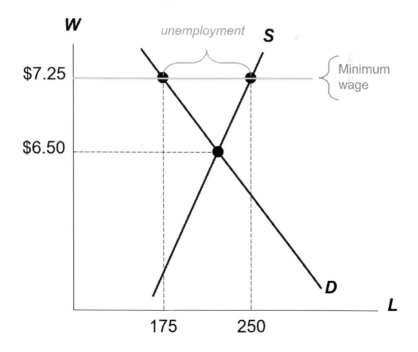

From our graph, the supply line stands for the supply of jobs, while the demand line stands for the demand for jobs. The horizontal axis measures the quantity of labor, while the vertical axis depicts the wage. The equilibrium wage of $6.50 is the point where supply and demand meet each other. Any wage point above the equilibrium creates the shortage of jobs, i.e., unemployment, since the number of jobs is not sufficient to meet the demand for jobs.

In most labor markets, companies have to compete for workers and offer prevailing market wages, which are often above the minimum wage. In these markets, the minimum wage laws do not prevent the wages from adjusting to balance supply and demand. At the time of this writing, the most recent BLS report identifies that 2.1 percent of all hourly workers earn wages at or below the federal minimum level.[404] For these workers, who are the least skilled and least experienced, such as teenagers, the minimum wage laws matter the most. The desire to help the working poor by setting the minimum wage ends up reducing the number of jobs and hurting those who cannot find a low paying job.

It is important to note that two individuals might be without work and actively looking for one, but the reason for their unemployment be completely different. One reason for unemployment might be the process of a job search, when workers are *searching* for the jobs that best suit their skills and preferences (frictional unemployment). The other reason for unemployment might be the process of *waiting* for jobs to open up (structural unemployment). In general, structural unemployment results from the wage being kept above the equilibrium level, regardless of whether it is because of minimum-wage laws, unions, or efficiency wages.

Unions and Collective Bargaining

A *union* is defined as a worker association that bargains with employers over wages, benefits, and working conditions.[405] Most workers in the US discuss and often negotiate with their employers on such issues as salary, benefits, and important work arrangements. Workers in a union do not discuss or negotiate on those issues as individuals but as a group. The process of negotiation to arrive at agreeable terms of employment is called *collective bargaining*.

A union has leverage in bargaining for higher wages, better benefits, and better working conditions, since it can organize a strike and temporarily withdraw the workers from work until the firm agrees with the union's demands. A company is likely to agree with paying higher wages since a strike has a direct negative effect on the company's level of production, which in turn reduces sales and profits. Some strikes do not end up as well for the company's workers, as has been the case with Hostess Brands, Inc. After a prolonged strike, the eighty-two-year-old company, based in Irving, Texas, posted the following announcement on its website: "sorry to announce that Hostess Brands, Inc. has been forced by a Bakers Union strike to shut down all operations and sell all company assets."[406] All 18,500 workers lost their jobs, even though only about five thousand of them were members of the Bakery, Confectionery, Tobacco Workers and Grain Millers International Union.[407] Most of the Hostess employees had approved a pay cut necessary for the company to stay open, but the members of the Bakery Union had voted against the pay cut.

Economists who study the effects of the union generally find that unionized workers receive ten to twenty percent more than similar nonunionized workers. A more recent Bureau of Labor Statistics report shows that employer costs for private industry workers are 42 percent higher for union workers compared with nonunion workers.[408] When a union calls for a higher wage than the equilibrium wage (found at the intersection of labor supply and labor demand curves), it raises the quantity of labor supplied and reduces the quantity of labor demanded, thus causing unemployment. Workers who remain employed are better off, but workers who lose their jobs are worse off. Those who remain unemployed can either wait for a chance to get a unionized job again or get a job in firms that are not unionized. It follows that when unions raise wages in some firms and industries, the supply of labor increases in nonunionized firms and industries, which leads to depressed wages for nonunion jobs. In sum, workers in unions reap the benefits of collective bargaining, while all the other workers bear some of the costs.

The idea of bargaining for higher wages efficiently and effectively has some merit, but the belief that unions can provide an answer for higher wages for all workers is a delusion, as Henry Hazlitt keenly notes: "The belief that labor unions can substantially raise real wages over the long run and for the whole working population is one of the great delusions of the present age. This delusion is mainly the result of failure to recognize that wages are basically determined by labor productivity."[409]

Efficiency Wages

The theory of efficiency wages suggests that paying above-equilibrium wages may be profitable for firms, because it raises worker productivity and helps firms operate more efficiently.[410] The reason for unemployment in the presence of efficiency wages is the same as it is with the minimum-wage laws or unions, the wage is set above its equilibrium point causing the surplus of labor. However, there is a striking difference as well. Minimum-wage laws and unions require the firm to pay the above-equilibrium wage even as it creates a surplus of labor; but with efficiency wages the firm does it voluntarily. It might seem counterintuitive that a profit-maximizing firm would want to increase its costs by keeping wages high, but there are several explanations as to why this might be a smart business strategy.

First, the theory of efficiency wages suggests that there is a strong link between wages and worker turnover. Turnover relates to the frequency with which a firm needs to replace the workers who quit their jobs. Workers quit their jobs for various reasons, and some of those have to deal with finding better opportunities elsewhere. Better opportunities often narrow down to better pay, and workers who are already receiving the above-equilibrium wage are less likely to find better-paying jobs and less likely to leave their present employer. High worker turnover involves the process of constantly finding and training new workers and that ties up firm resources, which could be used more productively somewhere else. Another downside of high worker turnover is that newly trained workers are typically not as productive as experienced ones. In sum, paying a high wage might not only reduce worker turnover but also raise the firm's profits.

Second, the theory of efficiency wages suggests that there is a strong link between wages and worker quality. All firms desire to have workers who are the best performers for the types of positions they offer. Setting the wage above its market equilibrium allows the firm to attract a larger pool of applicants, which in turn increases the chance of hiring more competent workers, which in turn raises the quality of the firm's workforce. If the link between higher wage and worker quality is strong enough, then it might be more profitable for firms to offer above-equilibrium wages.

Robert Bosch, the founder of Bosch—a German multinational engineering and technology company and a pioneer of introducing an eight-hour working day in 1906 and a free Saturday in 1910—is attributed as saying: "I don't pay good wages because I have a lot of money; I have a lot of money because I pay good wages."[411]

Third, the theory of efficiency wages suggests that there is a strong link between wages and worker effort. The exertion of effort at work is driven by the incentives workers are offered. If workers are not monitored and can get away with shirking their responsibilities, then less effort will be exhibited at work. Even if employees are being monitored, it is a costly and oftentimes imperfect way to deter shirking. If a company is paying just an equilibrium wage and employees know they are able to find a comparable job easily, then shirking may prevail even with monitoring systems in place. Companies may be better off by paying above-equilibrium wages to increase worker effort, since losing a higher-paying job may equate to settling for a lower-paying (equilibrium wage) job.

Henry Ford's five-dollar-a-day wage policy is a good example of how efficiency wages can be used to increase the firm's profitability. In 1914, paying five dollars a day was about twice the going wage, so

Ford could attract a greater number of workers than what he actually needed. Introducing the assembly line meant that workers were interdependent and if one worker was absent or worked slowly, it directly impacted the work of others. Ford's decision to pay efficiency wages helped to reduce worker turnover, boost worker effort, and improve worker quality, all of which contributed to production efficiency and higher profits. It was a smart business decision at that time and made Ford a desirable place to work.

Going back to the parable of the workers in the vineyard, we can observe the efficiency wages at play for those who were hired later in the day but got paid the full amount for the whole day's work. The master's explanation for paying a higher wage was that it was his own money and he could be more generous if he wished. From the perspective of the efficiency-wage theory, it is not just a generous act but could be a smart business strategy.

The objective to fight unemployment is taken very seriously by the Federal Reserve and is part of its so-called dual mandate, which is to maximize employment and stabilize prices. However, very low levels of unemployment can be an issue in itself. As we read in a *Wall Street Journal* article, "Conventional economic wisdom dictates that lower unemployment sparks wage inflation, which can spiral into wider inflation that is hard to tame."[412] In other words, the Fed has to perform a balancing act of maximizing employment and keeping prices at bay.

Should the Government Pay Unemployment Insurance?

The goal of unemployment insurance is to reduce income uncertainty, which arises when a worker loses his or her job and needs time to find a new one. Unemployment insurance (UI) falls under the jurisdiction of the US Department of Labor and aims to provide unemployment benefits to eligible workers who become unemployed through no fault of their own and who are actively looking for a job.[413]

Unemployment compensation is a social insurance program, which is unique in its kind since it involves a federal-state partnership.[414] It was created by federal law (Social Security Act of 1935), but is administered by state employees under state law. Total UI benefits paid in 2018 amounted to $27.5 billion, and the average weekly benefit per person amounted to $356.[415] Unemployment insurance benefits are funded almost totally by employer taxes (payroll taxes), so the burden of this expense falls primarily on the firms.

Typically a worker covered by unemployment insurance receives 50 percent of his former pay for twenty-six weeks. At the time of this writing, the maximum number of weeks covered by UI benefits varies from sixteen weeks in Florida to thirty weeks in Massachusetts.[416] At times of severe economic conditions and high levels of unemployment, the length of receiving UI benefits is typically extended. In March 2009 President Obama extended unemployment benefits by thirty-three weeks, and in July 2010 Congress passed the Emergency Unemployment Compensation Act, which extended benefits for up to ninety-nine weeks.[417, 418] Between those two dates, the unemployment rate increased from 8.5 percent in March 2009 to 9.5 percent in July 2010.[419, 420]

Unemployment insurance reduces the hardship that people face when becoming unemployed, but it also increases unemployment. We can also observe that after increases in unemployment benefits, the unemployment rate tends to go up, as by the end of 2009 it peaked at ten percent, and then again by the end of 2010 it peaked at 9.8 percent.[421] The explanation is based on the role of incentives, as it impacts the decision-making process and the subsequent behavior. Unemployed spend less time and effort in looking for a job, since finding a job results in losing the unemployment benefits. In addition, unemployed can spend more time looking for better jobs by turning down unattractive job offers.

Several studies looked into job-search efforts before and after UI benefits expire. They found that after UI benefits expire, the probability of finding a new job rises significantly.[422] The conclusion is that the search efforts in finding a job are not as strong in the presence of receiving unemployment insurance benefits. The majority of economists agree that eliminating UI benefits would reduce unemployment, but where they disagree is whether it would improve economic well-being.

In the Old Testament, the Israelites were instructed to provide for the worse-off members of society not through the established channels of authority but through the goodwill of other people. In Leviticus 19:9–10, God instructs the field owners not to harvest all the produce, but to leave some unharvested portions for the poor: "When you reap the harvest of your land, do not reap to the very edges of your field or gather the gleanings of your harvest. Do not go over your vineyard a second time or pick up the grapes that have fallen. Leave them for the poor and the foreigner. I am the LORD your God."

Charity was encouraged in support for those who could not find work or were not able to work. The poor of that day were expected to collect the remainder of the produce from the harvested field. In the book of Ruth, the main character went to the fields to gather the gleanings of the harvest in order to support herself and her mother-in-law. Ruth was a foreigner and a widow, which placed her at the bottom of the socioeconomic ladder. Ruth relied on the goodwill of the field owner to let her collect the leftovers, but she had to work hard and was even commended by the field workers for her diligent work. We can draw an analogy between the biblical command on gleanings and unemployment insurance, except in the former case a person had to work hard to pick up the gleanings of the harvest but in the latter the eligible unemployed worker has to be actively looking for work.

Consistent in spirit with our ten commandments of economics, we propose that the government should not require employers to pay for unemployment insurance. The economic command of "people should be free" elevates individual freedom over government intervention in limiting freedom for the sake of the greater good. In this case, the greater good is the unemployment benefit received by someone who lost his/her job, but the cost is a compulsory payroll tax placed on business owners. The benefit distorts the incentive of looking for a job diligently, which translates into longer times without a job and adds to the cost of paying for unemployment benefits. The cost of unemployment benefits places a burden on employers as well as employees. Employers pay for unemployment insurance and that adds to the overall costs of staying in business and lowers the wages and compensation benefits a company can offer to its employees. In the absence of such a tax, an employer could pay higher wages. We propose that unemployment insurance should be optional and that workers could choose between a job that offers unemployment insurance benefits and the one that does not. This freedom to choose would also result in a lower unemployment rate.

The relationship between unemployment benefits and unemployment rates can also be observed when comparing one country to another. In 2017, French President Emmanuel Macron proposed to extend unemployment payments to people who voluntarily leave their jobs to pursue other jobs, start their own businesses, or work on demand like driving for Uber.[423] Around the same time the UI claimants in France spent on average ten months receiving the benefits, while it was half that number in the US.[424] The results of more generous unemployment benefits also impact the unemployment rate in both countries. In June 2019, the unemployment rate in France was 8.7 percent, compared with 3.7 percent in the United States. In France, the state-backed insurance program has more than 33 billion dollars in debt, while in the United States only two states have an outstanding debt of about $1.7 billion, and twenty-nine states exceed the recommended minimum solvency standard.[425]

We conclude that work is good because God is seen as working. If humans are made in his image, they should work. We should have a distaste for policies that prevent work, such as minimum wage and labor unions. One of the basic assumptions of economics is "there is no free lunch." Thus, if a person is not working, someone is paying for that "lunch." The church is clearly assigned the job of taking care of widows and orphans, who can't provide for themselves. But for most others, the Bible teaches us that work is good, so we should do it.

Chapter 9

The Monetary System

Is Borrowing and Lending Biblical?

Borrowing and lending is such a predominant function of financial markets and a lubricant to a well-functioning economy that studying these concepts through the lens of the Scriptures is vitally important. Borrowing and lending are not treated the same in the Bible; our goal in this section is to examine the difference between the two and ponder on God's intent on treating them differently.

The book of Deuteronomy records God's commandments, which Moses received from the Lord and then conveyed to the Israelites, God's chosen people. Chapter 28 describes the consequences for obedience as well as disobedience in the treatment of God's commands. Verse 12 includes the blessings: "The LORD will open the heavens, the storehouse of his bounty, to send rain on your land in season and to bless all the work of your hands. You will lend to many nations but will borrow from none"; and the curses are found in verse 44: "They will lend to you, but you will not lend to them. They will be the head, but you will be the tail."

Borrowing is treated negatively in the book of Proverbs as well, which associates the borrower as a slave to the lender (Proverbs 22:7). The apostle Paul encourages believers not to be indebted to anyone in Romans 13:8: "Owe no one anything, except to love each other, for the one who loves another has fulfilled the law." It is not a sin to borrow, but borrowing and not paying back is treated as wickedness (see Psalm 37:1).

In the New Testament, Jesus often referred to financial matters in his teaching, especially in His parables. Jesus referred to money lending several times in His parables, and we can infer it was a common practice in those times. Oftentimes, people borrowed out of necessity in order to provide for their most basic needs. Jay Richards in *Money, Greed, and God* notes: "By modern standards, almost everyone was dirt-poor. Only the rich, a tiny minority, had any money to lend. Any money lending, then, would involve rich people lending to their poor neighbors, probably their kin, for a basic need like food."[426] Jesus encouraged his followers to give generously, expecting nothing in return: "And if you lend to those from whom you expect repayment, what credit is that to you? Even sinners lend to sinners, expecting to be repaid in full. But love your enemies, do good to them, and lend to them without expecting to get anything back" (Luke 6:34–35). Richards continues: "Jesus says that even sinners lend money, expecting to receive back the *same* amount. He says nothing about charging interest. Instead, he says we should lend *expecting nothing in return*. So he's admonishing gratuitous generosity, not denouncing banks for charging interest on business loans."[427]

Borrowing and lending can happen for different reasons, and in some instances borrowing is done out of necessity to pay for food and shelter, while in others the borrowing is used to engage in trade and commerce. Richards points out this fact: "It slowly dawned on people that money lent for capital was different from money lent to a poor neighbor out of need. . . . By lending the money, for instance, the bank is forgoing other opportunities to use the money, and it's taking a risk in lending the money in the first place."[428]

From the perspective of a bank or money lender, forgoing other opportunities implies that the amount of loanable funds is fixed at any point in time and that the loan to one party reduces the opportunity of lending to the other. If multiple borrowers are seeking a loan, but the pool of capital is not sufficient to provide for all then the bank has to implement a plan of prioritizing some borrowers over the others. The risk is another important consideration in money lending and is a key determinant on whether the loan will be issued and at what rate. Minimizing the risk by securing collateral and compensating for that risk by charging interest are the reasons to incentivize the holders of capital to part with it, albeit only temporarily.

In a financial sense, risk implies uncertainty about future outcomes; the greater the risk, the greater is the uncertainty of what the future outcome might be. If the borrower has a history of paying back on time and a collateral for the loan can be put forth, then the risk is minimized and chances of getting a loan are high. If the individual does not have a history of paying back on time and does not have collateral, then the risk is higher and the borrower might not be able to obtain the loan or be required to pay a higher interest rate.

In ancient Israel, the law had preferential treatment of the poor and commanded the lender to be lenient to the worst-off members of their society. Exodus 22:25–27 reads, "If you lend money to one of My people among you who is poor, you must not act as a creditor to him; you are not to charge him any interest. If you take your neighbor's cloak as collateral, return it to him by sunset, because his cloak is the only covering he has for his body. What else will he sleep in?" In the same vein of preferential treatment of the poor, Jesus commands to lend even to enemies and not to expect getting anything back. Jesus raises the bar higher. Rather than worrying about getting our money back, he teaches us to just give rather than lend. Jesus encourages us to be generous in personal dealings with those who are in need, but he does not oppose earning interest on the money, which is loaned out.

The parable of the talents in Matthew 25 and Luke 19 is an example where earning interest becomes an important distinction of being faithful. There are three servants in the story and each was given some money to invest. Richards notes, "He should have put it in a bank where it could bear interest. If you're looking for Jesus's views on interest, this is the best clue there is. Jesus isn't giving an economics lesson—the parable is about the kingdom of God. But he would never have told this parable if he thought it was always immoral to accept interest for lending money to someone. On the contrary, he treats risk, investment, *and* interest in a positive light, and trusts his listeners to do the same."[429] If earning interest is being encouraged, then the borrowers of money are also expected to engage in commerce and trade to generate profits. A servant in the story who kept the capital in a safe place and avoided taking on any risk was reprimanded harshly.

Jesus seems to draw a distinction between lending to the poor and lending for the purpose of generating profits. In the former case, Jesus encourages charitable giving rather than lending, but in the latter it is earning the interest that is encouraged. Jesus does not command to give someone else's money as charity, since the person whose money is taken away does not give the money voluntarily but under compulsion. The positive view of interest goes back to early Christian saints, as Samuel Gregg points out in *For God and Profit*: "It was thus possible for interest payments to become understood as a way of reestablishing the balance of justice between lenders and borrowers by *restoring* a lender's financial position to make up the difference (the Latin *interest* means "in between" and "difference") between what was likely to be returned and what was given. Thus, as prominent a medieval figure as the Dominican canonist St. Raymond of Penafort (1175–1275) was able to define interest as "not profit but the avoidance of loss."[430] Charging interest as a compensation for a possible loss is not unjust, but rather just; the greater the probability of a loss, the higher the interest rate.

Gregg also highlights that Christians were involved in banking and venture capitalism as early as we have records of these activities: "Some of the most famous international banking families and venture capitalists of the medieval and early-modern period, such as the Medicis of Florence and the Fuggers of Augsburg, were in fact, Christian and actively involved in the life of the church. After the reformation and until long into the eighteenth century, European and North American financial markets revolved around Calvinist and Catholic banking families in the Netherlands."

Going back to our original question on whether borrowing and lending is biblical, we assert that it is. Borrowing and lending should not be viewed in isolation from the general truths revealed in the Bible, but in conjunction with the overall message. Borrowing is portrayed negatively in the Old Testament, since borrowing represented deficiency and need, and the borrower was likely to use the funds for basic necessities like food and shelter. Borrowing for the purposes of commerce and trade is viewed positively as seen from the parable of the talents. Lending is viewed positively, since the ability to lend implied a certain degree of financial prosperity and blessing from the Lord (Deuteronomy 28:12). In the Old Testament, lending to the poor Israelites included special provisions of not charging interest, while in the New Testament Jesus encouraged to give even to enemies without expecting anything in return. In light of Jesus who gave His life for the sake of sinners, it is not surprising that charitable giving is preferred to lending. There is nothing that sinners can do to repay the gift of salvation, and in light of such a gift, the apostle Paul reminds believers in Ephesus the words of Jesus who said, "It is more blessed to give than to receive" (Acts 20:35).

What Is the Correct Interest Rate?

The interest rate is connected to our previous section on borrowing and lending. While in the previous section we discussed the differences between borrowing and lending in light of biblical passages, in this section we discuss the price of using someone else's money, which is measured by the interest rate. The price of money can range from zero to manyfold the amount being borrowed, and somewhere between those two extremes there is a correct interest rate.

First, we should mention that there is not just one interest rate, but hundreds of various interest rates that exist in a contemporary economy. To complicate matters even more, the interest rate does not stand still but is a constantly moving target responding to various factors and forces.

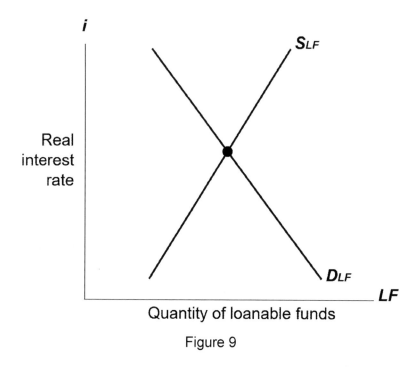

Figure 9

Individuals, firms, and government are all engaged in money borrowing and lending and the laws of supply and demand primarily determine the price of money.

The greater the number of market participants, the lower the chance that any single party has enough market power to set and then maintain the interest rate at a certain level. Consistent with our first economic commandment that people should be free, we believe that the equilibrium interest rate is the correct interest rate, since it jointly reflects the choices of individuals regarding lending and borrowing. The equilibrium interest rate is also consistent with using honest measures, our fifth economic commandment. Robert Sirico notes that one of the benefits of an equilibrium interest rate is that it encourages responsible behavior by rewarding those who save, while taking a fee from those who consume now.[431]

If we define the money available to be lent out as loanable funds, then the demand curve is representative of preferences by economic participants to borrow money at various interest rates. The downward-sloping demand curve indicates that as the interest rate goes up, the quantity of funds demanded goes down, as the rate declines the quantity demanded goes up. The supply curve is representative of investors or lenders who are willing to loan funds at various interest rates. The supply curve is upward sloping, which indicates that the amount of funds available increases as the interest rate increases and declines as the interest rate declines. The equilibrium interest rate is thus a market clearing rate that balances the quantity of loanable funds demanded with quantity of loanable funds supplied. Supply and demand model for loanable funds is depicted in Figure 9.

If policy makers decide to set the interest rate at a certain level, it creates a disequilibrium and results in a shortage or surplus of loanable funds, thus creating dishonest measures. Henry Hazlitt, in *Economics in One Lesson*, notes, "The effect of keeping interest rates artificially low, in fact, is eventually the same as that of keeping any other price below the natural market. It increases demand and reduces supply. It creates economic distortions."[432] A controlled interest rate is not able to send the true signal to borrowers and lenders about the actual conditions in the market and will result in actions driven by distorted incentives. For example, if the Federal Reserve pursues the policy of keeping the federal funds rate low, then lower interest rates distort a company's incentive as they move money from safer investments such as bonds into riskier investments such as stocks. Lower interest rates distort company's incentives as they fund projects that otherwise would be too risky or unfeasible. The interest rate that is purposefully kept low penalizes individuals who live off the conservative investments such as bonds, and it also delays the retirement of those who plan to live off the interest earned on fixed-income securities. Finally, lower interest rates do not attract customer deposits, which are used by banks to fund the loans, and thus banks might experience lower profits.

The use of interest rate caps does not guarantee that people are less likely to get into financial distress. On the contrary, Samuel Gregg writes, "France and Germany, which both have interest rate caps, had around five times the level of complete financial breakdown—such as bankruptcy—among people who had trouble with their debts. While the figure stood at only 4 percent in the UK, in France and Germany it was between 20 and 25 percent. This is a shocking statistic. Financial breakdown of this kind is often accompanied by difficulties in obtaining housing, employment and the purchase of essentials such as food."[433] Implementing interest rate caps does not guarantee that individuals who need a loan, can get one at that low rate. Gregg continues, "It also turns out that the number of those tapping into the black market for loans— which involves truly usurious interest rates and is often characterized by the use of violence to enforce payment—is much less in Britain than in France and Germany." The intention of keeping interest rates low in order to aid the economy often results in abuse of those who need help the most.

Is there a time for a zero interest rate? Yes, if it is an equilibrium interest rate. It is not uncommon in some markets for the seller of a product to provide financing for it. Some examples are car manufacturers who offer zero percent annual percentage rates (APRs) to sell their new cars, or credit card companies who offer zero APRs during a promotional period. Charging a zero percent interest rate is a strategy of boosting sales or increasing a customer base; where the company loses on financing it might gain on profit margins by selling more of their products.

Another instance of charging a zero interest rate is mentioned in Exodus 22, which commands the Israelites not to charge any interest to the poor. Another reference is in Deuteronomy 23:19–20 (ESV): "You shall not charge interest on loans to your brother, interest on money, interest on food, interest on anything that is lent for interest. You may charge a foreigner interest." The distinction is drawn between fellow Israelites and outsiders. George Robinson provides a likely explanation on that, "To some extent, it is the result of living in an agrarian society in which one's neighbors (likely to be fellow Jews) would seek out a loan to tide them over until the next harvest; by comparison, the non-Jew might well be an itinerant merchant who needed the loan purely for business reasons."[434] A practice of charging an unreasonably high interest rate is often referred to as usury. Gregg clarifies, "While usury was certainly seen as a serious sin, the question of its relationship to justice seems primarily to do with the abuse of the poor."[435]

To better understand the determinants of interest rates, we need to consider the following four factors: risk, production opportunities, time preference for consumption, and inflation. These factors directly impact the cost of money and jointly affect the supply and demand for loanable funds. In our previous section, we discussed that risk implies uncertainty about the future repayment of the loan; the greater the risk, the higher the interest rate. Companies decide which projects to accept by assessing the risk of each project and then discounting the anticipated future cash flows by the appropriate interest rate to see which projects generate the greatest value. Banks and other lending institutions assess the risk of individuals by reviewing their credit history, which is summarized by the credit score. Oftentimes lending money to a friend or a relative is based on whether that individual requested money in the past and was able to pay back on time as promised. In some cases, it is better to give than to lend, so that the money does not ruin the relationship. In other cases, it is better not to give if giving enables the person to rely on the bailout and discourages personal responsibility. Risk is a big factor in lending money and assessing that risk and pricing it accordingly helps to better estimate the correct interest rate.

Another factor that impacts interest rates is related to production opportunities. The economy goes through the cycles from recession to boom and the demand for loanable funds goes up when the economy is expanding and declines when the economy is contracting. Firms and individuals increase their borrowing when times are good and decrease spending and borrowing when times are tough or expected to be tough in the near future. When individuals feel secure in keeping their jobs, experience pay raises, and hear that other firms are hiring, they are more likely to spend or borrow in expectation that it will be easy to pay back. When firms see many viable business opportunities and feel optimistic about future economic growth, they are more likely to borrow to invest in various projects. Both of these responses by individuals and firms lead to greater demand for loanable funds, which leads to the upward pressure on the price of money, that is, the interest rate. When the economy is contracting then demand for loanable funds tends to decline, which leads to lower cost of money.

The third factor affecting interest rates is time preference for consumption, which reflects the preferences of individuals to spend immediately versus to delay spending by saving for future needs. Someone who prefers to spend immediately would need to be offered a higher interest rate as a nudge to save, compared to someone who can delay consumption. Time preference for consumption can be high or low relative to an average individual's preference. For example, if Bob cannot delay spending $100 because his rent payment is due, then he has a high-time preference for consumption. On the contrary, if Janet has an extra $100 she can save for later use, then she has a low-time preference for consumption.

Time preference for consumption can be measured at the aggregate level to compare one country with another. Developing economies have a higher preference for consumption since a larger portion of an individual's income goes to cover the immediate needs. Higher interest rates in developing economies also reflect the higher expected growth rates than in developed economies. The interest rate that can be used to reflect this preference at the aggregate level is the real risk-free rate, which is approximated by the Treasury-bill rate minus inflation. T-bill rate is a short-term rate that reflects the immediate tradeoff between waiting to consume and consuming now. Government securities have risk-free rates since the government can print money or raise taxes to pay off its debts. The three-month Treasury bill rate in the United States averaged at 3.5 percent over the last eighty-five years.[436] The real risk-free rate is lower than the T-bill rate because of inflation and is fairly stable over time.

The last factor that impacts interest rates is inflation, which is the tendency of prices to go up over time. If the inflation rate is expected to increase over the next year, then the one-year interest rate will reflect that expectation. Inflation erodes the value of money and thus lenders take inflation into account when determining the appropriate interest rate. The inflation premium is built into the interest rate and is based on the average expected inflation rate over the life of the loan. For example, if the nominal interest rate is five percent and inflation is expected to be six percent over the same time period, then the real value of money would decline and individuals would be better off in buying real assets that keep up with inflation. Since the mid-1980s the inflation rate has been fairly stable, and averaged at 2.6 percent from 1985 through 2018.

To recap, the equilibrium interest rate equates the level of needed funds with the level of supplied funds and informs the decisions of savers and borrowers regarding the funds they could either save (invest) or to consume (slow down on investing). The factors that impact the level of interest rates are risk, production opportunities, time preference for consumption, and inflation. As a general rule, the lower rates encourage borrowing and discourage saving, while the higher rates discourage borrowing and encourage saving. The interest rate cap or floor creates the shortage or surplus of funds, and thus distorts the incentives and behavior of market participants. In light of two economic commandments of people should be free and using honest measures, we assert that the equilibrium interest rate is the correct rate.

Should the Federal Reserve Increase the Money Supply?

Since 1977, the Federal Reserve has operated under a mandate from Congress to pursue three economic goals: maximum employment, stable prices, and moderate long-term interest rates. The first two goals are commonly referred to as the Fed's "dual mandate." The third goal can be achieved by pursuing the second, since long-term interest rates remain at moderate levels when prices are stable.[437]

The Fed does an excellent job in keeping prices stable but typically resorts to lowering short-term interest rates as an aid to the economy during recessionary periods. The process of lowering interest rates is primarily conducted by buying and selling Treasury bonds. This process is called open market operations (OPO), which is the primary channel through which the Fed increases or decreases the money supply.[438] To decrease interest rates, the Fed buys government securities such as Treasury bonds and thus injects money into the economy. To decrease interest rates, the Fed sells government securities and thus reduces the money available to be lent out by banks. The Fed is very effective in controlling the short-term rates via OPO, but the targeted interest rate is not the same as the equilibrium interest rate. The Fed's actions of setting interest rates distort incentives by injecting too much or too little capital into the economy and thus result in unintended consequences. Robert Sirico, in *Defending the Free Market,* writes, "The policies of our central bank seem to reinforce this habit by driving down interest rates to near zero and thereby denying people a material reward—in the form of interest on their banked savings—for foregoing consumption."[439] Denying people a material reward for earning the market interest rate on their savings is equivalent to using dishonest scales. As Proverbs 20:10 says, "Differing weights and differing measures—the LORD detests them both."

Money performs three different functions as a means of exchange, store of value, and unit of account. Individuals in any society are better off if they are given true measures of the money they use to exchange for goods and services. Inflation makes individuals worse off, since it reduces the ability of money to store value over time. It also distorts the ability of money to convey value of one good against the other as prices of various goods may rise at different rates. The federal government is the only entity that can print more money at will, thus the value of money directly depends on the actions conducted by the government.

The Fed has not always had a good grip on inflation, as the 1970s and early 1980s indicate. Shortly after Gerald Ford took office as president in 1974, he addressed Congress in a speech that targeted inflation as "public enemy number one." He proposed a failed initiative known as Whip Inflation Now (WIN) to curtail inflation through the actions of citizens in reducing energy use by carpooling, turning down thermostats, and planting vegetable gardens.[440]

At first glance, you might think that inflation hurts the rich more than the poor, because the rich have more money to be devalued. But the rich have advisors to help them move their money into inflation-secure investments like inflation-protected bonds or TIPS, stocks, gold, and land. And, they have the ability to delay purchases. The worst-off members of our society must buy bread and milk daily from the market. If the majority of their income goes to cover basic necessities like food and shelter, then increases in prices will hamper their ability to afford even some of the basic necessities. The poor suffer to a greater extent when inflation is rising, since their sources of income are fixed in the short term and cannot expand keeping pace with inflation.

In 2018, the Bank of Jamaica launched a public-education campaign and recorded upbeat reggae songs to explain economic concepts such as inflation targeting, monetary policy, and consistent GDP growth.[441] The reason for such a campaign is quite simple: for decades Jamaica's central bank kept interest rates low and printed money to finance a budget deficit, which resulted in multiple bailouts from the IMF. The IMF's assistance program calls for austerity measures, which are notoriously unpopular with the public, and music videos are used to build public support for a government policy designed to bring economic stability. Jamaica's central bank has not been independent from direct government control, and fifteen bailouts later their parliament plans to vote on a bill that would make their central bank independent of the elected government. They have one primary mandate—to control inflation.

Should the Federal Reserve Bank fight inflation? This is the first job of the Federal Reserve Bank: to match the supply of dollars with the value that's being created. If they just did that, and left the economy alone, it would be fine. Makes sense, doesn't it? The increase in the amount of dollars should match the growth in production of goods and services. When they match, inflation is zero. When there are too many dollars, relative to production, there is inflation. When there are not as many dollars, relative to production, there is deflation and the level of prices declines. The US economy has experienced deflation in 2008 and 2009 in the midst of the Great Recession. At first glance, consumers may like to see falling prices, but it also discourages spending because even lower prices are now expected. Firms are likely to see lower revenues and consumers are likely to get lower wages. Deflation increases the real value of debt, which makes it more difficult for consumers to pay off their loans. High inflation and deflation are both undesirable for the overall economy, but increasing money supply in step with economic growth ensures money will hold its value.

The Federal Reserve Act of 1913 established the Federal Reserve System as the central bank of the United States to oversee the monetary policy to achieve a more flexible, stable, and safer monetary and financial system.[442] The goal of achieving full employment (i.e., reducing unemployment) was added in the mid-sixties. That was probably a mistake. Employment is going to come and go and fluctuate around its natural rate. The failure of the Phillips curve shows this. The Phillips curve shows a tradeoff between inflation and unemployment, and higher inflation as a policy option may work to reduce unemployment. However, Milton Friedman among others suggested that additional inflation barely reduces unemployment since people become used to inflation at which point the Phillips curve shifts upward resulting in higher inflation but not lower unemployment. After the Great Recession of 2007–2009, the extended period of falling inflation and unemployment is not consistent with the Phillips curve model.

In a market-driven economy, the Fed manages the money supply to smooth the economic cycle from both extremes. But if we imagine a purely socialist economy, then no money would exist in that society. Goods and services would be owned and distributed by the government. In that scenario, believers would not be able to fulfill their commandment to give.

Is a Strong Dollar Good for America?

A strong dollar can be either good or bad based on the perspective of the person you ask. If you ask a person who plans to visit other countries then he or she would benefit from a strong dollar. Having a strong dollar makes it more affordable to travel as foreign goods and services appear relatively less pricey. If you ask an exporter who is trying to sell a batch of goods overseas, you may hear a different story. Having a strong dollar hurts industries that are heavy on exporting, since US goods appear relatively more expensive compared with their rivals.

An example might be helpful to illustrate these points. Imagine you are traveling to London and checking out hotel prices. You would like to stay at the London Bridge Hotel that costs 136 pounds per night, which is equivalent to $220 US dollars at a $1.61 per pound exchange rate. If the dollar strengthens to where it takes $1.22 to buy one pound, then the same hotel will cost about $166 per night. A US tourist is better off since each dollar goes further abroad and prices are relatively less expensive. From the viewpoint of the US manufacturer, the strengthening of the dollar might mean a lower volume of exports or/and lower profit margins. If the costs for US producers are incurred in dollars but the products are sold overseas in foreign currency, then the exchange rate plays an important role in estimating profits. If the cost of making an automobile is $18,000 to be sold in the UK market, then the lowest pound price would be 11,180 pounds at the exchange rate of $1.61 per pound. If the value of the US dollar goes up relative to the British pound, then $18,000 is equivalent to 14,754 pounds at the new exchange rate of $1.22/pound. If the US exporter raises the price in pounds from 11,180 to 14,754 to keep the same $18,000 inflow, then a US-made car is not as attractive of a purchase in the UK market since its cost just went up by 32 percent. A US exporter is worse off because his sales would plummet due to the law of demand, which states that as the price goes up, quantity demanded goes down. If the US exporter doesn't raise the UK's price by 32 percent, then he would experience losses for each sold car. The risk that cash flows are hard to predict due to fluctuating exchange rate is termed as exchange rate risk. Firms take several measures to reduce such risk, but it is a topic for another chapter.

Going back to our original question, there are clear winners and losers of a strong dollar and it is questionable whether a strong dollar is good for America. For example, an investor in the United States would benefit from a strong dollar, since return from dollar appreciation would be added to the return from the foreign investment itself. The government does not necessarily benefit from a strong dollar, however, since the government might care to reduce trade deficit and a strong dollar only works to increase trade deficit rather than decrease it. A trade deficit occurs when the value of imports exceeds the value of exports; a strong dollar only increases the price for foreigners, who buy American goods. The government might like the value of the US dollar to be sustained since it is easier to sell government bonds to sovereign funds and pay lower interest rates.

Should There Be Active or Passive Monetary Policy?

This question is easy for atheists. If there is no active God, there is only government run by humans, and therefore a more active monetary policy is better. As believers, we have to make a choice somewhere along the active-passive continuum.

In *The Red Sea Rules,* Robert Morgan puts us at the edge of the Red Sea with the escaping Israelites. The Pharaoh's troops are approaching with drawn swords. What do you do? Among the ten pieces of advice is Red Sea rule #5: Stay calm and confident and give God time to work. That's it? This turns the old phrase, "Don't stand there, do something," to "Don't do something, just stand there." Exodus 14:13–14 (NKJV) says, "Do not be afraid. Stand still, and see the salvation of the LORD, which He will accomplish for you today. For the Egyptians whom you see today, you shall see again no more forever. The LORD will fight for you, and you shall hold your peace." This Red Sea rule encourages a passive monetary policy, because there is an active God who will take care of things.

But Red Sea Rule #5 is followed quickly by Red Sea rule #6: When unsure, just take the next logical step by faith.

As a side note, that's what we have done in writing this book. We have found a gap: Christians don't understand biblical economics very well. How to fill that gap is where we have relied on this Red Sea rule. We have simply taken the next logical step by faith. God gave us knowledge of economics and the Bible. He gave us the ability to write, even though Sergiy is writing in his third language. We have continued to take the next logical step by faith. The book in your hand is the result.

OK, back to monetary policy. Red Sea rule #6 advises a more active policy. It cites Exodus 14:15 (NKJV): "Why do you cry to Me? Tell the children of Israel to go forward." One logical step at a time. That's because God is logical. He very seldom tells someone to take an illogical step. God could tell Dave to buy a ticket to Africa and serve indigent people there. But it's more likely that if Dave does end up in Africa, it's because he has a friend named Andy Perkins who established a feeding center in Liberia for undernourished kids. God typically uses your friends and acquaintances to tell you how to "move forward."

It's the same with monetary policy. It's hard for us to believe that God wants really aggressive monetary policy. That would indicate a lack of faith in God to affect our lives. If we believe there is a God who represents himself in the Holy Spirit to make our world better, we have to believe he is at work in monetary policy as well. That should encourage us to at least move to the relatively passive end of the spectrum.

Dave's swimming pool was twenty years old and in need of serious repair. Because he's cheap, he chose to do some of the work himself. With his cousin, he dug and moved the PVC pipes that serve the filter system. He found a grounding wire at the bottom of a three-foot hole, twisted it up, tossed it in the hole, and covered it with dirt, planning to reground the motor after extending the pipes forty feet. That night, the pool guy texted to remind him to extend the bonding wire. "Bonding wire? What's that?" As it turns out, when a pool is built wires are attached to the rebar in the pool to dissipate electrical surges. Dave had buried the bonding wire under three feet of dirt. The next day, the guys pouring the concrete deck buried it under another foot of dirt. The night before the concrete was to be poured, Dave and Ginger had multiple phone calls to experts and a trip to Home Depot in an attempt to produce an alternate plan to replace the buried wire. Then next morning, Dave and Ginger, the pool guy, and the cement guy gathered at the spot where cement was scheduled to be poured in an hour, further burying the bonding wire. As they stood together, Dave looked down and said, "What's this?" It was the bonding wire, laying on top of the ground. Dave and the cement guy looked at each other in disbelief. "Angels!" shouted the cement guy. Let's use this little episode to create three categories of belief in God's activity in our lives.

1. Angels moved the wire overnight. That requires a belief in a metaphysical power that moves physical things in our world.
2. Angels guided the hands of Dave and the cement guys without them knowing it. Could be.
3. The wire was there all the time. There is no such thing as a god who is active in our lives.

We could categorize the Christian view of monetary policy the same way. Those who adopt the first belief would not even favor a central bank, because they would believe God takes care of monetary policy. Those who adopt the second belief would say that God guides the hands of Federal Reserve Bank officials as they implement policy. The third is the atheist, who, as we mentioned earlier, has the easiest decision to make. Since there is no god, humans are alone in making policy.

Certainly, the Fed should be open and transparent about monetary policy, to remain in alignment with economic commandment #5: use honest measures. "Christian economists advocate monetary policy that is transparent; that is, the Federal Reserve should do its very best to ensure that no policy change comes as a surprise."[443]

Here's a brief explanation of monetary policy. It is the adjustment of the interest rate and money supply by the Federal Reserve Bank.

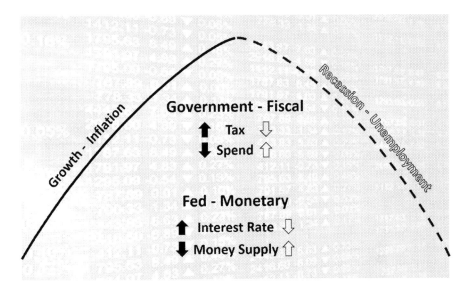

Figure 10. The Macro Model

The macro model shows that as the economy heats up, the top must be shaved off to avoid a steep rise followed by a crash. The economy is slowed down by increasing interest rates and decreasing the supply of money. Actually, a class exercise shows how those two actions are really only one.

Dave's macro class is divided into twelve "city groups," each one representing a city where there is a federal reserve bank. For this exercise, Dave invites a student from the New York group to the front of the class and puts a Federal Reserve Bank cap on him. "Jackson represents the president of the New York Federal Reserve Bank, and I represent a citizen," Dave announces. "At the end of the Federal Open Market Committee meeting the voting members turn to the president of the New York Fed and say, 'We've decided to change (let's say lower) the interest rate. Go increase the money supply, until the interest rate is in the range we want.'" At this point, Jackson, representing the New York Fed, is holding money and Dave is holding a Treasury Bond. Jackson gives the money to Dave, who gives the bond to Jackson. "There," Dave announces, "The money supply has been increased. Jackson will keep doing this until the interest rate is in the assigned range." It's as easy as that. Changing the money supply changes the interest rate (price) of money.

But how active should the Fed be? Let's return to the continuum created by Red Sea Rules #5 and #6: God's sovereignty, and man's responsibility. If God is sovereign, he could do anything he wants, without human intervention. But our Christian worldview states that he has called us to join him in this endeavor to redeem the broken world. So we're someplace in the middle. As Christians we want to honor our fellow believers on both ends, realizing that God moves differently in each of us. A sovereign God has called us to work with him to redeem the broken world. What a privilege and a high calling! But it should also humble us, so that we pray every time we consider adjusting monetary policy. If we believe there is an active God who is active in the world, we will seek his guidance on every monetary adjustment.

Claar and Klay take a more definitive tone: "Given the speed at which freely functioning markets direct resources to their most highly valued uses, monetary policymakers should never seek to actively manage the economy. Instead, the most important thing that the Federal Reserve can do to help the economy improve steadily over time is to make sure that we experience as few surprises as possible."[444]

Have we answered the question? How about this: *A biblical Christian economist will favor a less active monetary policy than an atheist, and a more active policy than someone who does not believe God called us to work with him.*

Samuel Gregg takes this view: "Beyond issues of inflation, governments can conduct monetary policy in ways that profoundly damage the common good. Excessive reliance on monetary policy to stimulate the economy instead of tackling deeper, more intractable, economic problems that may be politically unpopular to address can mean that a government is not facing up to its responsibilities to the common good."[445] He seems to be saying that monetary policy that is too active causes harm to the economy, and the Fed has shown this destructive tendency more than a few times.

The more we learn about economic history, the more it seems like there should be one monetary policy: Match money supply to GDP growth to maintain stable prices. This puts us in the group of Milton Friedman, who claimed the Fed's most important job was to control inflation. The second mandate, to control unemployment, is seen as an overreach to many economists, and we would put ourselves in that group. Employment always does seem to return. Is it the work of angels? Perhaps. And perhaps it is the ongoing work of an active God who guides the hands of those pulling the monetary levers of money supply and interest rates. Claar and Klay agree with us: "Therefore, freely functioning markets create the jobs necessary to maintain high levels of employment in an economy; active monetary policy—no matter how noble its makers' intentions—cannot reliably accomplish it."[446]

Forced to make a summary statement, we would say that biblical economics teaches us to be active in controlling money supply to limit inflation, but not active in attempting to control unemployment. We will leave that to God—and his angels, if he chooses to do it that way.

Chapter 10

Inflation

What Does the Bible Say about Inflation?

Christian economists tend to agree that inflation is not a desirable phenomenon, and that stable prices not only benefit an average member of society but especially those who are the most vulnerable: the poor. Samuel Gregg notes, "On the ethics of money, for instance, Messner stated that, from the standpoint of Christian ethics and natural law, 'the maintenance of the stability of the value of money is the fundamental obligation of justice.'"[447] Claar and Klay add, "Moreover, price instability is particularly harmful to the poor. Levin and Smith (2005) make a thorough case for helping the poor through the pursuit of stable prices."[448] Henry Hazlitt, who was not a professing Christian but one of the early defenders of the free markets back in the 1940s, wrote in *Economics in One Lesson*, "Inflation acts to determine the individual and business policies we are all forced to follow. It discourages all prudence and thrift. It encourages squandering, gambling, reckless waste of all kinds. It plants the seeds of fascism and communism. It leads men to demand totalitarian controls. It ends invariably in bitter disillusion and collapse."[449] In another place Hazlitt states, "Inflation is the opium of the people."[450]

Earlier we noted that increases in money supply that correspond with the rate of economic growth is healthy for the economy. Additions to the money stock do not necessarily result in inflation if more products are available to be purchased with extra money. However, if more money is printed than what would be supported by growth in GDP, then prices are bound to rise. Quantity theory of money asserts that the quantity of money determines the price level while the growth in the quantity of money determines the inflation rate. According to the quantity theory, the primary cause of inflation is the growth in the quantity of money. As Nobel Prize-winning economist Milton Friedman once said, "Inflation is always and everywhere a monetary phenomenon in the sense that it is and can be produced only by a more rapid increase in the quantity of money than in output." Since the government is the only entity given power to print money, then the primary cause of inflation lies in the actions conducted by the government.

Inflation Tax

When the government prints money to raise revenue, it imposes an inflation tax on its citizens. An inflation tax is not a tax that has to be paid to the government directly, but rather indirectly when the increased price level reduces the value of dollars kept in wallets and bank accounts. The inflation tax affects everyone who holds money and discourages people from saving money. Milton Friedman once said, "Inflation is taxation without legislation." Printing money raises revenue for the government just as taxes would, but the former does not require legislation to do it while the latter does. A very high rate of inflation is known as hyperinflation, typically defined as inflation in excess of 50 percent a month. Those governments that resort to printing money as a way to raise revenue usually suffer from high spending, inability to raise sufficient funds through taxes, and limited ability to borrow.

In the recent past, the inflation tax has been an insignificant source of revenue in the United States and accounts for less than three percent of government revenue.[451] However, in the 1970s and early 1980s the United States experienced periods of high inflation and the public viewed such periods as a major economic issue. An unusually high period of inflation in 1980 of 13.5 percent coincided with the year of presidential elections when Ronald Reagan defeated the incumbent Jimmy Carter in a landslide. Reagan pointed to high inflation as a major failure of Carter's economic policy. Since then, the average rate of inflation has been under three percent between 1981 and 2019, which has facilitated economic growth and provided a level of certainty about future prices to households and firms.

Tax Distortions

Most taxes distort incentives and lead to less efficient allocation of the economy's resources. Many taxes exacerbate these distortions in the presence of inflation. Inflation works to increase the burden of paying taxes on capital gains and income earned from savings because nominal values are used rather than real ones in assessing the size of tax. For example, if someone earned ten percent in interest income over the time period with an inflation rate of four percent, then the actual return would be only six percent. The tax is assessed on the nominal rate of ten percent even though someone only gained six percent in real terms. A capital gains tax is assessed on the positive difference between the sale price and the purchase price of an asset. If someone purchased an asset for $400 and sold it for $1,000 five years later, then a long-term capital gains tax on $600 would be assessed. However, if inflation over the same time frame was five percent per year, the real value of a $400 investment would be worth about $511; thus, the real gain would be the difference between $511 and $1,000, not $400 and $1,000. In other words, the higher the inflation rate, the greater the distortion between the real gain and the nominal gain on which the tax is assessed. In both scenarios, the tax imposed on capital gains and interest income discourages savings and investments—and this effect is magnified in the presence of inflation.

Living through Hyperinflation

An increase in prices leads to a decrease in the quality of life for many households. An extended period of high inflation not only discourages saving but also can erase a lifetime's worth of savings. Living through such a period can have a lasting effect. Sergiy recollects his own experience of living through a period of hyperinflation in Ukraine from 1993 to 1997. Sergiy's father, who kept the family savings at a bank, ignored the warning of upcoming inflation and paid the price of losing it all. At one point, the Ukrainian government froze all bank accounts and no money could be withdrawn during the inflationary period.

Sergiy's family is just one example from when an extended period of high inflation in Ukraine wiped out the savings of millions of households. It also affects the fabric of society, changing its thinking and habits regarding money. Sergiy's entrepreneurial brother-in-law Valeriy, who got to live through hyperinflation in his late twenties, was convinced even in his thirties and forties that saving money was always a bad idea; he would rather spend extra cash on new cameras and equipment for his photography business as soon as it was available.

The ingrained attitude of holding cash as a losing proposition results in lower savings and impacts the whole economy negatively, since the uncertainty in the ability of money to keep its value complicates fundamental business decisions regarding accessing capital, determining appropriate prices, and keeping track of rising costs. At times of high inflation, the families who live on fixed income or from paycheck to paycheck are hit the hardest. The incomes that do not rise in step with inflation create hard choices for families to pay for basic necessities such as food or shelter. In sum, the state gets richer at the expense of its citizens when it prints too much money.

Arbitrary Transfer of Wealth

A surprising period of high inflation arbitrarily transfers wealth from one group to another. A lender gets poorer, while the borrower gets richer during the time of high inflation. For example, if a borrower secures a mortgage at a fixed rate of six percent over the next thirty years, then any surprising period of high inflation works to arbitrarily transfer wealth from the lender to the borrower. In fact, a thirty-year mortgage at six percent and average annual inflation of four percent reduces the real cost of borrowing from six to two percent and equates to a transfer of $575 a month from the lender to the borrower on a $250,000 mortgage. If inflation is predictable then lenders would account for it in the interest rate that they charge, but a surprising period of high inflation arbitrarily redistributes wealth not based on need or merit. A deflationary period would work in the same way, except the wealth is transferred from the borrower to the lender since the real value of the loan to be repaid at times of falling prices goes up.

Regardless of whether prices go up or down, a surprising change in the purchasing power of money creates winners and losers and works to reduce economic activity. Lenders will reduce lending activity and start charging higher rates accounting for added risk of surprising inflation. Countries with higher average inflation experience more variation in the inflation rate from year to year and suffer more from arbitrary transfers of wealth. Countries with lower average inflation benefit from stable prices and increased economic activity because of the predictable nature of future price changes.

Changing the Unit of Account

Money is used as a unit of account, store of value, and medium of exchange. As a unit of account, money helps people to decipher relative values of different goods and services and provides a way to measure the value of assets, liabilities, labor, and income. Money as a stable unit of account works similarly as other conventional ways of measuring lengths, weights, time, etc. Can you imagine arbitrarily changing the number of minutes in an hour from sixty to one hundred? It would create nationwide confusion and result in a strong pushback from the public. Likewise, when government prints too much money, it distorts the value of money and creates confusion regarding old versus new prices, prices of some goods compared to those of other goods, and expenses in relation to income. It becomes much harder to allocate the resources to their optimal use within the economy since the best performers are harder to identify.

As investors evaluate companies based on their performance, they have to spend more time and effort in determining which companies are profitable and which are not. At times of high inflation, it becomes increasingly hard to estimate profits, since revenues and costs are measured in dollars with different real values. For example, a company's cost of goods sold could have been $100 million and the sales worth $200 million, leaving the company with a net operating income of $100 million. The real value of net operating income could be much less if the costs were incurred at old prices, but the revenues were made with new inflated prices. The allocation of resources to their best economic use is hindered in the presence of inflation, since managers, debtholders, and investors might not be able to estimate accurately the real value of firms' profits and compare the performance of one firm to the next.

Shoe Leather and Menu Costs

Economists typically cite two other costs of inflation, which are shoe leather and menu costs. Shoe leather costs capture the time spent, effort exerted, convenience sacrificed, and other related costs which are incurred in reducing someone's money holdings; the more literal meaning comes from the wear and tear on someone's shoes because of more frequent trips to exchange money for other goods and services. Shoe leather costs are not significant in the US, since for almost four decades the inflation was kept at a moderate level. However, those countries that go through hyperinflation experience a significant waste of resources as people are trying to spend or convert money to a more stable currency as soon as they get paid. As people make more frequent trips to the marketplace, they are more likely to face instances of fraud and theft.

Sergiy remembers that during such a time in Ukraine in the '90s, many currency speculators or "money changers" would appear roaming marketplaces or standing in front of department stores or train stations calling out: "Dollars, rubles, zloty . . ." Those times were ripe for such activity, since the official currency exchangers were not keeping up with real changes in exchange rates; street money changers were able to offer much better rates. Oftentimes, you could spot several money changers right outside the official foreign currency exchange window trying to lure the customers by offering better rates. The risks of using money changers were high, since you could be fooled with fake banknotes or your money could be simply taken away. Law enforcement agencies either looked the other way or did very little to stop the fraudulent activities. However, there are cases when fraud was prosecuted, and Sergiy became a witness to one such case.

In the spring of 1999, as Sergiy and his friend walked past the police department on the way to their next class at the university, they were stopped by a police officer dressed as a civilian who asked them to participate in the witness trial and offered an excuse note for missing a class. A part of the process was to watch a video where apparently a money changer took the money from another individual on a busy street and ran off. After playing the video, several individuals were brought in the room one by one, and Sergiy and his friend were asked to identify the individual who appeared in the video.

By the early 2000s, as the exchange rate became more stable and the inflation rate somewhat moderate, the money changers started to disappear in Ukraine. Their services were no longer needed, as the value of Ukrainian hryvnia has stabilized and more competitive exchange rates were available at the official money exchangers. It was not just bad reputation but the laws of supply and demand which helped to end the phase of street money changers in Ukraine. In general, high rates of inflation breed black markets and impose other costs on society such as higher instances of fraud and theft.

Limited Access to Capital

Another disadvantage to society with higher average rates of inflation are borrowing costs. Even in periods of lower inflation, banks will charge higher interest rates in anticipation that inflation may increase in the future. It prices out many families from being able to afford a mortgage, which has been a longstanding way to assess capital in the developed nations. As of this writing in January 2020, a fixed thirty-year mortgage rate in the United States is 3.88 percent and a fifteen-year rate is even lower at 3.30 percent. Conventional mortgages have some flexibility in the amount of the down payment, typically ranging from five to twenty percent from the purchase amount. At the same time, the mortgage rates in Ukraine start at 19.99 percent with a minimum 30 percent down payment and a maximum twenty-year term. For the sake of comparison, someone taking a loan for $100,000 in the United States at 3.88 percent for twenty years would pay about $600 a month, and an equivalent loan in Ukraine at 19.99 percent would require about $1,700 a month. It is true that the inflation rate in Ukraine is much higher at 7.9 percent in 2019, compared with 2.3 percent for the same year in the United States. If we adjust the interest rate for inflation in both countries, then the payment in the United States would be equivalent to $486, and in Ukraine $1,107. Higher average inflation in Ukraine reduces the ability of the middle class to afford a mortgage and start building equity. Access to capital for startup firms is equally hard to obtain, and economic activity which could enrich the country does not happen. The inflation raises the level of uncertainty about the future and reduces the number of transactions, which could have happened in a more stable economic environment.

A Lesson from Joseph

As we have established, the main cause of inflation is when a government prints too much money. However, the other cause of rising prices should be recognized: when the production level drops, holding all else equal.

The story of Joseph found in the book of Genesis 37–50 highlights the rise in dominance and power of the Egyptian pharaoh as a result of the prolonged famine. Joseph predicts the time of famine, which follows the time of plentiful harvest. Pharaoh appointed Joseph to collect a portion of the harvest during the prosperous times, so it could be stored and later sold during the times of famine. When famine struck the land, Joseph not only accumulated great wealth for Pharaoh, but also the land and the people. During the famine, the Pharaoh became the sole owner of the resource everyone desired and as a result he could charge the high price. The agrarian societies highly relied on the good harvest, since that was their sustenance for the rest of the year. No harvest for one year could be bad enough to wipe out the family savings, if it had any. No harvest for multiple years results in high prices for food and famine throughout the land. Joseph's father Jacob, who had accumulated great wealth, had resources to send his sons to Egypt to buy grain. Pharaoh became the monopolist in selling a scarce resource—grain—and thus could charge higher prices. He increased his dominance not only in Egypt but also among other nations. Famine led to scarcity, and scarcity to higher prices.

Wilhelm Röpke, in *Humane Economy*, notes how much success Germany got to experience shortly after World War II when they turned their near-bankrupt economy to follow the tenets of market economy and monetary discipline: "The world was treated to a unique and instructive example of the paralysis and anarchy which can afflict an economy when utterly mistaken economic policies destroy the foundations of economic order and of how quickly and thoroughly it can recover from its fall and start on a steep, upward climb if only economic policy recognizes its error and reverses its course."[452]

Another aspect of keeping inflation at bay is to not stimulate employment through government spending. Claar and Klay point out, "As Keynes and his critics both pointed out, policy actions designed to stimulate employment today will lead to greater inflation tomorrow."[453] Hazlitt echoes a similar sentiment, "Inflation gives birth to a thousand illusions. The most persistent is that it will bring full employment. This argument in its cruder form rests on the immemorial confusion between money and real wealth. What inflation really does is to change the relationships of prices and costs."[454]

In summary, Christians who have concern for the poor should dislike inflation. The first job of the Federal Reserve Bank was to create "stable prices," which is another way of stating "controlled inflation." It is our stance that the addition of the dual mandate—to also limit unemployment—has weakened the Fed's concentration on their first responsibility. In terms of the Ten Commandments of Economics, inflation also violates the concept of honest measures. Prices that are inflating every day are not a reflection of the honest value of dollars, nor of the products and services they buy.

Chapter 11

Fiscal Policy

Economic humanism is the assumption that humans are in charge of the world. This is an easy decision for atheists: since they believe there is no god, humans are responsible for everything. But for Christians—and any religious believers—we have a tough decision to make: What decisions do we trust to God, and what do we do ourselves? This can be seen as two extremes: God's sovereignty on one end of the spectrum, and man's responsibility on the other. God could take care of the economy if he chooses to. But we believe he calls us alongside to act as his "viceroys" to work with him. So even as we rely on God for our sustenance, we work for some of it. Monetary policy (chapter 9) and fiscal policy are subject to this Christian decision-making. As Christians, we are going to favor less economic humanism than the atheist. How much? Let's consider that question together.

Should the Government Practice Stimulus Spending?

Stimulus spending only works in the short term, yet you can only do it in the long term.

First, the long term. Economic humanism was exemplified by the American Recovery and Reinvestment Act of 2009, the $800 billion stimulus was the largest economic recovery program in history. Adjusted for inflation, it was nearly five times more expensive than the Works

Progress Administration. It was bigger than the Louisiana Purchase, the Manhattan Project, the moon race, and the Marshall Plan.[455]

When President Obama campaigned for the stimulus package at the start of his presidency in January of 2009, he and others in his administration repeatedly insisted the investments would go to "shovel-ready" projects—projects that would put people to work right away. In August of 2010, local governments were still facing delays spending the money they had been allocated.

The economy moves quickly, and governmental entities are notoriously slow. Unemployment remained near ten percent nearly two years after President Obama signed his economic stimulus package. Mr. Obama acknowledged in an hour-long interview with *The New York Times* that, despite his campaign promises, "there's no such thing as shovel-ready projects."[456] Economists knew there were no shovel-ready projects when the first announcement was made in 2009. There is a lag between proposing programs and implementing them. Stimulus can be proposed in the short term, but it can only be spent in the long term.

Now, the short term. Can you trade off inflation for reduced unemployment? Yes, in the short term, but that term closes before the government can get the money spent. The administration bragged that by March 2011—two years after the stimulus bill was passed—$633 billion of the $787 billion had been spent. There are very few projects where 80 percent is considered a success, especially when the objective is to spend money.

As we write this section, the US is entering a probable recession from the coronavirus pandemic. President Trump is suggesting a fiscal policy of sending checks directly to citizens, perhaps as big as $1,200. President George W. Bush did the same thing in 2008. That does provide some mitigation of the time-lag problem, but it does not prevent the debt that is incurred as a result of the stimulus.

First, there is a problem of recognizing we're in a recession. Students are often surprised to find that economists don't know where we are until we've been there. So there is a recognition lag, often a few months.

Then there is the implementation lag, which in President Obama's case took more than two years. That means, much of the stimulus money gets spent in a growth phase of the economy, where the government should be doing the opposite: withdrawing spending. So fiscal policy runs the risk of doing exactly the opposite of what it should be doing. Due to its lengthy recognition and implementation lags, fiscal policy proves less reliable in pursuing macroeconomic goals than monetary policy.[457]

The Phillips curve alleges you can spend your way out of a recession by increasing spending and trading off inflation for reduced unemployment. It has been proven wrong. You get the inflation, but employment returns to its natural level. And, you get the debt from the spending. So this produces two conflicts with our Ten Commandments of Biblical Economics.

Henry Hazlitt, in his 1978 update of *Economics in One Lesson*, wrote, "More than 40 years after the publication of John Maynard Keynes' *General Theory* and more than twenty years after that book has been thoroughly discredited by analysis and experience, a great number of our politicians are still unceasingly recommending more deficit spending in order to cure or reduce existing unemployment."[458] Governments just don't get it. Why not? Most economic myths stem from a denial of the fallen nature.

The Fall

Presidents like to spend stimulus money because *they* do the spending. When road development expenditures were made from the 2009 stimulus package, they were accompanied by large road signs that included President Obama's name. You have to wonder if he would have approved the stimulus if the name of his political opponents were put on the signs.

Stimulus spending is also rife with corruption and insider dealing. Think about it: $787 billion needs to be spent quickly. Based on the assumption of the fallen nature, would you expect this to increase or decrease corruption? To paraphrase Lord Acton, "Spending money tends to corrupt, and the more that's spent, the greater the corruption."

Denial of the fall is the supporting argument to justify big government. It is a myth that big government provides vital assistance to the average American. In this chapter, we will show how that is a myth. Instead of helping the average person at the expense of the wealthy, bigger government taps into the fallen nature and encourages fiscal policy makers to serve themselves at the expense of others. When used as a panacea for society's problems, fiscal policy fails. As government grows more powerful via fiscal policy, it becomes more aligned with the fallen nature of the centers of power in society.[459]

Don't Steal

This is "spending" in the macro model. If the government could spend from its resources, it would not be stealing, and a Christian economist would favor it. But the government has no money. It only has money that has been confiscated from successful, free-market capitalist entities. First, because the government only *distributes* scarce resources, it does not *create* them. It can only redistribute profits that are made by free-market participants. It cannot make its own profits. So money that is spent in stimulus programs has been taken from the profits of individuals and corporations. It is simply redistributing those profits from their place of value creation to a place where government officials believe they will create more profit. This is the elitist attitude at work. To believe that government officials, with their limited view of the market, can more accurately distribute wealth than the market, where everyone votes, is the height of narcissism and economic humanism.

Second, the government does not have the money in hand so it has to borrow it, which increases the national debt. Consuming goods without paying for them is stealing. Stimulus spending increases the debt, which we will discuss later. That debt is owed by the next generation, and that's why it is theft. The next generation does not consume the goods that are bought in the stimulus, but they must pay for them.

Honest Measures

Let's look at the facts of the 2008 recession and the subsequent 2009 recovery. The economy shrank by 4.4 percent in the first quarter of 2009 and 0.6 percent in the second quarter, then grew by 1.5 percent in the third quarter and 4.5 percent in the fourth quarter. These are dishonest measures, because they confuse correlation with causality. They assume the economy would not recover on its own. That's not consistent with the historical record. The economy has gone down eleven times since World War II, and it's come back up eleven times. It always recovers. What economists measure is the speed of the recovery. And, even though the 2009 recovery was supported by historically strong monetary policy and a $787 billion stimulus, it still set a record for the slowest recovery of the eleven since World War II. So, if you're using only correlation, it is honest to state, "The $787 billion stimulus *correlated* with the slowest economic recovery in eighty years." That's an honest measure. It is dishonest to say the stimulus *caused* the recovery. And even if it did, it caused the slowest recovery in modern history.

Should the Government Have Debt?

Henry Hazlitt had the correct view of deficit spending, way back in 1946: "The public works seem to be created out of new purchasing power. For the moment, the nation seems to have got something for nothing. The government cannot keep piling up debt indefinitely; for if it tries, it will someday become bankrupt."[460]

We are rather astounded at seemingly reputable economists who claim that government debt does not matter. We are reminded of the cartoon where Wile E. Coyote runs off the cliff, then freezes in space before he realizes there is no ground underneath him. If economic rules work, and we're quite sure they do, debt is not a Christian ideal.

People Should Be Free

When debt creates leverage, it can have a positive economic outcome. We encourage our students to limit their college debt, but they are confident that the certificate they receive at graduation will increase the human capital they supply to society, and they will be rewarded for their value creation activities. Reliable data shows that college graduates make about $20,000 a year more than non-college grads. Thus, the investment in a college degree should pay measurable dividends and increase their freedom.

If the government could show that the estimated $1.1 trillion deficit spending in 2019 was an investment in assets that could increase the future wealth of the nation, there could be a Christian argument for an increase of freedom. But there seems to be no evidence of those assets existing. If the government could show a new interstate highway system that would improve distribution of goods, or perhaps a high-speed internet system that would increase data transfer, those investments would benefit the future resource capability of citizens. But no such claims are made. Thus, we have to consider that almost all national debt is really intergenerational theft.

Don't Steal

In an earlier section on stimulus, we pointed out that stimulus produces debt, but not economic growth. The US debt clock shows that you *do* get the debt that arises from the spending. It is currently just over $22.5 trillion. Then-senator Barack Obama accused President George Bush of being unpatriotic by raising the debt per citizen from $20,000 to $30,000—then *President* Obama raised it to more than $60,000.

Economists are concerned that the debt as a percentage of GDP has gone from 57 percent in 1990 to 105 percent today. Consuming goods without paying for them is a reasonable definition of stealing, and that's what's happening. Seen in that light, it's the oldest game in politics: to take from those—like widows and orphans—who can't defend themselves from the theft. For the approximately 25 percent of Americans under the voting age, government debt is taxation without representation. Via fiscal policy, the government has taken future wealth from children because they can't vote, and given it to adults because they can.

Pope Benedict XVI argued that the readiness of so many governments to take on such high amounts of debt may mean that "we are living at the expense of future generations."[461] The Pope is interpreting economic rules correctly: there is no free lunch. Someone, sometime, has to pay for the current level of debt.

In warning the people of Israel against a king, Samuel predicted that a king would accumulate land for himself, and require forced labor to work it.[462] That's what government officials have done to future generations of widows and orphans.

Honest Measures

We are astounded at how economists seem to dismiss the current level of national debt as the cost of running a successful country. We feel like a prophet in the wilderness, warning that these debts will eventually have to be paid.

A *Wall Street Journal* article in June 2019 warned "How Washington Learned to Love Debt and Deficits: Political support for taming federal debt has melted away, and the US is testing just how much it can borrow." The article went on to explain, "The theories about debt and deficits and whether they matter—once widely shared in Washington, on Wall Street and in academia—have fundamentally changed. Political support for taming deficits has melted away, with Republicans accepting bigger deficits in exchange for tax cuts and Democrats making big spending promises around 2020 election campaigns."[463] These are not honest measures.

There are even leading scholars who debate whether large federal debt and deficits might be tolerable. Voters are less concerned than they used to be. Estimates are that the government will spend more on interest in 2020 than on Medicaid and more in 2025 than on national defense.

These are simple scarcity rules at play: if you spend money on interest, you can't spend it on something else, like taking care of widows and orphans.

We are concerned that the eleven years of economic growth from 2009–2020 have lulled people to sleep. They don't know what a recession is. When the next one comes, spending on safety-net programs like unemployment insurance will increase, and tax receipts will fall. Government policy makers will be pressured to increase spending or cut taxes to stimulate growth, as described in the previous section, so when the economy sinks, already large deficits will soar.

We refer again to the husband-wife team of economists, Christina and David Romer of the University of California, Berkeley, who found that countries with high debt before economic crises have weaker recoveries, partly because policy makers pull back on stimulus quickly for fear of pushing debt levels too high. We think they are correct. We are mortgaging our future by spending today.

Our fellow citizens seem to dismiss the problem: A January 2019 Pew Research Center survey found 48 percent of Americans said deficit reduction should be a priority, compared with 72 percent in 2013.

Love Your Neighbor

From 2008 to 2016, the national debt soared from just over 10 trillion to almost 20 trillion dollars. Per citizen, it went from $34,000 to $61,000. That means each of your neighbors gained $27,000 in debt. That's not love.

Take Care of Widows and Orphans

The increase in national debt means that you and your neighbors will have fewer resources to use when keeping the command to care for widows and orphans. Deficit spending, once embarked upon, creates powerful vested interests which demand its continuance under all conditions. Inflation is a form of taxation. It is perhaps the worst possible form, which usually bears hardest on those least able to pay. It is tantamount to a flat sales tax of the same percentage on all commodities, with the rates as high on bread and milk as on diamonds and furs. The poor are usually more heavily taxed by the inflation caused by debt, in percentage terms, than the rich, for they do not have the same means of protecting themselves by speculative purchases of real equities.[464]

Should There Be Active or Passive Fiscal Policy?

For an atheist, this is not even a question. If it's "just us humans," without a God, then humans are solely responsible, and there should be active policy. But if you believe there's a God, then you need to determine how much we rely on his providence, and how much we practice. That's sometimes considered being on the horns of a dilemma between God's sovereignty and man's responsibility.

Creation

Just think of a diagram with "God's Sovereignty" on the left side, and "Man's Responsibility" on the right. Atheists don't believe in God, so their decision is made. For those who believe there is a Creator God who made the world and still works in it, we have some difficult decisions to make. But clearly, we are pulled somewhere from the right end of this spectrum.

We recall Robert Morgan's Red Sea Rule #5: stay calm and confident and give God time to work. Yet Red Sea Rule #6 suggests the opposite: when unsure, just take the next logical step by faith. So what do we do: Wait or walk?

Good question. But it's interesting that rule #6 doesn't tell us to sprint illogically. There are three qualifiers here: *logical, step,* and *faith. Logical* means there are fiscal policies that a Christian approves of; we wrote about those in chapters 1 and 2. We found biblical support for taxing and spending, when it meets with our Ten Commandments of Biblical Economics. But we don't find reliance in fiscal policy. We find only the use of money as a means of exchange, which agrees with the economic definition of money. When fiscal policy is used to increase human flourishing, we support it. But we find most Christian Economists favoring the left side of the diagram.

In *The Commanding Heights*, Daniel Yergin and Joseph Stanislaw ask the same question, using different terms. They ask whether you see the economy as a force of nature (left side) or a machine (right side).[465] Christians tend to operate more on the left side. We believe a Creator God made and sustains the earth, so we rely on His providence more than on our intelligence.

People Should be Free

John 11:47–48 reads: "Then the chief priests and the Pharisees called a meeting of the Sanhedrin. 'What are we accomplishing?' they asked. 'Here is this man performing many signs. If we let him go on like this, everyone will believe in him, and then the Romans will come and take away both our temple and our nation.'" The Pharisees were concerned that a powerful government was going to take away their form of worship and their nation. This scripture calls for a passive government. Some economists want a larger, more active government, and they want a larger, more active economic policy, because they assume people can't take care of themselves. Others want a smaller, less active government that increases individual freedom. The New Testament is clearly aligned with the smaller government position and a less active fiscal policy.

Take Care of Widows and Orphans

Revelation 3:20 reads: "Here I am! I stand at the door and knock. If anyone hears my voice and opens the door, I will come in and eat with that person, and they with me." This scripture indicates that the individual makes the decision to accept or reject the invitation of the greatest being humans have ever conceived of: God. It calls for a smaller role for the government, and greater responsibility for the individual. People who support larger governments with more active fiscal policies believe widows and orphans should be taken care of by the government. Others assume that individuals should be allowed responsibility for their decisions and that widows and orphans should be cared for by individuals and the church.

Conclusion

Claar and Klay summarize their view of fiscal policy succinctly, "Due to the limited ways in which we now believe that economies respond to active economic policy actions, there is no reason to believe that fiscal policy—the taxation and spending policies of the government—can perform any better than monetary policy actions in improving on our attainment of macroeconomic goals. Activist policies designed to expand or stabilize the economy cannot work, whether those policies are fiscal or monetary."[466]

Societal breakdowns have one thing in common: a selfish failure to look beyond our own lives and how our fiscal policies affect others. The attitude is perfectly summed up in the words of the economist whose misguided theories have done so much to steer many nations into bankruptcy. John Maynard Keynes said, "In the long run we are all dead." In that single sentence he captured everything that was missing from his economic worldview and much of what's wrong with America and the world today.[467]

Let's focus on the pronoun "We." If "we" are all dead, that means the "we" who consumed the stimulus spending go happily to our graves, leaving the debt to some other "we"—in this case, our grandchildren. Our government has created a scheme whereby we can consume goods without paying for them, and pass the bill to the next generation. That's politically appealing, but biblically and morally wrong.

Hazlitt's *Economics in One Lesson*[468] strives to look at policy from two points of view: all parties involved, and the second- and third-tier effects of fiscal policies. When we use his two tools, we find that Keynes was encouraging selfish and shortsighted policies.

Since Keynes uttered his famous phrase, we have found that in the long run, active fiscal policy produces very little positive economic results, and catastrophic debt. As we mentioned earlier, the catastrophe has not yet struck, but the old economic rule that states, "There is no free lunch" will revisit itself on a later generation.

Chapter 12

Income Inequality

Are the Rich Paying Their Fair Share of Taxes?

> Give to everyone what you owe them: If you owe taxes, pay taxes; if revenue, then revenue; if respect, then respect; if honor, then honor. (Romans 13:7)

Pharisees trying to trap Jesus asked him whether it was the right thing to do to pay the imperial tax, which was highly unpopular among the people. Jesus' response did not condemn paying the tax to Caesar, but emphasized that we ought to give the things that belong to God, which is everything. Lawrence Reed points out: "Jesus said, 'Render unto Caesar the things that are Caesar's, and unto God the things that are God's.' But that has absolutely nothing to do with high taxes or wealth redistribution. It was the seed for the idea of separating church and state. It certainly wasn't the same as saying that whatever Caesar says is his must then be so, no matter how much he demands or what he intends to use it for."[469] At the time of Jesus, the imperial tax resembled the flat tax and was levied on individual incomes.[470] Flat tax does not disproportionately penalize the incomes of the wealthy, since all contribute an equal share of their incomes.

Wealth can be acquired in several ways, one of which is without compromising someone's conscience or breaking moral laws, while the other is and involves an unjust way. In the New Testament, Jesus makes the statement that it is hard for a rich man to enter the kingdom of God (Matthew 19:24), but then he adds that it is impossible for a man to be saved on his own but with God all things are possible. Jesus did not condemn wealth but rather elevated trust in God above the trust in riches. In the Old Testament, wealth is often seen as a blessing from God. Kerby Anderson notes in *Christians and Economics*, "Wealth is not condemned in the Old Testament. We read in Genesis 13:2 that Abraham had great wealth. In Job 42:10, we see that God once again blessed Job with material possessions. In Deuteronomy 8:22, Proverbs 22:2, and Ecclesiastes 5:19, wealth is seen as evidence of God's blessing."[471]

The reality of unequal outcomes is troubling to some, and one example of it is the evolution of the concept known as "social justice." With the progression of the social justice movement, an answer to the question of whether the rich are paying their fair share would seem to be always a "no," since having the rich would imply that unequal outcomes are still in place. Defining justice—or rather, social justice—based on equal outcomes competes with God's view on justice and places humans as an ultimate judge of good and evil. Communist regimes replaced God with the state, which also necessitated a complete obedience of its subjects to the state's agenda. In that view, the Church had to either support the state's agenda or be altogether eradicated. Social justice elevates the role of the state to achieve a desirable outcome—the outcome that places humans in God's place of judging good and evil.

John Bolt comments on the work of Thomas Sowell, who highlights a distinction between justice and social justice:

> What is this new understanding of social justice? We gain clarity when we use Thomas Sowell's preferred term "cosmic justice." Whereas traditional justice is about unbiased and fair processes (in legal terms, due process), no matter what the outcome, cosmic

justice is driven by a distress about unequal outcomes. "Playing by the same rules" is not enough when the results reflect disparities that are morally troubling to some. "Through no fault of their own" is a key phrase in the pursuit of cosmic justice. . . . Sowell's main objection against such an expanded notion of justice is that it attempts to put humans in the place of God.[472]

Some politicians in their appeal to the electorate target the "1%" by implying that the very wealthy are not paying their fair share. The distinction is needed in terms of top earners and top holders of wealth, since the two are not the same. Wealth is what someone has accumulated, while income is what someone has earned in a particular year. It is much easier for someone to be in the top one percent of earners and not be in the group of the top one percent in terms of net worth. For example, in 2019 the individual income for the top one percent is about $330,000, while the individual net worth of the top one percent is about ten million dollars.[473] If someone just crossed the threshold of entering the top one percent using the measure of annual income, then it would take him or her thirty years in saving all of that income year after year to cross the threshold of the top one percent of holders of wealth.

Regardless of which measure we use to define the top one percent, it is important to realize that in free economies the income is the reward for making someone else better off. For example, an entrepreneur who takes a risk of starting a new business and invests all of his money and energy in creating a new product or service is only rewarded when that product or service appeals to the customer who is willing and able to pay for it. The profits are just the result of making consumers richer, that is, creating consumer surplus.

In the third quarter of 2019, the top one percent of households and nonprofit organizations held 32.2 percent[474] of all net worth in the United States, while the bottom 50 percent held 1.6 percent[475] of total wealth. Wealth includes the values of homes, automobiles, personal valuables, businesses, savings, and investments minus the value of all debts.

In *Defending the Free Market*, Robert Sirico notes, "It's businesses that make up most of the wealth of the 1 percent. Confiscating that wealth and giving it to the other 99 percent would mean shifting much of that wealth from investment and production to consumption, since the poor and middle class consume a far higher percentage of their income than the wealthy do. This sudden shift from investment and production to consumption would demolish the infrastructure that makes jobs, goods, and services possible."[476]

Another way to look at income disparity is to compare the incomes of the top ten percent with the bottom ten percent of income earners. Using 2019 data, an individual in the top ten percent would be making more than $116,250 a year, while someone in the bottom ten percent would be making less than $8,507.[477] To make a fair comparison, we would need to account for tax liabilities for both groups and monetary and nonmonetary transfers of wealth to the poor such as the value of housing assistance, food stamps, Medicaid, TANF, SSI, etc.[478] Progressive tax brackets and standard deductions would also reduce the gap between top and bottom incomes. For example, in 2019 someone making $8,507 would be in a 10 percent tax bracket but after a single deduction of $12,200 would owe no tax. Someone making $116,250 after a single deduction of $12,000 would owe about $19,146, which effectively reduces the income to $97,104.

The Cato Institute conducted a study where they looked at a typical welfare family with two children that receives benefits from the seven most common welfare programs, and estimated the value of these benefits would vary from $16,984 in Mississippi to $49,175 in Hawaii.[479, 480] Michael Tanner, in debunking the myth that inequality in the United States has never been worse, writes: "What the pundits, politicians, and others fail to understand is that the US tax and transfer system is already highly redistributive. Taxes are progressive, significantly so. The top 1 percent of tax filers earn 19 percent of US income, but in 2013 they paid 37.8 percent of federal income taxes. . . . The wealthy pay a disproportionate amount of taxes."[481] Typically incomes go up with age, so part of the inequality is attributed to increased levels of education, job training, and relevant experience that workers acquire over time. Based on survey data from the Bureau of Labor Statistics and the Census Bureau, the average income of a twenty-year-old is about $18,000; a thirty-year-old, $48,000; a forty-year-old, $67,000; and a fifty-year-old, $77,000.[482] Thus, the burden of progressive taxes largely falls on those who are in the prime of their working careers and it disproportionately penalizes those who through their experience and training became the most valuable contributions to the for-profit and not-for-profit organizations.

Michael Tanner from the Cato Institute wrote a paper on "Five Myths about Economic Inequality in America," where he exposes some of the misconceptions about inequality and how those misconceptions or myths tend to hurt the poor, not help. To summarize his findings, he notes, "Contrary to stereotypes, the wealthy tend to earn rather than inherit their wealth, and relatively few rich people work on Wall Street or in finance. Most rich people got that way by providing us with goods and services that improve our lives. . . . Few fortunes survive for multiple generations, while the poor are still able to rise out of poverty. More important, there is little relationship between inequality and poverty. The fact that some people become wealthy does not mean that others will become poor."[483]

Michael Strain, in *The Wall Street Journal*, adds, "Data from the US Census Bureau from 1967 through 2018 shows a 12 point drop in the share of households with inflation-adjusted income between $35,000 and $100,000. The share of low-income households—those earning less than $35,000—has also fallen over this period, from 36% to 28%. And the share of households earning over $100,000 has tripled, rising from 10% to 30%."[484]

Most individuals wish they could earn more, but those who earn greater incomes tend to work more and have less leisure time. Nobel Prize-winning psychologist Daniel Kahneman shows in his research that most people believe that they would be happier if they were richer, but evidence is largely inconsistent with that belief. Kahneman concludes,

"When someone reflects on how more income would change subjective well-being, they are probably tempted to think about spending more time in leisurely pursuits such as watching a large-screen plasma TV or playing golf, but in reality they should think of spending a lot more time working and commuting and a lot less time engaged in passive leisure."[485]

Higher tax rates on the rich do not necessarily translate into higher incomes for the poor. A study by Gale, Kearney, and Orszag in 2015 finds that a significant tax hike on high-income families and corresponding transfer to low-income families does not have a significant effect on reducing inequality.[486] Advocates of increased taxes on the rich seem to realize that higher taxes would do little to reduce poverty.[487]

Politicians who target inequality seem to be more concerned with punishing the rich than lifting up the poor. Bernie Sanders is quoted as saying, "We will no longer tolerate the greed of corporate America and the billionaire class—greed which has resulted in this country having more income and wealth inequality than any other major country on earth."[488] In another statement he said, "We will not accept a society in which the very rich get richer, while almost everyone else becomes poorer."[489] Hillary Clinton argued that fighting inequality requires a "toppling" of the one percent.[490] Michael Tanner concludes, "The ultimate losers of such policies are likely to be the poor. Economic growth, after all, depends on people who are ambitious, skilled risk-takers. We need such people to be ever-striving for more in order to fuel economic growth. That means they must be rewarded for their efforts, their skills, their ambitions, and their risks."[491]

The top quintile makes 73 percent of the nation's income and pays 84 percent of the taxes; just under 50 percent pay no income tax at all. Some people claim that is not progressive enough, but it is important to realize that rich people can live where they want. As an example, Paris experienced a new outflow of 12,000 millionaires in 2016 alone mainly because of high taxes.[492] AfrAsia Bank's Global Wealth Migration study reports that in 2017 and 2018 the top countries that experienced the outflow of high net worth individuals (HNWIs) were China, Russia, India, and Turkey, while the top two countries in receiving HNWIs were the United States and Australia.[493] Another study showed that when California raised its income tax rates in 2012, it caused a substantial migration of wealthy residents to lower-tax states.[494]

Christians are instructed to give generously and to care for the poor, but not being coerced in doing so. A desire to give and to care is a response of a redeemed heart of each believer, who acknowledges that God was the first who gave generously and cared for his creation. An early church community described in the book of Acts shared a unique experience of helping each other: "And all who believed were together and had all things in common. And they were selling their possessions and belongings and distributing the proceeds to all, as any had need" (Acts 2:44–45, ESV). Montero, in *All Things In Common,* writes, "Christians were obliged, morally, to share things in common, but they were not coerced to do so. To not do so would not be a legitimate exercise of freedom; but rather, a moral error."[495] A distinction is important here in sharing *some* or *all* things in common. The Acts text suggests that only some things were shared, not all things, since believers continued to gather in their own houses and sell additional plots of land when needed. Hay in *Economics Today* notes, "As the church spread outside Judea, there is little evidence, in the epistles at least, that the experiment in radical community living was repeated in the new churches. But the ideal of the church as a new people of God, a new community rooted in Christ, is very strongly emphasized."[496] Giving should result from the redeemed heart of each believer and not be replaced by a compulsory tax from the state in achieving an arbitrary distribution of wealth from rich to poor.

Should the Government Redistribute Wealth?

Exodus 20:17 reads: "You shall not covet your neighbor's house. You shall not covet your neighbor's wife, or his male or female servant, his ox or donkey, or anything that belongs to your neighbor." Wealth redistribution violates these and several more economic commandments. Redistributing wealth involves three parties: the party whose wealth is taken away, the party that receives that wealth, and the party that takes from one group and gives to another. The party whose wealth is taken away represents those who pay the highest marginal tax rates. The party who receives that wealth are those who benefit from public assistance programs such as Medicaid, food stamps, subsidized housing, etc. The third party that does redistribution is the government that legislates laws supporting progressive income tax brackets and public assistance programs, collects the money, and then redistributes it to the poor.

If a party that receives the benefits can outvote the party whose wealth is taken away, then redistribution is one step away from being outright theft. Stealing is defined as taking another person's property without permission or legal right and without intending to return it. Stealing is morally wrong even though it can be legislated. The Tax Foundation, in summarizing data from the Internal Revenue Service (IRS), finds that in 2016 the top 50 percent of all taxpayers paid 97 percent of all individual income taxes, while the bottom 50 percent paid the remaining three percent.[497] If the top 50 percent of taxpayers pay most of the tax, then the motivation to work by those who are the most productive in economic terms is eroded. Progressive tax systems punish those who make more and work more. Work is good, and if those who work more are taxed more, then income taxes discourage individuals from working and generating value to those around them. In 2016, the share of reported income earned by the top one percent of taxpayers was 19.7 percent, but their share of federal individual income taxes was 37.3 percent.[498] Those who make more contribute a bigger share in taxes than the share of income they receive.

Another economic commandment that is not supportive of wealth redistribution is "do not covet." The purpose of the government is not to punish the wealthy but to lift up the poor. Wealth redistribution does little to lift up the poor in any sustainable way, but it does a lot to punish the rich. Focus on someone else's wealth for purposes of taking it away is breaking the tenth commandment of Mosaic covenant, which is also one of our ten economic commandments. Desire to help the poor is an honorable aspiration, but if the accomplishment of that desire requires taking someone else's property or possessions, it is a concealed covetousness.

There are many biblical commands to give. There is no command to take. We shouldn't do it in the country, for the same reason we don't redistribute grades in our DBU classes—it rewards slackers and punishes productive students. Soon, they will all be slackers. Some will argue that the poor spend more of the money given to them, so it stimulates the economy. But you have to take before you can give, and there is no biblical command to take. Even if you could get around that one, it's like eating sugar for energy: you get a short-term boost, but a long term flabby belly. Economists call the flabby belly lower productivity and higher debt.

Making the rich poor doesn't make the poor rich. As a matter of fact, it does just the opposite. Making the rich poor hurts widows and orphans. Let's say you're jealous of a Texas Rangers pitcher who has a salary of $3.6 million because that's 100 times what you make at QuikTrip. But, your $36,000 is 100 times what a billion people make in the world: one dollar a day. How can you demand that some of the $3.6 million be redistributed to you but that none of your $36,000 be redistributed to the billion who make 100 times less than you? Does morality stop at the border? And if it does, then it's not a moral issue, is it? It's a political issue. And it's a violation of the tenth commandment.

Thomas Sowell points out that ordinary folks have benefited more from Western capitalism than the wealthy of ancient Greece or Rome:

Industrial progress, mechanical improvement, all of the great wonders of the modern era have meant relatively little to the wealthy. The rich in ancient Greece would have benefited hardly at all from modern plumbing: running servants replaced running water. Television and radio—the patricians of Rome could enjoy the leading musicians and actors in their home, could have the leading artists as domestic retainers. Ready-to-wear clothing, supermarkets—all these and many other modern developments would have added little to their life. They would have welcomed the improvements in transportation and in medicine, but for the rest, the great achievements of Western capitalism have redounded primarily to benefit the ordinary person.[499]

Redistributing wealth ignores the fact that those who assessed the wealth have done so by improving the lives of others. Sowell writes on this point in *Wealth, Poverty, and Politics*:

> By focusing on the *rewards* received for achievements, redistributionists ignore the benefits of those achievements for *others*, which is the very reason that those others—whether employer, patient, customers, or other recipients of the goods or services that people with these achievements produce—are willing to pay their own money to receive those benefits. As in many other contexts, *productivity* vanishes into thin air by verbal sleight of hand, when discussing the "income distribution" that results from that productivity. It is as if all that matters is the income difference between A and B ignoring the benefits of their respective achievements for C, D, E and many others. Ultimately, it is as if the internal distribution of the fruits of production is more important than the amount of production itself—on which the standard of living of a whole society depends.[500]

The motive of wealth redistribution is often rooted in envy, which the Law of Moses and Jesus both condemned. Lawrence Reed points out, "Jesus never endorsed the forced distribution of wealth. That idea is rooted in envy, something that he, and the tenth commandment, rail against."[501]

Jesus would not attempt to redistribute wealth when he was asked to do so. In Luke 12, someone asked Jesus to intervene in a family dispute about inheritance. In his response, Jesus not only declined to do so but warned the man to be on his guard against any type of greed. Next, Jesus gave a parable of a rich man who accumulated great wealth and said to himself: "I have it made! I can relax and take it easy for years! So I'll just sit back, eat, drink, and have a good time!" (Luke 12:19, VOICE). Little did he know that it was his last night and while he laid up great treasures on earth, he was not rich toward God. Jesus condemned being covetous toward someone else's wealth but rather to be rich toward God in good deeds.

Larger income gaps result from the policies designed to redistribute more wealth. Growth-oriented policies create opportunities for entrepreneurs to start new businesses, and thus increase the number of jobs available for those who may desperately need them. Patrick Garry points out that impact of big-government versus growth-oriented policies can be seen on state by state level in measuring inequality: "A state-by-state analysis shows that states with big-government policies have larger income gaps than do states whose more limited governments follow growth-oriented policies. So, at the minimum, redistributionist policies like raising tax rates or the minimum wage fail to achieve greater income equality. And at worst, such policies actually worsen the inequality by dampening economic opportunity and mobility."[502]

A state can lift more people out of poverty not by income redistribution but by uplifting the values, which are aligned with a Christian worldview. Garry writes, "People who marry before having children, avoid substance abuse, graduate from high school, stay out of jail, and hold even minimum-wage jobs for at least a year, virtually never end up living in poverty."[503] Putting to practice these principles does not guarantee that someone will never experience falling below the poverty line, but the chances of that happening are greatly reduced. Living by biblical principles not only affects personal income but also improves the overall quality of life.

Redistributing wealth may appear as a feasible thing to do for someone who is idealistic and cares for the poor. After all, if someone has great wealth and someone can barely make ends meet, then an easy solution to the problem of the poor would be for the rich to share. However, involuntary redistribution of wealth from rich to poor leads to the outcome that is worse off for the poor. Father Robert Sirico tells the story of his "a-ha moment" regarding redistribution of wealth. In the 1970s he was participating in marches and demonstrations calling for the redistribution of wealth from the rich to the poor. Then a friend asked him, "After you redistribute the wealth, then what happens?" The friend made this important point: The rich don't keep their wealth in cash. A large percentage of it is invested in companies. So after you force them to close their manufacturing plants, distribution facilities, and retail locations, where will the poor take their redistributed money to buy goods?[504]

Kaiser points out the same point in *For the Least of These*, "The 'Robin Hood' approach to solving the problem has never proven consistently effective. In all economies where such forceful redistribution of wealth has occurred, the standard of living for all has dropped."[505] Regardless of how noble someone's motives are, taking from one group in order to give to the other breaks the two commandments prohibiting stealing and coveting.

Another issue that arises with wealth redistribution involves the fallen nature of men who do the redistributing. Kotter writes, "A problem with redistribution is the temptation to corruption among those who serve as middlemen between the rich and the poor."[506] Acknowledging we all share a fallen nature makes it naive to assume that there is an impartial third party who can take on the role of God in deciding who pays too much and who pays too little and redistributes wealth without personal biases or conflicts of interest. Corruption of government officials will lead to a predictable outcome every single time: the wealth will be taken away from those who have it and it will end up with those who have the power to redistribute. It happened before with the rise of communism in Russia and other parts of the world, in Sub-Saharan Africa with their long-lasting leaders, in Latin America with widespread corruption cases, and the rule of monarchies in the Middle East.

The Israelites living under the Law of Moses were instructed to return the land to the previous owner during the year of Jubilee. It is not uncommon that Israelites who sold their land did so out of dire economic need, so returning the land back to them would appear as a mechanism of wealth redistribution. However, as Bradley and Lindsley write in *For the Least of These*, "The primary intent of the Jubilee is not economic equality at all. God wanted to prevent Israelite families from losing their ability to enjoy the Promised Land."[507]

Poverty cannot be eradicated by wealth redistribution, since the moment wealth is redistributed actions of free people will lead some back to the place where they have started. John Bolt notes in *Economic Shalom*, "The Bible simply does not call for redistribution from the wealthy to the poor as its answer to the problem of poverty. Rather it places responsibilities and obligations on all of us, including the poor themselves."[508] Once we accept the fact that choices of free people lead them to different occupations and those occupations have different monetary rewards, then the differences in pay should not be the focus of our attention but rather the ability of the worst-off members of society to improve their standard of living. Doug Bandow, in *Counting the Cost*, notes, "Increasing gains of the poor, not reducing the gaps between different income levels, should be the principal concern of public policy."[509]

If some poor move from the bottom quintile to the very top, it might not affect the measure of inequality. In fact, it might even deteriorate if the gap between the remaining poor and the old poor who are now rich is wider than the previous gap between rich and poor: "Worrying about income inequality is not a good idea. One would like to think that it is unambiguously good that more than a third of the poorest citizens see their incomes grow and converge to levels enjoyed by the richest people in the world. And if our indexes say that inequality rises, then rising inequality must be good and we should not worry about it!"[510]

We believe in the framework of creation, fall, and redemption to aid us in understanding human origin, the problem of evil, and the path to restoration. We play our role but the stage has been set for us long before we came into being. The fallen nature of the current state of affairs cannot be fixed by human ingenuity or a grand plan. John Bolt states in *Economic Shalom*: "Individuals and nations do not have equal access to the gifts and resources of creation. . . . Global judgements about unfairness, along with grand schemes to 'fix' things, are attempts by finite and fallible human actors to play the role of God."[511]

Wealth redistribution not only violates the rights to private property but also results in more poverty, not wealth. Robert Sirico, in *Defending the Free Market*, writes, "Each scheme of redistribution that has defied the right to private property has created more poverty. The right to private property is not absolute, but it is a basic human right. When and where that right is respected, people and whole societies flourish."[512] Living in the Soviet Union right at its collapse proved that state's ownership of all resources results not only in systematic violation of private property but also in the inevitable demise of the entire state-run economy. Privatization of homes, apartments, and small and large state-owned enterprises was a big step forward toward market-based economy, but it also advanced the emergence of a new social class, the oligarchs. The 1990s for the former Soviet Republics became the period of the Wild West, where entire industries were privatized, and often at the helm emerged a small group of individuals, aka the oligarchs. Pekka Sutela writes about those times in Ukraine: "Sometimes the dividing line between legitimate capitalists and plain criminals is blurred, and elected politicians may be little more than covers for their interests."[513] Privatization process mired with corruption schemes contributed to public dislike of new ruling elites, and it was portrayed in newspapers, TV shows, and anecdotes people shared with each other. Elderly and children were hit the hardest during the transitionary period. High rates of unemployment, widespread alcoholism, and drug addiction affected the children who were often neglected, abused, or left without parents.

A great story of rescuing homeless children is depicted in the documentary *Almost Holy*, which follows the life and ministry of Gennady Mokhnenko from Mariupol, Ukraine. Gennady adopted more than thirty homeless children and emerged as a contemporary hero by defending homeless children from being abused and neglected and promoting adoption to others through his round-the-world bike tour, World Without Orphans.

The elderly were also hit hard, since the safety net that the state previously provided was abruptly severed and many experienced intense hardship in order to adapt to a new way of living. Fiscal issues created extended delays in paying wages to some government employees such schoolteachers, nurses, doctors, etc. The lesson from the Soviet Union is that the government doesn't give up its powers voluntarily; it takes a major event such as an economic collapse to initiate a change of the regime, and even then the transition to a more market-based economy is mired with challenges.

Donald A. Hay in *Economics Today* came to the conclusion that "an economist who is a Christian must abandon welfare economics as a tool for policy recommendation."[514] Jay Richards succinctly concludes, "Wealth isn't the problem. Poverty is."[515] In another place, he writes "When government takes the property of one person and gives it to another, it sets up a lose-lose game disguised as a win-lose game. One group is coerced; the other is degraded."[516]

Samuel Gregg reminds us, "Scripture doesn't criticize the wealthy because they are richer than others. They are criticized, often fiercely when they are engaged in fraud, when they forget their real and direct responsibilities to the poor, or when their wealth becomes their God."[517] Criticizing the rich in the Scriptures, just like any other people group for their sinful ways, does not give the right to take away their wealth in order to distribute it to some other people group.

Should the Government Attempt to Provide Equality of Income?

God's original plan for his creation is to thrive on earth, which includes a provision for basic human necessities like food and shelter. God placed Adam and Eve in the garden where all their needs were met, including their physical needs. Even after the fall, God shows his care for Adam and Eve by providing the coverings for them made out of animals' skins. God shows his concern for the Israelites, who were enslaved by the Egyptians, by setting them free and leading them to a bountiful land. Moreover, God promises: "But there will be no poor among you; for the Lord will bless you in the land that the Lord your God is giving you for an inheritance to possess" (Deuteronomy 15:4, ESV). God's intent for the Israelites was to eradicate poverty. His intent was not to distribute the wealth from rich to poor, but to provide the land where each Israelite could achieve a certain level of prosperity.

In the parable of the talents (Matthew 25:14–30), Jesus does *not* morally condemn the unequal distribution of talents and the resulting outcome of earned interest. In fact, the servant who had the most was given even more by taking from the one who had the least.

The Bible does not approve of taking by force from the rich and giving to the poor. In contrast, it affirms a personal initiative in taking care of the needy and less fortunate members of society. God elevates the care for the poor as a sign of spiritual maturity and proper religious practice.

In James 1:27 (CSB), we read, "Pure and undefiled religion before God the Father is this: to look after orphans and widows in their distress and to keep oneself unstained from the world."

Our concern for the poor should not be sidetracked by focusing on the income gap between the rich and the poor, but on whether there are plenty of opportunities for the poor to climb out of poverty and become fulfilled members of our society. The tenth commandment warns us that covetousness of what our neighbor has is a serious sin and that we should guard ourselves against envy.

Equality of income is not a feasible outcome, given that people bring different skills and experiences to the marketplace. The Communist ideology tried to achieve equality of income and eradicate the divide between the rich and the poor. They excelled in making all people equally miserable and poor. In contrast, the United States offers one of the best examples of economic mobility, where the poor can change their lot by hard work and personal initiative and the rich can find themselves in need. According to one study, about four out of five millionaires achieved their success on their own; only one in five millionaires inherited their wealth.[518]

Equality of income is not a goal we should aspire to, given the free choices people can exercise regarding their education, work, and leisure. Claar and Klay, in *Economics In Christian Perspective,* write, "However, it is not clear to us that income inequality by itself ought to be a special concern for Christians. . . . [M]any Christians believe that income differences reflect free choices people make about education, risk taking, flexible schedules, and leisure. They are simply the result of people exercising their gifts, opportunities, and responsibilities before God in different ways and to different degrees."[519]

Leviticus 25 describes the Jubilee year, every forty-ninth year where land was returned to the original owner. That's because, in an agrarian society, land was the means of creating wealth. In an information society, the means of creating wealth are described in *Free Agent Nation* by Daniel Pink as "Digital Marxism." Everyone owns the means of creating wealth: a computer and a cellphone. Thirty-two percent of Americans living below the poverty line own a computer. Eighty-one percent of families in poverty have a cellphone. All of them have access to free computers and internet service at their local library. The means of creating wealth is available to everyone.

We should also distinguish between temporary versus persistent poverty. Based on Greg Mankiw, about one in four families may fall below the poverty line over a ten-year period, but only three percent of families remain in poverty for eight or more years. The experience of poverty is only temporary for the majority of households who find themselves below the poverty line.[520] Fifty-three percent of American families spend at least one year among the top ten percent of income earners.

In sum, it should be the equality of opportunity, not the equality of income, that we should strive to achieve. Economists who really care about widows and orphans concentrate on the income of the lowest quintile, not the gap between the rich and poor. The US has the "richest poor" in the world. Of those in poverty in the US, 99 percent have a refrigerator, 98 percent have a TV, while 65 percent have two TVs. Eighty-three percent have air conditioning, almost the same as the national average. The average family living in *poverty* in the US has more living space than the average family in Europe.

Thomas Sowell, in *Wealth, Poverty, and Politics,* notes that achieving equality of income comes at a cost of gaining more poverty: "Since the reduction of poverty and the closing of economic gaps are competing goals, on what basis can we choose between them?"[521] The question is whether we spend our time and effort on reducing inequality or reducing poverty. The answer would be to focus on helping the poor in such a way that would be sustainable. One way this can be done is by investing in the growth of the economy. Again, Thomas Sowell points out, "People in general, and the poor in particular, seem to 'vote with their feet' by moving to where there is greater prosperity, rather than where there is greater economic equality. Rising standards of living, especially for those at the bottom economically, have resulted not so much from changing the relative sizes of different slices of the economic pie as from increasing the size of the pie itself."[522]

Focusing on income inequality is counterproductive. It leaves us with less growth and more inequality. *The Wall Street Journal*'s article from July 5, 2019 shares the same sentiment: "The Federal Reserve's bond purchases and near-zero interest rates for eight years drove up asset values and let corporations borrow cheaply while the Administration's punishing regulations bred business uncertainty that depressed investment in human and physical capital. Those with financial assets prospered more than middle-class wage earners. The Obama Democrats talked constantly about inequality rather than growth, and the result was less growth and more inequality."[523] Inequality is more effectively addressed by enhancing the skills and education of those workers who would benefit the most, "The goal of policy makers, in education and the labor market, should be to bring up the skills of the lower half of wage earners so that they compete more effectively with the top. Only narrowing the skills gap can address the problems of the working and middle classes."[524]

There are multiple ways of measuring people's wellbeing that do not focus on measuring the inequality of incomes. In *Counting the Cost*, Art Lindsley and Anne Bradley note, "Instead of Gini, we should use other measures of economic freedom, happiness indices, life expectancy, or GDP per capita."[525]

From other developed countries we learn that less inequality works to suppress the incomes of the most valuable workers within the economy. The GDP per capita in 2018 for Sweden is at 86 percent of that for the United States, while GNP at PPP dollars is at about 85 percent. Both of these measures indicate that an average citizen in the United States is better off than his counterpart in Sweden. The average annual growth of GDP per capita in the United States over the last ten years has exceeded that of Sweden, and more people have benefited from this growth. The number of people who live in the United States is about thirty-three times greater than that of Sweden. Claar and Klay note:

> Sweden is such a country, where the tax and transfer system is much more extensive than that of the United States. It is not surprising, therefore, to find that GDP per capita in Sweden (tied with Belgium for the lowest ratio of CEO compensation to factory worker, at less than four times) is only about 68 percent that of the United States (data taken from GNP in purchasing power dollars for 1999). Apparently, the Swedish electorate has opted for less inequality of compensation (and incomes), accepting a somewhat lower standard of living as a necessary price for their social values.[526]

Advocating for income equality ignores the fact that our free choices lead us to use the resources we have in different ways. Each one of us should be considering the best way we could utilize the gifts God has given us. Claar and Klay note, "one of the wonderful paradoxes of the great abundance God provides is this: great abundance necessitates making choices. In all things, whether we are blessed with time, talents, spiritual gifts, financial resources or any other resource, the mere possession of a valuable resource occasions a decision: How then shall I use this gift?"[527] In market-based economies, application of some gifts will yield a higher reward than of the others. In order to honor God with the gifts he gave us, we should strive for freedom to exercise these gifts, not the equal reward for doing so.

Individuals go through various stages in life, and their incomes typically follow those stages. Young adults tend to borrow more to invest in education or buy their first car or home. Middle-aged adults tend to make and save more, since gains from education and additional years of experience help their wages rise. Older adults who enter their retirement years may not have any income from work but live off savings. The gaps in income are typical during different life stages, but the ability to borrow and save can smooth the differences in the standard of living. Another important consideration is not the current income but the ability to increase that income given the individual's aspirations and hard work. Bradley and Lindsley note in *For the Least of These*, "What matters is not so much how wide the gap is, but the ability to move from one quintile to the next, and the relative prosperity of those in the bottom quintiles."[528]

Equality of income is not part of a biblical narrative. "Any attempt to correct or fix income inequality will fall flat, because egalitarianism is antithetical to our God-given anthropology."[529]

Income inequality is not as much of an issue when opportunities for creating wealth are not systematically abused by those who are in power. Unfortunately political power, like any other power, tends to corrupt. Lindsley and Bradley write, "Cronyism is a form of corruption and institutionalized theft that results when the rich and powerful rig the system so they can curry favors at the expense of the less powerful and less well-connected. This crony-led income inequality is not a problem of capitalism; it is a problem of political power, and can be seen wherever there is such power, from democracies to more centrally planned societies."[530]

Capitalism is not a perfect system—nor is any other system devised by humankind—but given its track record of lifting people out of poverty and aligning individual incentives with those that benefit the society at large, it is the best invention that people have been able to conceive. *The Wall Street Journal* recently featured an article about two captains of industry who show concerns about the future of capitalism: James Dimon, chief executive of JPMorgan Chase & Co., and Ray Dalio, founder of hedge-fund manager Bridgewater Associates. It states: "Mr. Dalio and Mr. Dimon love capitalism and aren't apologizing for it. But they recognize the system isn't working for everyone, and they have ideas for fixing it, some of which might require rich people like themselves to pay more tax. Yet they fear the federal government is hamstrung by intensifying partisanship."[531] The online edition of the article had a conversation section with a question: Are business leaders today helping or hurting the case for capitalism? Robert Shaw, one of the article's readers, posted a comment which earned many likes:

> Capitalism doesn't need help from business leaders since progressives are doing the job quite nicely—revealing to us how alternatives to capitalism are so much worse! Progressive arguments about income inequality are valid only if there is no labor or income mobility and when the government, not customers, pick winners and losers. In a free market environment, someone's higher income doesn't mean mine is lower. Similarly, wealth is not uniformly created because people are free to have different propensities to spend, save or invest—freedom to choose leads to different outcomes according to our preferences. Of course, this only makes sense to those willing to take responsibility for their actions.[532]

Diversity and equality do not go hand in hand, and pursuit of one comes at a cost to the other. Robert Sirico notes, "When you think about it, the rage for income equality is rather curious in the contemporary social climate. 'Diversity' is celebrated and individuality praised, yet so many are looking to equality as a prescription for human flourishing. All of people's varied talents, interests, and backgrounds—all of the rich diversity that makes human beings so interesting—renders egalitarian utopianism unworkable."[533]

To answer our original question on whether the government should provide equality of income, we will use the quote from Thomas Sowell, "What is truly …. the blood of millions."[534] We get on a dangerous path when we treat those who have less as victims of those who have more. Instead of focusing on the income gap between rich and poor, we are better off by enhancing creative capacities of each individual, which are best fostered in free market economies and with little government intervention.

Chapter 13

Social Economics

Is Social Security a Biblical Role for the Government?

Finding "security" in anything other than our salvation through Christ is against Christian principles. We're not secure, and never will be on this side of heaven. Finding security in money—or any form of material goods—is not in the Christian belief system: "Do not store up for yourselves treasures on earth, where moths and vermin destroy, and where thieves break in and steal. But store up for yourselves treasures in heaven, where moths and vermin do not destroy, and where thieves do not break in and steal. For where your treasure is, there your heart will be also" (Matthew 6:19–21).

Finding security in our social system is not biblical either, because that violates the first commandment, "You shall have no other gods before me" (Exodus 20:3). As Christians, we wonder why it was called "Social Security" in the first place—because it doesn't come from society, and it doesn't provide security.

Social Security has been a redistribution scheme from the beginning. The Social Security Act was passed on August 14, 1935. The first recipient of a monthly payment was Ida May Fuller of Vermont, who received a check for $22.54 dated January 31, 1940. Over her lifetime, Ms. Fuller received a thousand times more than she paid in. Thus, it was a transfer of wealth from people who were working productively to those who were not working.

Ms. Fuller had some Christian economic insight into the program. When a Social Security increase was proposed in 1970, Ms. Fuller opposed it, on the basis that it was as high as it should go. She realized that every time it was increased they had to raise the amount taken from working people.

Ms. Fuller was citing our third economic commandment: don't steal. Redistribution schemes like Social Security transfer wealth from productive members of society to nonproductive members. We honor retirement (although it's not mentioned in the Bible) and Ms. Fuller should be cared for. But we can't find anything in the Scriptures that calls for the government to do so.

The government must take before it can give. We have found lots of scriptures that command us to give, but we can't find any that tell us to take. A student approached Dave after class recently and said, "The government has the money, so . . ." Dave interrupted, "No. The government has no money. It only takes from productive sectors of society and gives to unproductive sectors." That's correct. The money government spends comes from somewhere.[535] It is a transfer agent. And that's what it's doing with Social Security.

In 1978 Hazlitt wrote, "The Social Security system must stand today as a frightening symbol of the almost inevitable tendency of any national relief, redistribution, or 'insurance' scheme, once established, to run completely out of control. Practically all government attempts to redistribute wealth and income tend to smother productive incentives and lead toward general impoverishment. It is the proper sphere of government to create and enforce a framework of laws that prohibits force and fraud. But it must refrain from specific economic interventions. Government's main economic function is to encourage and preserve a free market."[536]

The government extracts money from young people by force, and gives it to older people. Even if the end was positive, the means are not. Taking money by force is stealing.

Social Security also violates economic commandment #1: people should be free. Social Security denies the working individual the freedom to use their personal goods (money) as they wish. It interrupts the market. People flourish when markets are allowed to develop. Markets work only when there is freedom to participate in them. If workers were allowed to invest their earnings as they wish, there would be a greater diversity of investments that would perform better. Clearly, Social Security is making bad investments of peoples' earnings. Since 1968, the government has been dipping into the Social Security Trust Fund and spending the money on non-Social Security expenses. Social Security had an unfunded liability of $43 trillion as of February 2020. In 2020, the system started paying out more than it was taking in, and it is expected to be out of money in 2035.

That takes us to economic commandment #5: use honest measures. Lots of economists will try to convince you that the money is still there in the hands of the government. But that's not using an honest measure. When you open up the "bank vault" of Social Security, you find IOUs from other governmental agencies. Dave has told his students, "That's like your mom borrowing from your dad, and claiming the family is rich. The family is not rich, and neither is the Social Security trust fund. It has unfunded IOUs."

Next is economic commandment #8: take care of widows and orphans. The Social Security scheme attempts to do this, but we don't find any scriptures designating the government to do so. We've already mentioned there are many commands to give, but none to take. We find specific directions about how widows and orphans are to be taken care of. The procedure is specifically described in James 1:27: "look after orphans and widows in their distress." That message is meant for the church, not for the government.

Then there's economic commandment #10: honor those in power. This means we should pay Social Security as the law demands. We don't suggest you try not paying. That would be against the law and would not only violate the Scriptures but get you in serious legal trouble. But those in power have committed a serious ethical and Christian violation of Scripture by forcibly taking money from people for one stated cause, and then using it for another. It really is one of the major governmental crimes of the late-twentieth century and continues today. Our college-age students are paying into Social Security, and their payments are being transferred to others. Our students will probably never receive a Social Security payment—or if they do, it will not be anywhere near what they have paid in.

Should the Government Pay Agricultural Subsidies?

The government should probably not provide subsidies to any industry. When it does so, it is choosing winners and losers, and removing freedom from the market to make those choices. The market is where people vote. When a governmental entity favors one industry over another, it is denying the vote of the people. Let's take it from a more systematic view: worldview, then the Ten Commandments of Economics.

Christian Worldview

The cover of Dave's little book *Economics and the Christian Worldview* has three panels. The first, representing creation, is a bountiful apple tree. The second, representing the fall, is a single apple after Adam and Eve took a bite. The third panel represents redemption, and is a diagram of a house under construction. The apple tree was "redeemed" to its original creational intent when the wood was used to build a house to shelter humans.

The same is true for all food. God created apple trees and wheat and corn stalks. Creative humans (because they're made in the image of God) improve the plants through research and testing. They are using God's creational energy to make the plants more productive for their neighbors. Because they love their neighbors as they love themselves, farmers produce more food to feed more of their neighbors at a lower cost.

Today, two percent of Americans have become so productive that they are able to feed all of us, and more, because the US exports agricultural products. Food comes first. A country's citizens have to eat. But as the percentage of those working in agriculture went from 90 to two percent, 88 percent were freed to perform other value-creating activities that enrich our lives—like the computers we are using to write this book, the chair you're sitting in as you read, and the lamp next to you. Increases in agriculture—discovering how God intended us to create food more efficiently and productively—has economically enriched our lives.

It's generally true that very few of us have eaten anything in our lives that was not some form of a hybrid that made the food more efficient to produce. Every apple, strawberry, piece of bread, corn, and hamburger was hybridized, fertilized, and processed in a way that made the food production system more efficient and lowered the cost of food for the poor.

You might be asking "But is that what God intended?" That's the question all of us are asking. And we won't get a clear answer on this side of heaven because we continue to look through a glass darkly. But it's quite clear that God intended for humans to make improvements to His creational foodstuffs. Food production is a great example of humans using their creative nature to lower the cost of food for poor people.

When government gets in the way of the voting system of the market, it throws the market out of balance. Typically then, the industry overproduces. That's how schools end up with surplus peanut butter. The Acton Institute has an impactful video titled "Poverty Inc.," where they explain how US government subsidies encourage the agricultural sector to over-produce. Tariffs keep even cheaper food products from being imported into the US, and then US food products are shipped overseas, destroying the local market. The introduction of "Poverty Inc." profiles how US policies destroyed the rice production and distribution market in Haiti. That's just one case.

The Ten Commandments

Don't steal. The subsidies that are paid to farmers have to come from another productive part of society. Those dollars are forcefully expropriated from productive sources, and awarded to less productive sources. That's stealing. It has the perverse effect of discouraging the productive parts of society from being more productive, and encourages recipients to be less productive. When Dave was in high school, many farmers in his community received government subsidies for idle acres that is, leaving ground unplowed to reduce the supply and increase the price of food products. Any society that pays its citizens to not produce is stealing from one entity to give the proceeds to another entity. And that society will be poorer as a result.

Honest measures. As explained in the scheme about "idle acres," the price of food products is not honest. The prices are artificially increased above the equilibrium price. Poor people spend a higher proportion of their expendable income on food than the rich. Thus, agricultural subsidies are a regressive tax. And the strange thing about food prices is, food is really cheap anyway. Think how cheap it would be if consumers were allowed to keep their tax dollars that are expropriated from them, and use them to buy food. That would drive the relative cost of food even lower. If the market were allowed to operate on a competitive basis, as other productive markets are, consumer prices would be even lower.

Trade is good. Free trade is even better. Agricultural products don't trade on an internationally free market. As we are writing this, President Trump has put tariffs on steel and aluminum from Argentina and Brazil, because those countries have low currency valuations, which make their agricultural products cheaper in the US. President Trump is noting, correctly, that those low prices harm US farmers. But the low prices of those food items lower the cost of food for America's poor. Why would a US president favor rich farmers over poor consumers? Especially when it comes to food, because food comes first.

Take care of widows and orphans. Much of the practice of caring for the poor is providing food products for them. Because as we've written so many times, "Food comes first." But the price of providing that food is artificially increased when the government pays farmers to limit their production. The US government gave out $60 billion in food stamps to almost 40 million Americans in 2019. Taking care of widows and orphans would be even cheaper if the government didn't increase prices with one policy while buying those products with another policy.

We wish we had more space to comment on "fair trade," but we don't see it as Christian. As one of Dave's children explained to the other, "Fair is an annual celebratory event." What's fair? It depends on who you ask. As you've noticed so far in this book, we like to ask the market, where everyone votes. The market determines what's fair (equilibrium price), then some egotistical do-gooder comes along and says, "That's not fair!" and overpays for a product, often coffee. If the do-gooder really wanted to do good, wouldn't she help the oppressed producer find a way to meet the market instead of beat the market? We will join with Jay Richards on this issue: "Farmers in fair-trade schemes are deprived of market information. It's in the long-term interest of some of these farmers to start growing more-competitive products or even to move out of agriculture altogether. Moreover, the small percentage of farmers in fair-trade schemes are being favored arbitrarily over farmers in most places, who don't have access to such a scheme."[537] In this case, instead of government choosing winners and losers, powerful buyers like Starbucks choose winners and losers. Isn't the market a better mechanism for determining winners and losers?

Should Genetically Modified Crops Be Banned?

If evidence shows they cause harm to humans, absolutely, yes. As of the writing of this book, there is no evidence that genetically modified crops harm humans. In economic terms, they certainly help poor people, by lowering the cost of food.

Christian Worldview

In the previous section, we explained how just about everything you've eaten in your entire life has been modified in some way by creative humans, whom we believe were acting on God's creational intent to increase production and lower the food cost for their neighbors.

There are many statistics, but perhaps only one is necessary. In 1960, Americans spent fourteen percent of their income on food. Today, they spend six percent. Americans are much richer today because of the lowered cost of food. Genetically modified crops will lower the food cost even more, which benefits the poor more than the rich.

Ten Commandments of Economics

People should be free. There is a lot being printed and said these days about agriculture companies who have patented GMOs and raised the price. They should be free to charge the market price. If farmers see enough value in the GMOs they will pay the price, and make themselves richer. If farmers don't see the value, they will not pay the price and the GMO seed supplier will go out of business. The ag company should be free to benefit from their creative inventions. The market should be free to choose to purchase or not purchase the seeds.

To some extent, the market is taking care of this problem. There is increased voluntary labeling of food products, so consumers can choose to buy GMO products or non-GMO products. The market is a very effective system for rewarding and punishing what the public wants. Freedom of markets is one of the most purely democratic forms of decision-making, because everyone consumes from the market.

Work is good. All the work that has increased the supply of foodstuffs is good work. We should appreciate every bit of food that has been hybridized, fertilized, and efficiently brought to market at a historically low cost. To those who disagree with the efficient system: consult the previous section on freedom. You are free to buy from another system, or to grow your own food. But we should appreciate the work that's gone into lowering the price of food for the poor. While GMOs are in a different category than previous food improvements, they are an improvement that increases the supply, and thus lowers the cost of food for the poor.

Recall our story in Chapter 7 about Norman Borlaug, "The man who saved a billion lives." He did it through crop improvements. Borlaug is one of many humans who reflect the image of God when they discover means of redeeming the fallen world, back to God's creational intent.

Honest measures. GMO products reflect the honest price of food production. To limit the use of GMOs would increase food prices to a dishonest measure.

Love your neighbor. A supplier who loves his neighbor provides goods and services demanded by the neighbor, and provides them at the lowest cost. Denying poor people the freedom to buy low cost food from GMO plants does not show love toward your poor neighbors.

Be a Good Samaritan. Good Samaritans provide food for the poor. GMO products enable the Good Samaritan to provide even a greater quantity of food, at a lower cost. GMOs encourage more Good Samaritan activity.

Should Population Be Controlled by Abortion?

This is one of the easier questions for Christians. No.

This answer is found in our Christian worldview. If you believe people are created, then you should not kill the innocent among them. A fetus is created, and should not be killed. While this seems so simple to most Christians, apparently it's not, because "about 29 percent of self-identified Christians—almost one in three—do not consider themselves to be pro-life on the issue of abortion. How is it possible for such a large swath of believers to support such evil? Is it even possible to be a faithful Christian and support abortion?"[538]

Let's explain the wording here. There are sins of commission and sins of omission. We are going to maintain that not standing against the evil of abortion is a sin of omission.

Here's the even darker aspect of abortion: one-third of US blacks have been killed by the Democratic party policy of abortion. Here are the numbers:

> Abortion: Since 1973, about 63 million babies have been aborted. Let's round it to 60 million to make the math easy.
>
> Black abortions: Blacks make up thirteen percent of the US population, but have 36 percent of the abortions. Let's round that to 33 percent to make the math easy. That means twenty million black babies have been aborted.
>
> Black population: The current black population in the US is 42.5 million. Let's round that to 40 million to make the math easy. There are 40 million live blacks and twenty million dead blacks. That's one third.

Now, who favors abortion? There used to be support for pro-life policies on both sides of the aisle. The Democratic party clarified their position when presidential candidate Pete Buttigieg stated he was firmly in the pro-abortion camp during the Iowa caucus race in January 2020. The following statement was made by Susan B. Anthony List president Marjorie Dannenfelser, "The modern Democratic Party is the party of abortion on demand through birth, paid for by taxpayers, and even infanticide."[539]

There is only one Democrat in Congress who is solidly pro-life. His name is Daniel Lipinsky, from the Illinois Third District. He barely survived a primary challenge staged by his own Democrat party against him in 2018. Many Catholics from Ohio and Indiana went door to door in his district to preserve the only remaining pro-life Democrat. He lost the primary election in 2020 because his own party used Planned Parenthood money to defeat him.

So the choice is becoming very clear: The Republican party is pro-life and the Democrat party is pro-death. The argument was settled when Lipinsky lost the 2020 primary election.

The economics of the abortion issue are easy also: the more people there are, the more minds there are to solve problems. The United Nations Millennium fund disagrees. They see humans as mouths to be fed. The Christian worldview sees them as creative minds to work. Don't miss the word "creative." We are made in the image of the Creator. As such, we inherit the creative nature of our Creator. This is a longstanding discussion that has been clearly solved by economic testing. There are currently 7.7 billion people in the world, and the world is in much better shape than it's ever been. (See the appendix, "Life is Better Now Than Any Time in History," for some facts.) We will only mention one in this section: food. In 2020, there are more people on the planet than there has ever been, and there is more than enough food for everyone. It will continue to be so.

Abortion is perhaps modern society's greatest separation from virtue. The value of virtue to a market was effectively explained by Samuel Gregg in *For God and Profit*:

No less than the founder of modern economics, Adam Smith, understood that market economies need to be immersed in a culture of virtues. Self-interest, even rational self-interest, isn't enough. As his life drew to a close, Smith added a new section entitled "Of the Character of Virtue" to the sixth and final edition of his *Theory of Moral Sentiment*, published in 1790. The first edition of this book was written seventeen years before his more famous *Wealth of Nations* (1776). Smith's reasons for making this addition to the *Theory of Moral Sentiments* may never be fully known. But perhaps Smith understood that as capitalism began to spread across the globe, fueled by banks based in London and Amsterdam, people needed to be reminded that the "moral capital" that facilitates the workings of commerce, industry, and finance needed to come from somewhere "outside" the market.[540]

Should College Be Free?

Wouldn't it be nice if education was free for all? Wouldn't it be nice to graduate from college debt-free and not have to pay student loans decades later? These sentiments especially appeal to college-age students, who often struggle to pay for college and resort to taking on ever-increasing levels of student debt. While the cost of education is a real concern for students and their parents, making college free is not part of the solution.

Making college free would not make it free to *provide*. A popular statement in economics is, "There is no free lunch." College professors, administrators, and staff still have to be paid, as well as utilities, maintenance, cafeterias, etc. If college was free to attend, then more students would enroll, which is the prediction derived from the Law of Demand. Additional inflow of students would further increase the cost of providing "free" education. If students are not sharing in covering these costs, then who is? Someone may suggest that the government should or the very wealthy, but each of these propositions has fatal flaws.

The primary source of government's revenue is from collecting taxes. Increasing tax rates to pay for free college education places a substantial burden on the taxpayers and hampers economic growth. Economic growth is what frees widows and orphans from poverty. State and federal governments are already investing substantial amounts in higher education. The federal government's current total debt of twenty trillion dollars will have serious repercussions for future generations of widows and orphans.

Placing a burden on the wealthy to pay for free higher education will have a negative effect on low- and middle-income homes. The very wealthy provide capital for businesses to explore new ideas and create new jobs. Once their ability to invest is hampered by a heavy tax burden, it would work to slow down the growth of the economy and limit the number of jobs available for widows and orphans who manage to graduate from college.

The fallen nature is at work in governmental desires to control more of the business landscape, as exemplified in their intrusion into higher education. The subsidies that have been granted to higher education have been captured, often for dubious purposes like hiring administrators, who have multiplied faster than instructional staff. Massachusetts Senator Elizabeth Warren laments that in her day college was much cheaper, yet the prime reason it's more expensive is federal subsidies and student loans. For every new dollar a college receives in subsidized loans, colleges raise tuition 60 cents, according to an analysis from the Federal Reserve Bank of New York.[541]

Is college too expensive? Attending junior college in Texas costs $55 a credit hour, but by the time you add in fees, it should be calculated at about $80. Fifteen credit hours each of two semesters is a fulltime college student load. $80 x 30 = $2,400. If a student is making just over minimum wage, at eight dollars an hour, she would have to work 50 weeks at six hours a week. That's too much? That's before federal, state, and local scholarships and grants. You could make a good argument that tuition is too low. Students who have no personal investment treat the college experience as not valuable. They miss classes, make poor grades, and drop classes. That lowers the level of quality in the classroom.

Another reason against free college education is a high dropout rate. Based on the National Student Clearinghouse report,[542] one-third of college students never finish their degrees, almost a quarter are still enrolled after six years, and the remaining 43 percent of students complete their degrees within six years. Dropouts are much more likely to default[543] on their student loans, which makes borrowers and lenders worse off than they were before. Social pressure to go to college and lack of discipline to succeed is part of the problem. Proverbs 4:7 reads "The beginning of wisdom is this: Get wisdom. Though it cost all you have, get understanding." The wisdom literature found in the Bible advises us to be ready to pay a high price in getting understanding and wisdom. Instead of focusing on making college education free, we ought to promote the value of wisdom and understanding, which once obtained will help widows and orphans make better choices not only in regard to college education but to life as a whole.

In conclusion, price is an efficient way of connecting those who value the product the most and those who can provide it in the most efficient way. Deviating from the equilibrium price by making college free would only increase the cost of education and place a heavy burden on society.

Should the Government Provide Healthcare as a Right?

If we believe God has a perfect plan for humans, then either the founders of Christian hospitals were wrong or the recent calls for nationalized healthcare are wrong. Both can't be right. The government is not mentioned in the Good Samaritan story. Thus, we conclude that Christian healthcare is more in line with God's creational and biblical intent than government healthcare. We redeem the fallen world when we support church-based programs than when we favor government-based healthcare programs.

People face trade-offs, even when accepting something that is seemingly free. When economists evaluate costs, they consider an opportunity cost, which includes the value of the next best alternative. If access to free healthcare is a right, then someone has the obligation to provide it. If the government takes on the role of providing free healthcare, it has to either raise money or obligate someone to provide it free of charge. The money it takes to provide healthcare could be spent on other worthy goals, or never taken from the taxpayers in the first place.

It is a fact that the cost of providing healthcare has a negative impact on the economy at large. The Congressional Budget Office (CBO) estimates that the Affordable Care Act (ACA) costs the US economy 0.5 percent growth every year, which is an equivalent of $92.5 billion given the size of US GDP at $18.5 trillion. If we assume that widows and orphans would accept a beginning annual salary of $25,000, that's 3.7 million jobs a year that are not created because of ACA. That's greater than the population of Iowa, Arkansas, or Mississippi. Every year. There are only 13.5 million unemployed people in the US. Four years without the ACA and the number of unemployed widows and orphans would be zero.

While the ACA has decreased the number of uninsured from 48 million to 28 million, it was written to fail. Insurance is based on the assumption that healthy people pay for the sick. The ACA was written so that sick people have a greater incentive to join the program, while healthy individuals have a disincentive to join. That causes higher premiums, which causes fewer people to join. As fewer join, the premiums go up. As premiums go up, fewer join. That's the definition of a death spiral.

The *Journal of Health Affairs* published a report[544] in which it projects that health spending in the US will represent twenty percent of the total economy by 2025. The spending on major healthcare programs[545] includes the spending on Medicare, Medicaid, the Children's Health Insurance Program, as well as outlays to subsidize health insurance purchased through the marketplaces established under the Affordable Care Act. Based on the CBO projections if current laws remain mostly unchanged, they would lead to growing budget deficits, which would account for 150 percent of GDP in 2047. The CBO's 2017 Long-Term Budget Outlook concludes that the prospect of such large and growing debt poses substantial risks for the nation and presents policymakers with significant challenges. There is no easy solution in fixing the healthcare system and making it free will only exacerbate the problem. We are not short of examples when good intentions lead to disastrous outcomes.

We believe the market—where everyone votes—is a Christian principle for distributing scarce goods and services. Healthcare is not a free market, as explained by Robert Sirico: "The problem is the dominance of third party payment throughout the health care system. This separation between the payer and the consumer is at the root of most of the problems of our health care system, including rising costs. The deplorable lack of knowledge we have about the real cost of the medical care we choose is the single greatest reason for the unsustainably steep climb in health care prices."[546]

A moving image of compassion and help of one human being to another is found in the story of the Good Samaritan. It provides a compelling illustration of how the needs of the hurting can be met through the personal initiative and free will and not through the coercion imposed by the government. We need more Good Samaritans in the world today, and we can make a difference in that regard by choosing to be one.

Should the Government Provide Incentives for Renewable Power?

Solar and wind are more expensive than electricity made from fossil fuels. Which is better for the widows and orphans? If solar and wind are so cheap, why are tax incentives offered for them? Those tax breaks have to be made up by widows and orphans. Germany has led the way in building of windmills and solar plants. They had to abandon the project in mid-2016, because it was going to break the nation financially. Dave pays ten cents per kilowatt hour for power in Texas. Germans pay thirty-five to forty cents, depending on the dollar-to-Euro exchange rate. Widows and orphans in Germany pay five to seven times as much for electricity as those living in Texas. The poor spend a higher percentage of their income on electricity than the rich, so it's a regressive tax on the poor.

A quest for renewable energy is a noteworthy undertaking, which signifies human ingenuity. After all, it is more desirable to continue on generating the energy we need without fear of completely depleting our natural resources. A fear of running out of natural resources is not new to our generation. St. Francis is the patron saint of ecology, because of his great love for creation. But you may not have known that St. Francis is also the patron saint of merchants, who are responsible for caring for the earth's resources and turning them to productive use.[547]

Economics is about the production and distribution of scarce resources. Jay Richards takes a very economic point of view on the matter: "Remember the economic trade-off. According to an article in *National Review*, 'Earth got about 0.7 degrees Celsius warmer in the twentieth century while it increased its GDP by 1,800 percent, by one estimate. Even if we caused all the warming, that's a great bargain.'"[548]

In fact, the level of farm output has experienced a steady increase while the farm inputs—such as the energy, land, and chemicals increased hardly at all over the last 65 years.[549] Farm production in the US has increased by 270 percent from 1948 to 2013.[550] Despite the growth in agricultural productivity, the share of US GDP accounted for by agriculture declined significantly from 37.5 percent in 1869 to 1.1 percent in 2016. In sum, US farmers are more productive using less land and other resources and can support a greater number of people, reaching even those who live outside of the national borders.[551, 552]

Advances in technology have similar effects on energy production as they do in agriculture. With the disruption of crude oil supply in the 1970s, many thought that this natural resource would be soon depleted. However, the innovations in technology resulted in more fuel-efficient vehicles and at the same time led to innovations in exploring shale oil. The Texan electricity consumer mentioned earlier pays 6.9 cents for a kilowatt of energy. In New York, where fracking is not allowed, they pay just over twenty cents. It's tough to be a widow or orphan in New York.

The well-known Ehrlich challenge is worth mentioning here. Economist Julian Simon publicly bet one thousand dollars that over the next ten years the real prices of any five commodities would go *down*, not up. Ehrlich and his team took up the challenge and picked five commodities: nickel, tin, tungsten, chromium, and copper. Ehrlich's team lost the bet. Over time, virtually any natural resource you can think of—oil, copper, mercury, coal, whatever, *has gotten less scarce, more plentiful, and thus, less expensive.*[553]

What's the best way to encourage people to conserve resources? People care for what they own, not what they don't own. There is an old quip, "No one ever washed a rental car." That's because you don't own it. Private property is the best preserver of creation, and no greater environmental spoilage has been witnessed than in the old socialist Eastern bloc countries, where private property was abolished. Indeed, the communist regime in China has also had a horrendous track record on environmental protection.[554]

Scarcity and incentives play a huge role in the study of economics. Scarcity of resources works as a restraint of human wants, which are unlimited. Human creativity and resourcefulness that are cultivated in free markets allow society to find new ways of solving the existing issues, whether they are related to the limited nature of natural resources or using the existing resources in new ways. It is more desirable to let renewable sources of energy to become more cost-efficient via innovation, not government intervention. Government subsidies come at a cost of higher taxes, which place a greater burden on widows and orphans.

There are two answers to the scarcity of energy problem: economics and Christianity. Since this is a book about Christian economics, we will look at both.

Economics

A basic rule of demand is that when commodities become scarcer, the price goes up and consumers use less. That has happened with every scarce resource, so there's good reason to predict it will happen with fossil fuel. Here's how Klay and Claar describe it: "By the time oil becomes so scarce that no one can afford it, no one will want to buy it anyway because we will soon be discovering better, cheaper, cleaner technology that will allow us to abandon oil as an input in many of our world's economic activities."[555]

Jay Richards has a similar view: "Every predicted global environmental catastrophe based on current trends has proved false. If we look at long-term historical trends, in contrast, the evidence of declining energy costs, increasing energy abundance, and growing prosperity provides no basis for such pessimism."[556]

Christianity

In *Economics and the Christian Worldview*, Dave writes, "There is a limited amount of land and God isn't making anymore. But he IS making creative humans who find ways to use it more efficiently." The creator God made humans in His own image. That's where our creativity comes from. Think about it: How could we be creative without a Creator? As Christians, we believe this creative part of our nature enables humans to discover more efficient ways of using scarce resources. The third part of the Trinity is the Holy Spirit, who we believe guards and guides humans. We believe the Spirit guides the hands of creative human beings as they research and develop everything from autonomous vehicles to robot surgery.

Chapter 14

Conclusion: Biblical Economic Policy in the Twenty-First Century

The Economy in the Twenty-First Century

Does a first-century book tell Christians how to respond to twenty-first-century macroeconomic policies? We believe it does.

First, the Christian worldview tells us that God created a perfect world, human sin has caused scarcity, and we can find redemption by accepting the offer of Christ to join in the redemption of the earth back to God's creational intent.

Next, we believe God gives us Ten Commandments of Biblical Economics that can be used to guide our stance on macroeconomic policies. In the ten years leading up to 2020, extreme poverty fell from 18.2 percent of the world's population to 8.6 percent. In the trailer for the documentary movie *The Pursuit*, Arthur Brooks factually states, "Two billion people have been pulled out of starvation-level poverty," then shouts into the camera, "What *did* that?" The simple answer is: free-market capitalism. It's our view that the Bible tells Christians to practice free-market capitalism.

Humans, acting as God's viceroys, make themselves and their neighbors richer. Thus, the more humans there are, the richer we get. Since

1800, the population of the world has multiplied six times, yet average life expectancy has more than doubled and real income has risen more than nine times.[557] We're living longer, richer lives, because we have answered God's command to steward the earth and to love our neighbors as we love ourselves.

On almost every measure, we are healthier than we have ever been, and our environment is cleaner than it has been even in the recent past. Over time, we use more efficient and less environmentally destructive forms of energy. A United Nations report titled *State of the Future* began: "People around the world are becoming healthier, wealthier, better educated, more peaceful, more connected, and they are living longer."[558] The document even goes so far as to admit that these improvements are the fruit of free trade and technology.

Products and services that encourage human flourishing emerge where man and matter meet. And just as human ingenuity leads to new resources in a market economy, so too it can forge solutions to real environmental problems.[559] Life *is* better than almost any time in history, and it's going to get better.

We now expect prices to get lower as time goes on, which is the total opposite of what an ecologist would expect. If we are using up the earth's resources, prices should be getting higher, not lower. Yet, we expect that when a new item hits the market, we can wait a couple years and buy it cheaper. Dave bought a sixty-five-inch flat-screen TV in 2005 for $2,150. He just replaced it for $398. Life is getting better, because prices are getting lower.

Texas has a deregulated electricity market, so we change our suppliers about every six to twelve months. In the summer of 2020, we were paying ten cents per KWH, while New Yorkers were paying nineteen cents, and French and German citizens were paying forty-two cents. New York does not allow fracking of gas wells, and the French and Germans have increased the price of electricity by overbuilding windmills and solar farms.

If you're going to be poor, the US (particularly Texas) is a good place to be poor. Among those in poverty in the US, 99.6 percent have a refrigerator, 97.7 percent have at least one television, 32 percent have more than two TVs, 81 percent have a microwave, 78 percent have air conditioning, 63.7 percent have cable or satellite television.[560] Life is better, for rich and poor, when scarce goods are allowed to be distributed by the free market.

Christians are called to care for the poor, namely widows and orphans. So we should seek the economic means that provide the best care for them. The free market provides much greater benefit to the poor than the rich. In previous centuries, only aristocrats enjoyed such pleasures. Capitalist wealth has made them available to vastly more people.[561] The wealthy have always had running water (they had slaves carrying jugs) but now, most of the world has running water, rich and poor.

Jonah Goldberg estimated that worldwide poverty would be eliminated by 2030.[562] If that's going to happen, we will need to determine the roles of each element of society. Here's how we see those roles, based on our reading of the Ten Commandments of Biblical Economics.

The Role of the Church

If God's people in both the Old and New Testaments had a concern for the poor during eras of relative economic equality, what are we to conclude about God's desire for the church today?[563] Our reading of Scripture indicates that the role the church played at the beginning of the twentieth century was correct. Churches developed hospitals, scout troops, treatment for alcohol addiction, orphanages, and much more. That role has been taken from the church by an ever-increasing federal government that threatens to control all aspects of our lives. The church needs to get this role back.

If we believe God has a perfect plan, then either the founders of church-based hospitals in the early 1900s were wrong or today's call for socialized medicine is wrong. They can't both be right. If you don't believe in God, then this rational thinking does not apply to you. Or if you are a Christian but don't believe God has a perfect plan, then you can disregard this logic. But we would wonder why you've spent hours reading a book about biblical economics if you don't believe either of those assumptions.

We are calling for the church to recapture its biblical command in society. It's what Alexis de Tocqueville termed "mediating institutions"— groups that occupy the space between the individual and the state. In the United States and in much of Western civilization, the Christian church has been a vital—one might argue the most significant—mediating institution.[564] Without mediating institutions, individuals are left to partition the ever-growing huge government mechanism on their own. An individual who tilts at those size windmills will not win. In *The Storm Before the Calm*, George Friedman[565] actually laments the loss of political bosses who played the role of the mediator a hundred years ago. We agree with Friedman that a mediator is necessary; we simply disagree about who should be the mediator.

In *All Things in Common*, Roman Montero calls for the church to revisit the role of mediating institution and caregiver. Writing about the Acts 2 condition, he says, "What we can derive from this fact is that this was not a small-scale, short-term, experimental commune; or just a spontaneous out-breaking of sharing and personal philanthropy. This was—and was meant to be—long-term, institutional, widespread, and organized; and it was firmly based on a moral framework of mutual obligations."[566] We agree with his point that the church should take a larger role in caring for widows and orphans.

There is a social price to pay for the church's abdication. It is no surprise that child abuse, classroom violence, and fatal interactions between police and individuals are escalating, despite all the government programs and education policies. What controlled and guided human behavior for centuries has been cast aside for big-government rules that command no allegiance. Big government has proved incapable of being a reliable moral compass.[567] That's because government has no moral compass. Because governmental officials are fallen, they will serve their own needs at the expense of those they are assigned to serve. The religious term is "the fallen nature," while the economic term is "self-interest," and the management term "agency." As we've pointed out throughout this book, the fallen nature is punished by competitive, free-market capitalism, but coddled and protected by state-sponsored centrist policies.

The early church was one of the early examples of inclusiveness. One of the most striking features of the economic practices of the early Christians would not have necessarily been that they practiced forms of informal and formal communism, but that these were practiced cross-culturally, and across ethnic and class lines.[568] Institutions that have a monopoly can discriminate against minorities: public schools, police departments, and other governmental agencies. But discrimination cannot exist in a competitive environment. Or more effectively stated: businesses in a competitive environment are allowed to discriminate, but the customers who are discriminated against will flee to another supplier. That's the demand side, but the supply side is true also. It's laughable that people still claim, "Women make 78% of the wages of men." Then why don't institutions, in a competitive environment, hire all women to gain a 22 percent cost-of-labor advantage over their competitors?

We are called to care for widows and orphans. Government does this very badly, but churches do it quite well. What has crippled the poor today is the disappearance of their social and cultural support systems. Economist Thomas Sowell has observed, "The black family survived centuries of slavery and generations of Jim Crow, but it disintegrated in the wake of the liberals' expansion of the welfare state."[569] And the late senator Daniel Moynihan wrote, "It cannot too often be stated that the issue of welfare is not what it costs those who provide it, but what it costs those who receive it."[570] There is no free lunch. "Free" is the opposite of "freedom." What it costs them is the freedom to manage their own affairs. It costs them the pride of work well done and belonging to a community where they love their neighbor (by providing goods and services they demand) while they love themselves (by making a profit).

In Chapter 1, we commented on the story of the Good Samaritan. First, the Samaritan had earned his own money. Jesus does not criticize this; as a matter of fact, he praises it. Remember, in a purely socialist economy, the Good Samaritan would have no money, only goods that were provided by the government. Second, he gave his own goods and money to care for the poor. This is the only way we can meet the biblical command to give, without taking. The government must take before it can give. The capitalist Samaritan gave of his own goods that he had earned in a capitalist environment, and Jesus praised him. The Good Samaritan represents churches who gain resources by free will gifts and use the resources to care for widows and orphans.

The Role of the Christian

The role of the individual Christian is to love the Lord your God with all your heart, with all your soul, and with all your mind, and to love your neighbor as you love yourself (Mark 12:30–31). If you love your neighbor, you will supply them with products and services they demand. If you love yourself, you will make a profit.

Dave was waiting for his wife Ginger, as she reviewed drug test results at a kidney dialysis clinic. In his boredom, he wandered into the conference room and wrote on the whiteboard, "Fear God. Tell the truth. Earn a profit." He had seen the quip on the wall of his Congressional representative Joe Barton, in Washington, DC. A few weeks later, a new doctor was joining the practice, having left a medical practice that did not tell the truth. As the new doctor completed the paperwork, his eye wandered to the saying on the whiteboard. He sought out the medical director to ask about it. The director knew nothing about the saying, and asked the new doctor why he was inquiring about it. "Because," he responded, "That's why I'm here."

The economic role of the Christian is to "earn a profit." As we've explained, profit (or wages) are a good measure of how much value you're creating for your neighbors. Jabez prayed that his territory would be increased (1 Chronicles 4:10). We make the same prayers for our DBU graduates: that they will do as much good as possible in serving their neighbors. That means some of our graduates will earn more than others. We're not prosperity preachers, but we fully understand that some people will earn more than others, because of inherited traits, learned skills, and providential good luck.

We are continually surprised at how often our fellow Christians—even well-read, highly educated believers—think there is something wrong with income inequality. "Equality of outcomes as a fact in the real world is not what poses a danger. It is the perpetually frustrated attempts to achieve this unachievable goal which produce such poisonous by-products as unprovoked lashing out at people who have more."[571] Thus, our fellow Christians are encouraging people to violate the tenth commandment (and our fourth commandment of biblical economics), against covetousness.

God made a world with scarce resources, and made unequal humans to inhabit it. That means some will become richer than others. We see no problem with that. As we pointed out in a previous chapter, Jesus distributed the gospel unequally. Thomas Sowell says it clearly and definitively:

No explanation of glaring economic differences by geography, demography, culture, or other impersonal factors has ever enjoyed the sudden worldwide acceptance and devotion as Marxism had in the twentieth century—a theory, belief system and agenda based on the assumption that the poor are poor because the rich exploit them. Yet none of the Communist countries established around the world ever achieved a standard of living for ordinary people equal to that in a number of capitalist economies. Even after communist countries became generally discredited by the end of the twentieth century, the idea that the wealth of the wealthy derived from the poverty of the poor continued to influence both beliefs and goals.[572]

In chapter 1, we posed a warning about concentrating too much on outcomes, at the expense of inputs. But on this issue, Sowell is correct about both: people should have freedom on the input side, and better outcomes—that he writes about—on the output side of the equation.

The Role of the Government

The government should encourage free-market capitalism, not socialism. Socialism is simply defined as "government control of the production and distribution of scarce resources." It's hard for us to understand how Christians would want fallen humans to have this kind of control. "What has always made the state a hell on earth has been precisely that man has tried to make it his heaven," writes Johann Holderlin.[573] In a fallen world, there are no perfect systems. Competition is more effective than government at dampening the fallen nature. That's because, in a free-market competitive environment, you have two fallen people competing against one another. In a socialist economy, you have one fallen person acting in her own self-interest. Lord Acton said it accurately: history is not a web woven with innocent hands. Among all the causes which degrade and demoralize men, power is the most constant and the most active.[574] The role of the government is to *control* the fallen nature, and it has been clearly shown in economic history that the most effective way to do that is via free-market competition.

Market systems don't exist in abstraction; they are always part of a larger social system, which needs to be carefully maintained by government policy. It is certainly *not* the case that societies that rely extensively on market systems *ignore* inequalities and injustices. Individuals, private groups, and governments regularly use the wealth that market systems generate to provide many kinds of assistance to persons who have fared poorly in those systems.[575] Let's think about this: The government has no money of its own. It can only take money from productive members of society. Have the socialists thought ahead to the second-level effect: After they destroy the market system, where are they going to get the resources to care for the poor? There won't be any!

Free markets are the only means of producing profit that can be used to care for the poor. Profits are sometimes called "excess value." Then, shouldn't we do more of that? That calls for the government to use its power to maintain competition, not to stifle it. *Free markets are the only means of producing "excess value" that can be used to care for the poor.*

The role of the government should not be to run the economy in a socialist manner. "Socialism always begins with a great promise and ends in disaster. It has failed every time and everywhere it was tried. Let's not throw away American prosperity so that a few leftists can give it another go."[576] Venezuela voted for socialism in 1998. By 2014 opposition leaders were arrested. It's been said, "Socialism: You can vote your way in, but you have to shoot your way out." Venezuela has the largest oil reserves in the world, yet there is not enough food on the shelves, and twenty percent of the population has fled the country. Christians should be concerned about what caused the fall of Venezuela, which in 1992 was the third richest country in the hemisphere, behind only the US and Canada. Venezuela is only the most recent example of how governmental controls can ruin a thriving economy. It always happens, because human nature has not changed. Fallen governmental leaders who seek their own self-interest through socialism have always ruined thriving societies.

Jesus cared about helping the least fortunate, but he did not endorse the government doing so. He never would have approved anything that undermines wealth creation. And the only thing that has ever created wealth, and lifted masses of people out of poverty, is free-market capitalism.[577] Thus, Jesus was not a socialist, according to Lawrence Reed: "Read the New Testament" he writes, "The plain meaning of the text is loud and clear. Jesus was not a Socialist. He couldn't be. He loved people, not the state."[578]

It is this love of power through state socialism, rather than love of freedom through free-market capitalism, where some Christians get it wrong. They fail to see the limitations of government control, because they deny the fallen nature of government officials. They are quite good at seeing the fallen nature of businesspeople, but somehow fail to see the same characteristics in governmental officials. They drive for an ever-expanding professional bureaucracy to manage government, denying the fallen nature of its staff. This bureaucracy in turn devotes itself to further expanding government and to cementing its control over the economy. Thus, a mutually reinforcing circle occurs—the formation of a political class, which then contributes to bigger government, which then requires a larger political class, and so on and so on. The bigger that government becomes, the more distant it is from the public, and the more an elite political class controls it.[579] Jesus did not endorse that type of system.

Most economic myths stem from a denial of the fallen nature. We're not surprised when nonbelievers support centralized government control. It just makes sense: if you believe there's no god, then humans have to do everything. But we are disappointed when fellow believers call for more centrist governmental control of the economy. While there aren't many of them left, they have outsized influence over society. The few remaining communists are cloistered mostly in places like Harvard and Havana.[580]

We hear a lot about the brutish, competitive nature of capitalism, about winners and losers, survival of the fittest, and all that; maybe we have even downloaded a podcast about it on an iPod. We hear far too little about the miracles of free cooperation and interdependence that free markets have made possible—that have helped make things like the iPod possible. Whatever the other vices in the market, we should take no critic seriously who does not first recognize this virtue.[581] Because we assume businesspeople are fallen, we make them compete against one another to serve us. In that free-market situation, the neighbor gets served first, the supplier gets served second.

Adam Smith would be astounded by the wealth that had been created by what he considered the invisible hand of the market. It transcended human limitations, and should be seen by Christians today as an expression of God's benevolent and providential governance of human society, since it created a more harmonious order than we would otherwise expect.[582] Friedrich von Hayek said the market was "spontaneous order," meaning it came out of nowhere. But that's because he was an atheist. Christians should easily see it as God's providence.

In 1978 Hazlitt wrote, "There are marked signs of a shift in the intellectual winds of doctrine. Keynesians and New Dealers (who favor more centrist control of the economy) seem to be in a slow retreat. Conservatives, libertarians, and other defenders of free enterprise are becoming more outspoken and more articulate. And there are many more of them. Among the young, there is a rapid growth of a disciplined school of 'Austrian' economists. There is a real promise that public policy may be reversed before the damage from existing measures and trends has become irreparable."[583] Hazlitt would be dumbfounded that a socialist almost won the Democratic nomination for president of the United States in 2016 and 2020. We are too. The Christian worldview of creation-fall-redemption clearly calls for a free-market economy and limited government intervention.

The Role of the Nation

The nation should encourage policies that promote production—because, that's what separates rich countries from poor countries.

Open Trade

The nation should encourage open trade with other countries. The best way to care for the poor in other countries is to open the country to international trade. That's how countries develop and grow their economies. Therefore, Christians should not be very concerned about income inequality between nations. But to the extent they are, international trade has been shown as the greatest power to reduce inequalities. All international and intranational effects considered, more globalization has meant less world inequality.[584]

We hear a lot about the colonial or imperial operations of powerful European countries during the sixteenth and seventeenth centuries. In economics, we call that mercantilism. It's when the mother country takes commodities from the colony and forces it to buy finished goods from the mother country. The idea is that the mother country gets rich at the expense of the colony. Spain exemplifies why that does not work.

During its golden age in the sixteenth and seventeenth centuries, Spain received other countries' products in exchange for the gold and silver it took from peoples it conquered in the Western Hemisphere. But Spain lagged behind other contemporary Western European countries in such human capital as both craft skills and scientific advances. Moreover, the disdainful attitudes toward productive work that developed in Spain under these conditions were negative human capital, as was the mass export of human capital by the expulsions of Jews and later Moriscos, both of whom had skills largely lacking in the general population of Spain. By contrast, the economies of Scotland and Japan rose dramatically by acquiring the human capital of other cultures rather than by importing their consumer products.[585]

In his book, *Imagine There's No Country: Poverty, Inequality, and Growth in the Era of Globalization,* Indian economist Surjit S. Bhalla provides stunning evidence of shrinking income gaps between first- and third-world peoples, along with closing gaps in literacy, infant mortality, life expectancy, educational achievement, and political and civic liberties.[586] Most remarkable is that the greater share of these improvements has occurred during the era of globalization (1980–2000) compared to the preceding two decades (1960–1980)—the opposite of what antiglobalization claims.[587] Open trade has allowed the poorest countries to enrich themselves by learning how to "grow rich," which is our next subject.

"Get Rich" vs. "Grow Rich"

Thomas Sowell shows us why our operating principle is correct: Scotland and Japan had policies that promote production, while Spain did not build productive capacity. The Spaniards showed us how to "get rich," but not how to "grow rich." It's a continual process of production that enables countries to grow their economies in a way that enables them to remain rich. Dave and his wife Ginger were visiting the tiny country of Luxembourg, whose GDP per capita is among the world's highest at $106,000; in comparison, Americans average $57,000. A local explained that Luxembourg was rich because of the rich mineral soil that was used to make steel in the early twentieth century. That explains why they were rich one hundred years ago. It does not explain why they are rich today. The answer: they are a tax haven for corporations. The negative point is made by Spain, who was able to "get rich" but not "grow rich." Luxembourg "got rich" via steel, and "grew rich" by becoming a tax haven. A tax haven has lower taxes than its neighboring countries.

Globalization has caused countries to become closer together in GDP per capita. That's quite different from what the media likes to tell us, "The rich countries are getting richer at the expense of the poor countries." That old axiom is not true theoretically, as Milton Friedman stated: "Most economic myths grow out the zero-sum fallacy." And it's not true factually, as shown by the very insightful Thomas Sowell:

> Among nations, as among individuals and groups, there is a fundamental difference between measuring what is happening over time to particular statistical categories and what is happening over time to specific sets of human beings. For example, data from the World Bank show that in 1960 the average per capita income of the 20 nations with the highest incomes per capita was about 23 times the average per capita income of the 20 nations with the lowest incomes per capita—and that this ratio rose to about 36 times as high by the year 2000. This fits the familiar notion of a growing gap between "the rich" and "the poor." But, comparing the *same* set of nations initially in the top and bottom categories, and following those particular nations over the same years, leads to the directly *opposite* conclusion, for the ratio between the per capita incomes of the particular nations initially in each category fell from about 23-to-one to less than 10-to-1.[588]

Sowell goes on to write about "growing rich." "Nevertheless, the status quo is by no means predestination, and the histories of particular very poor and very backwards nations of the past that have moved to the forefront of human achievement and prosperity show what can be done. The dramatic rise of Scotland in the eighteenth century, Japan in the nineteenth century, and Singapore, Hong Kong and South Korea in the twentieth century all show what can be done—and to some extent, how."[589] That "how" is policies that promote production.

Don't Send Aid

What does tax money sent from one government to another have to do with speeding up the creation of wealth? Nothing. No developing country ever got rich that way.[590] That's because aid attempts to help a country get rich, by skipping the details contained in how a country should grow rich.

Policies that promote production are the greatest poverty-reduction program in the history of mankind. Capitalist-induced economic growth has been the most important force for poverty alleviation in world history.[591] That's because they produce economic development that is sustainable for the long term. Most governmental aid acts like a sugar high. The country gets rich but doesn't grow rich. The long-term problem produces debt for the contributing country, and a lack of growth for the receiving country.

According to the Brookings Institution, 70 million people—about the population of Texas and California together—are lifted out of poverty every year. Between 1981 and 2005, the World Bank reported the number of people living in extreme poverty decreased from 52 to 26 percent. In one generation, poverty has been cut in half, not through charity but through job creation—not through getting rich, but by growing rich. Economic heavyweights like China, India, and Brazil have fueled the reduction of poverty. China went from an 84 percent poverty rate to 25 percent from 1981 to 2005. Brazil went from 17 to 8 percent, and India from 60 to 40 percent.[592]

Policies that promote production are what enable poor countries to grow their economies. Those types of policies encourage the development of human capital, which is in fact the biggest difference between ourselves and the caveman.[593] To phrase it in biblical terms: the resources to build the smartphone were in the earth during the time of Moses. Think about it: The people of ancient times had the same creational resources we have today: the same sun rays, the same earth, the same human and animal muscle power. It's the human capital—knowing how to *use* the resources more efficiently—that separates our lives from those of our ancestors.

Almost the whole wealth of the modern world, nearly everything that distinguishes it from the preindustrial world of the seventeenth century, consists of its accumulated capital. This capital is made up in part of many things that might better be called consumers' durable goods: automobiles, refrigerators, furniture, schools, colleges, churches, libraries, hospitals, and above all, private homes.[594] And they are all made from the same resources that have existed since creation.

In the 1990s it was the Asian Tigers—Taiwan, South Korea, Hong Kong, and Singapore—who showed great economic growth. Since 1961 it's been China's growth to the second-largest economy in the world. None of the numerous heartening examples of dramatic economic rises were due to the international transfers of wealth known as "foreign aid." Nor were these economic rises due to "nation-building" by outsiders, whether foreign governments or various experts supplied by international agencies such as the World Bank or the International Monetary Fund. Despite the many attempts to blame the poverty of some nations on exploitation by other nations or by foreign investors, it would be hard to find many nations that rose from poverty to prosperity by ridding themselves of colonial overlords.[595] It was open trade and "Policies that Promote Production" that enabled countries to "grow rich."

Economic Growth Is Good

There are some modern writers (like poet Wendell Berry), social activists, and theologians who suggest that the best Christian response to the uncomfortable speed and mobility of life today is to shun painful change in favor of returning to "simpler" lives in the village, where everyone knew each other and nobody was without work. (Even the village simpleton provided comic relief on dreary days.) This would mean a radical reduction in living standards everywhere. Furthermore, it is impossible to extract oneself from the intricate web of specialization, interdependence, and change that characterize the modern world. Who would buy Berry's books if communication were by talking drums or Pony Express? Who would have time to write poetry if others did not specialize in producing food for sale? Who would even know about the "world out there" to critique it (like those theologians who are skeptical about markets) if the only transportation were by foot?[596]

Grateful or Guiltful?

If I am born into a happy Christian family, nurtured in the faith, and grow up to be a disciple of Jesus, then my circumstances spiritually privilege me over a child born in India to Hindu parents. I can respond to this in one of two ways: 1) consider the privilege as a gift of God's providence, one of the means of his sovereign grace and be grateful; or, 2) think that the privilege is unfair, feel some measure of guilt for it, and pursue ways to level the playing field. Either response, of course, could lead one to obey our Lord's missionary call to share the gospel. But it makes a difference whether our missionary impulse is fueled by gratitude or guilt. Gratitude encourages us to share our abundant gift; guilt leads us to disparage the gift we have been given. In that case, even if we do not intend it, our ingratitude dishonors the Giver who has providentially made the gift possible and bestowed it on us.[597]

Christianity and Capitalism in the Twenty-First Century

Toward the end of Dallas Federal Reserve Bank president Robert Kaplan's interview of economist Gregory Mankiw, Kaplan asked, "What do you know about economics that you want others to know?" Mankiw's answer was simple, "That we are the luckiest nation in history."[598] That's all he had to say, because he assumed his audience knew about Angus Deaton's first line, "Life is better now than almost any time in history."

We would add that a providential confluence of ideologies came together to make us "lucky." What nonbelievers call luck, Christians often identify as providence. That is the view of Michael Novak, in his groundbreaking work *The Spirit of Democratic Capitalism*: "three dynamic and converging systems functioning as one; a democratic polity, an economy based on markets and incentives, and a moral-cultural system which is pluralistic and, in the largest sense, liberal."[599]

This integration of politics, economics, and the Judeo-Christian value system is truly a providential binding of three unique strands that has made America the richest nation in the world. No less than the founder of modern economics, Adam Smith, understood that market economies need to be immersed in a culture of virtues. Even though he was a deist, he believed that our self-interest, even rational self-interest, isn't enough. As his life drew to a close, Smith added a new section entitled "Of the Character of Virtue" to the sixth and final edition of his book *Theory of Moral Sentiments*, published in 1790, which had originally been written seventeen years before his more famous *Wealth of Nations* (1776). Smith's reasons for making this addition to the *Theory of Moral Sentiments* may never be fully known, but perhaps he understood that as capitalism began to spread across the globe, fueled by banks based in London and Amsterdam, people needed to be reminded that the "moral capital" that facilitates the workings of commerce, industry, and finance needed to come from somewhere "outside" the market.[600] It had to come from virtuous people—and that virtue was contained in the Judeo-Christian value system Smith saw operating around him. Man, Lord Acton believed, for all his propensity to evil, was a free agent capable of choosing the good, and although original sin was always there to dog his steps, it did not always succeed in tripping him up.[601] This gives us hope that a virtuous society can care for widows and orphans through the value created by free-market economies.

But free-market economies work only in a value-based Christian framework, as Röpke writes in *A Humane Economy*: "We can save ourselves only if man finds the way back to himself and to the firm shore of his own nature, assured value judgements, and binding faith."[602] If humans are to continue to thrive and grow, and care for widows and orphans, Christians will have to live out the Ten Commandments of Biblical Economics, to maintain a free-market capitalist system that enables us to serve our neighbors.

Appendix

Life is Better Now Than Any Time in History

Extreme poverty fell from 18.2 percent of the world's population to 8.6 percent in the last decade. In the 1980s, it was 44 percent.

Globally: The gap in basic living standards is narrowing.

Child mortality is at a record low. Fifteen thousand children died around the world in the last twenty-four hours. But in the 1990s, it was 30,000 each day.

Famine has virtually gone extinct.

Malaria, polio, and heart disease are all in decline.

Half of the world is now middle class or wealthier.

Mortality rates for women and children have been halved since 1990.

The global mortality rate for children under five declined from 5.6 percent in 2008 to 3.9 percent in 2018.

Primary education has become near-universal in nearly all the world.

US: 73 percent in the top 20 percent at some time, 56 percent in the top 10 percent.

Natural resources are more abundant and affordable than any time in history.

Energy—the master resource—is superabundant. My freshman pay 25 percent less for gas (cost-adjusted) than I did, and they get 50 percent more miles from it.

Air and water are cleaner.

There is no Malthusian nightmare of overpopulation.

Global per capita food production is 40 percent higher today than 1950.

In 1800, 90 percent of the population worked in food production. In 1900, it was 60 percent. Today, in the US, it's 2.5 percent.

The rate of death from physical destruction and natural disasters or severe weather has plummeted over the last fifty to one hundred years.

Malaria deaths have been halved since 2000.

Rich countries use less aluminum, nickel, copper, steel, stone, cement, sand, wood, paper, fertilizer, water, crop acreage, and fossil fuel every year. Consumption of sixty-six out of seventy-two resources tracked by the US Geological Survey is now declining.

US CO_2 from electrical production peaked in 2007.

Polio has been 99 percent eradicated since 1988.

Global life expectancy has gone from 29 in 1770 to 71 today. (It's falling in the US.)

Literacy has gone from 10 percent in 1820 to 80 percent today.

In 1820, 1.5 percent of the world lived in a democracy; today it's more than half.

Since 1990, 2.6 billion people have gained access to clean water. It's now 91 percent of the world's population.

Child labor has gone from 246 million to 107 million, just since 2000.

US: Disposable income spent on food has gone from 14 percent to 6 percent since 1960.

People in poverty in the US have more square feet of living space than the average European.

In seven hundred years, the homicide rate in Western Europe has gone from about forty per 100,000 to almost zero.

About 1990, there were more than fifty violent crime victims per thousand people in the US. As of 2009, it was fifteen.

Globally, 86 percent of all one-year-olds have been vaccinated against diphtheria, tetanus, and pertussis.

The last decade has been one of the most peaceful in history.

Notes and Sources

Chapter 1

1. Adam Smith, *An Inquiry into the Nature and Causes of the Wealth of Nations*, M. G. Spencer, ed. (Ware, England: Wordsworth Editions Limited. 2012), 477.

2. Anne Bradley, *Be Fruitful and Multiply: Why Economics Is Necessary for Making God-pleasing Decisions* (McLean, VA: Institute for Faith, Work & Economics, 2006), 24.

3. Jay Richards, *Money, Greed, and God: Why Capitalism is the Solution and Not the Problem* (New York: HarperCollins, 2010), 5.

4. Ludwig von Mises, *Human Action: A Treatise on Economics*, Scholar's ed. (Auburn, AL: Ludwig von Mises Institute, 2008).

5. Anne Bradley and Art Lindsley, *For the Least of These: A Biblical Answer to Poverty* (Grand Rapids, MI: Zondervan, 2015), 343.

6. Gregory Mankiw, "Global Perspectives," presentation at the Federal Reserve Bank of Dallas, March 7, 2019.

7. Victor Claar and Robin Klay, *Economics in Christian Perspective: Theory, Policy and Life Choices* (Downers Grove, IL: InterVarsity Press, 2007), 69.

8. John Bolt, *Economic Shalom: A Reformed Primer on Faith, Work, and Human Flourishing* (Grand Rapids, MI: Christian's Library Press, 2013), 12.

9. Joe Galindo, "Business in the Scriptures," presentation at the Lion's Den, Dallas Baptist University, March 22, 2019.

10. Donald Hay, *Economics Today: A Christian Critique.* (Vancouver, BC: Regent College Publishing, 2004), 63.

11. Francis Bacon, *Of Atheism*, in C. W. Eliot, ed., *Harvard Classics, Volume III, Part 1: Essays, Civil and Moral*, https://www.bartleby.com/3/1/16.html.

12. David Naugle, *Worldview: The History of a Concept* (Grand Rapids, MI: Wm. B. Eerdmans, 2002), xvii.

13. C. S. Lewis: *The Chronicles of Narnia, The Magician's Nephew* (Houndmills, Basingstoke, Hampshire: Palgrave Macmillan, 2012).

14. Steve Corbett and Brian Fikkert, *When Helping Hurts: How to Alleviate Poverty without Hurting the Poor—and Yourself* (Chicago: Moody Publishers, 2009), 57.

15. Donald Hay, *Economics Today: A Christian Critique* (Vancouver, BC: Regent College Publishing, 2004), 122.

16. Kenneth Barnes, *Redeeming Capitalism* (Grand Rapids, MI: Wm. B. Eerdmans, 2018), 138.

17. Bradley, *Be Fruitful and Multiply*, 13.

18. Albert Wolters, *Creation Regained: Biblical Basics for a Reformational Worldview*, 2nd ed. (Grand Rapids, MI: Wm. B. Eerdmans, 2005), 14.

19. Bolt, *Economic Shalom*, 110.

20. Hugh Whelchel, *How Then Should We Work?* (McLean, VA: Institute for Faith, Work & Economics, 2012), 13.

21. Robert Sirico, *Defending the Free Market: The Moral Case for a Free Economy* (Washington, DC: Regnery Publishing, 2012), 161.

22. Angus Deaton, *The Great Escape: Health, Wealth, and the Origins of Inequality* (Princeton, NJ: Princeton University Press, 2015).

23. Jim Denison, The Daily Article. "The New Royal Family and Nelson Mandela," Denisonforum.org, May 7, 2019, https://www.denisonforum.org/columns/daily-article/the-new-royal-baby-and-nelson-mandela-answering-the-call-to-be-selfless.

24. Richards, *Money, Greed, and God*, 209.

25. Sirico, *Defending the Free Market*, 31.

26. Claar and Klay, *Economics in Christian Perspective*, 57.

27. Richards, *Money, Greed, and God*, 75.

28. Hay, *Economics Today*, 123.

29. Erik Brynjolfsson and Andrew McAfee, *The Second Machine Age: Work, Progress, and Prosperity in a Time of Brilliant Technologies* (New York: W. W. Norton and Company, 2016), 29.

30. Bolt, *Economic Shalom*, 172.

31. Fred Gottheil, *Principles of Microeconomics*, 7th ed. (Mason, OH: South-Western Cengage Learning, 2013), 1.

32. Whelchel, *How Then Should We Work?*, 84.

33. Wolters, *Creation Regained*, 44.

34. Gertrude Himmelfarb, *Lord Acton: A Study in Conscience and Politics* (Chicago: University of Chicago Press, 1952), 196.

35. Austin Hill and Scott Rae, *The Virtues of Capitalism: A Moral Case for Free Markets* (Chicago, IL: Northfield, 2010), 10.

36. Wolters, *Creation Regained*, 59.

37. Kerby Anderson, *Christians and Economics: A Biblical Point of View* (Cambridge, OH: Christian Publishing House, 2016), 5.

38. Dennis Bakke, *Joy at Work: A Revolutionary Approach to Fun on the Job* (Seattle: PVG, 2005), 260.

39. Richards, *Money, Greed, and God*, 186.

40. Kelsey Grant, "Regulate Me," Morning Brew, March 31, 2019. https://www.morningbrew.com/daily/stories/2019/04/01/zuckerberg-regulate.

41. Patrick Garry, *The False Promise of Big Government: How Washington Helps the Rich and Hurts the Poor* (Wilmington, DE: ISI Books, 2017), 39.

42. Ibid.

43. David Horowitz, Radio interview with Mark Davis on AM 660, March 20, 2019.

44. Sirico, *Defending the Free Market*, 87.

45. Art Lindsley, *Free Indeed: Living Life in Light of the Biblical View of Freedom* (McLean, VA: Institute for Faith, Work & Economics, 2016), 32.

46. Roman Montero, *All Things in Common: The Economic Practices of the Early Christians* (Eugene, OR: Resource Publications, 2017), 22.

47. David Naugle, *Worldview: The History of a Concept* (Grand Rapids, MI: Wm. B. Eerdmans, 2002), 16.

48. Wolters, *Creation Regained*, 67.

49. Anderson, *Christians and Economics*, 6.

50. Art Lindsley and Anne Bradley, eds., *Counting the Cost: Christian Perspectives on Capitalism* (Abilene, TX: Abilene Christian University Press, 2017), 372.

51. Bolt, *Economic Shalom*, 172.

52. Lindsley and Bradley, *Counting the Cost*, 369.

53. Jonathan Witt, "Capitalism and the Cultural Wasteland," in Lindsley and Bradley, *Counting the Cost*, 340.

54. Garry, *The False Promise of Big Government*, 40.

55. Bob Briner, *Roaring Lambs: A Gentle Plan to Radically Change Your World* (Grand Rapids, MI: Zondervan, 1995), 31.

56. Richards, *Money, Greed, and God*, 32.

57. Friedrich von Hayek, *The Road to Serfdom*, 50th anniversary edition (Chicago: Chicago University Press, 1994).

58. Anderson, *Christians and Economics*, 43.

59. Hay, *Economics Today*, 64.

60. Richards, *Money, Greed, and God*, 115.

61. Ibid., 125.

62. Anderson, *Christians and Economics*, 32.

63. Richards, *Money, Greed, and God*, 164.

64. Ibid., 32.

65. Claar and Klay, *Economics in Christian Perspective*, 102.

66. Bolt, *Economic Shalom*, 19.

67. Sirico, *Defending the Free Market*, 176.

68. Robert Morgan, *The Red Sea Rules: 10 God-given Strategies for Difficult Times* (Nashville: W Publishing, 2014), 1.

69. Bradley, *Be Fruitful and Multiply*, 5.

70. Arthur Holmes, *The Idea of a Christian College* (Grand Rapids, MI: Wm. B. Eerdmans, 1987), 7.

71. Whelchel, *How Then Should We Work?*, 45.

72. Richards, *Money, Greed, and God*, 209.

73. Lindsley, *Free Indeed*, 3.

74. John Lynch, Bill Thrall and Bruce McNicol, *The Cure: What If God Isn't Who You Think He Is and Neither Are You?*, 3rd ed. (Phoenix: Trueface, 2016).

75. Whelchel, *How Then Should We Work?*, 5.

76. Himmelfarb, *Lord Acton*, 184.

77. Hay, *Economics Today*, 64.

78. Lindsley, *Free Indeed*, 13.

79. Bakke, *Joy at Work*, 260.

80. David Kotter, "Remember the Poor: A New Testament Perspective on the Problems of Poverty, Riches and Redistribution," in Bradley and Lindsley, *For the Least of These: A Biblical Answer to Poverty*, 68.

81. Bradley, *Be Fruitful and Multiply*, 13.

82. Whelchel, *How Then Should We Work?*, 122.

83. Lindsley, *Free Indeed*, 5.

84. James Davison Hunter, *To Change the World: The Irony, Tragedy, & Possibility of Christianity in the Late Modern World* (New York: Oxford Press, 2010).

85. Whelchel, *How Then Should We Work?*, 119.

86. Corbett and Fikkert, *When Helping Hurts*, 55.

87. Bradley, *Be Fruitful and Multiply*, 23.

88. Smith, *Wealth of Nations*.

89. John Maynard Keynes, *The General Theory of Employment, Interest and Money* (London: Macmillan, 1936).

90. von Hayek, *The Road to Serfdom*.

91. Whelchel, *How Then Should We Work?*, 93.

92. Hugh Whelchel, "How Then Should We Work?" presentation at Dallas Baptist University, October 21, 2018.

93. Röpke, *A Humane Economy*, 8.

94. Anderson, *Christians and Economics*, 12.

95. Gottheil, *Principles of Microeconomics*, 19.

96. J. Blair Blackburn, *A City on a Hill: Dallas Baptist University—An Architectural History* (Dallas: Dallas Baptist University, 2014).

97. Wolters, *Creation Regained*, 74.

98. Richards, *Money, Greed, and God*, 214–15.

99. Os Guinness, *Last Call for Liberty: How America's Genius for Freedom Has Become Its Greatest Threat* (Downers Grove, IL: IVP Books, 2018).

100. Sirico, *Defending the Free Market*, 108.

101. Claar and Klay, *Economics in Christian Perspective*, 35.

102. Whelchel, *How Then Should We Work?*, 122.

Chapter 2

103. Anderson, *Christians and Economics*, 29.

104. Bolt, *Economic Shalom*, 148.

105. Hay, *Economics Today*, 68.

106. Lindsley, *Free Indeed*, 19.

107. Anderson, *Christians and Economics*, 29.

108. Himmelfarb, *Lord Acton*, 219.

109. Lindsley, *Free Indeed*, 9.

110. Anderson, *Christians and Economics*, 41.

111. Joy Buchanan and Vernon Smith, "Who Benefits in Capitalism?" in Lindsley and Bradley, *Counting the Cost*, 190.

112. Bolt, *Economic Shalom*, 94.

113. David Horowitz, *Dark Agenda: The War to Destroy Christian America* (West Palm Beach, FL: Humanix Books, 2019).

114. Henry Hazlitt, *Economics in One Lesson* (Baltimore: Laissez Faire Books, 1962), 146.

115. Mary Anastasia O'Grady, "Socialism vs. the Person," *The Wall Street Journal*, April 21, 2019.

116. Samuel Gregg, *For God and Profit* (New York: Crossroad Publishing, 2016), 94.

117. Richards, *Money, Greed, and God*, 130.

118. Ibid., 131.

119. Ibid., 206.

120. Wayne Grudem and Barry Asmus, "Do Global Corporations Exploit Poor Countries?" in Lindsley and Bradley, *Counting the Cost*, 279.

121. Guinness, *Last Call for Liberty*, 44.

122. Richards, *Money, Greed, and God*, 163.

123. Lindsley, *Free Indeed*, 1.

124. Sirico, *Defending the Free Market*, 25.

125. Guinness, *Last Call for Liberty*, 240.

126. Richards, *Money, Greed, and God*, 209.

127. Marvin Olasky, *The Tragedy of American Compassion* (Washington, DC: Regnery Gateway, 1992).

128. Daniel Yergin and Joseph Stanislaw, *The Commanding Heights* (New York: Simon & Schuster, 1999).

129. Samuel Gregg, *For God and Profit*, 93.

130. Richards, *Money, Greed, and God*, 98.

131. Anderson, *Christians and Economics*, 8.

132. Whelchel, *How Then Should We Work?*, 2.

133. Hay, *Economics Today*, 74.

134. Kotter, *Remember the Poor*, 71.

135. Richards, *Money, Greed, and God*, 209.

136. Claar and Klay, *Economics in Christian Perspective*, 240.

137. Os Guinness, *The Call* (Nashville: W Publishing, 1998), 183.

138. Whelchel, *How Then Should We Work?*, 84.

139. Guinness, *The Call*.

140. Whelchel, *How Then Should We Work?*, 64.

141. Bolt, *Economic Shalom*, 155.

142. Max Weber, *The Protestant Work Ethic and the Spirit of Capitalism* (New York: Scribner Publishers, 1958).

143. theologyofwork.org.

144. Hay, *Economics Today*, 16.

145. Stephen Pinker, *Enlightenment Now: The Case for Reason, Science, Humanism, and Progress* (New York: Penguin Books, 2019).

146. Sirico, *Defending the Free Market*, 146.

147. Gregg, *For God and Profit*, 48.

148. Sirico, *Defending the Free Market*, 117.

149. Gregg, *For God and Profit*, 48.

150. Peter Greer and Chris Horst, *Mission Drift: The Unspoken Crisis Facing Leaders, Charities, and Churches* (Bloomington, MN: Bethany House, 2018).

151. Arthur Brooks, *Who Really Cares? The Surprising Truth about Compassionate Conservatism* (New York: Basic Books, 2006).

152. Richards, *Money, Greed, and God*, 151.

153. John Dickerson, *Jesus Skeptic* (Ada, MI: Baker Publishing, 2019).

154. Whelchel, *How Then Should We Work?*, 84.

155. Bakke, *Joy at Work*, 74.

156. Whelchel, *How Then Shall We Work?*, 5.

157. James Davison Hunter, *To Change the World: The Irony, Tragedy, & Possibility of Christianity in the Late Modern World* (New York, NY: Oxford Press, 2010), 3.

158. Dave Arnott and Bobbie Martindale, "Christianity & Capitalism: Correlation or Causality?" Christian Business Faculty Association meeting, October 1996.

159. Garry, *The False Promise of Big Government*, 62.

160. Timothy Keller, *Every Good Endeavor* (New York: Dutton Publishers, 2012), 211.

161. Sirico, *Defending the Free Market*, 37.

162. Montero, *All Things in Common*, 56.

163. Hazlitt, *Economics in One Lesson*, 54.

164. Ibid., 195.

165. Ligonier Ministries, *The Tenth Commandment*, www.Ligonier.org.

166. Thomas Sowell, *Wealth, Poverty and Politics* (New York, NY: Basic Books, 2016), 422.

167. Sirico, *Defending the Free Market*, 37.

168. Hazlitt, *Economics in One Lesson*, 142.

169. Dave Arnott, *Corporate Cults* (New York: AMACOM Publishers, 2001).

170. Montero, *All Things in Common*, 123.

171. Anderson, *Christians and Economics*, 52.

172. Bolt, *Economic Shalom*, 140.

173. Dennis Prager, *The Key to Unhappiness*. www.Prageru.com.

174. Bolt, *Economic Shalom*, 133.

175. Gregg, *For God and Profit*, 71.

176. Bolt, *Economic Shalom*, 138.

177. Kenneth Barnes, *Redeeming Capitalism* (Grand Rapids, MI: Wm. B. Eerdmans, 2018), 138.

178. Gregg, *For God and Profit*, 132.

179. Claar and Klay, *Economics in Christian Perspective*, 153.

180. Gregg, *For God and Profit*, 71.

181. Gregory Mankiw, interview at Dallas Federal Reserve Bank (attended by author), March 2019.

182. Nicole Gelinas, "Why Rent Control Hurts Renters," PragerU video at www.PragerU.com.

183. Bill Hammond, "Banishing Profit Is Bad for Your Health," *The Wall Street Journal*, March 18, 2019.

184. Bradley, *Be Fruitful and Multiply*, 24.

185. Sirico, *Defending the Free Market*, 82.

186. Montero, *All Things in Common*, 98.

187. Gregg, *For God and Profit*, 5.

188. Claar and Klay, *Economics in Christian Perspective*, 47.

189. Ibid.

190. Lindsley and Bradley, *Counting the Cost*, 152.

191. Richards, *Money, Greed, and God*, 77.

192. Claar and Klay, *Economics in Christian Perspective*, 157.

193. Poverty Cure Video, The Acton Institute.

194. Lindsley and Bradley, *Counting the Cost*, 371.

195. Hay, *Economics Today*, 167.

196. John McNerney, *Wealth of Persons: Economics with a Human Face* (Eugene, OR: Cascade Books, 2016).

197. Richard Doster, "The Kingdom Work of the Corporate World," crosswalk.com, December 20, 2009, https://www.crosswalk.com/family/career/the-kingdom-work-of-the-corporate-world-11624289.html.

198. Smith, *Wealth of Nations*.

199. Richards, *Money, Greed, and God*, 214.

200. Bolt, *Economic Shalom*, 156.

201. Whelchel, *How Then Should We Work?*, 52.

202. Sirico, *Defending the Free Market*, 136.

203. Hay, *Economics Today*, 30.

204. Gregg, *For God and Profit*, 168.

205. Hay, *Economics Today*, 57.

206. Lindsley, *Free Indeed*, 77.

207. Kotter, *Remember the Poor*, 89.

208. Montero, *All Things in Common*, 73.

209. Doug Bandow, "Capitalism and Poverty: Economic Development and Growth Benefit the Least the Most," in Lindsley and Bradley, *Counting the Cost*, 220.

210. Marvin Olasky, "Alleviating Poverty in the Abstract," in Bradley and Lindsley, *For the Least of These*, 211.

211. Corbett and Fikkert, *When Helping Hurts*, 44.

212. Sirico, *Defending the Free Market*, 118.

213. Hay, *Economics Today*, 52.

214. Montero, *All Things in Common*, 46.

215. Bolt, *Economic Shalom*, 142.

216. Richards, *Money, Greed, and God*, 35.

217. Corbett and Fikkert, *When Helping Hurts*, 39.

218. Claar and Klay, *Economics in Christian Perspective*, 34.

219. Richards, *Money, Greed, and God*, 45.

220. Montero, *All Things in Common*, 59.

221. Sirico, *Defending the Free Market*, 3.

222. Montero, *All Things in Common*, 54.

223. Bolt, *Economic Shalom*, 151.

224. Hay, *Economics Today*, 76.

225. Claar and Klay, *Economics in Christian Perspective*, 210.

226. Richards, *Money, Greed, and God*, 47.

227. Kotter, *Remember the Poor*, 86.

228. Himmelfarb, *Lord Acton*, 157.

229. Eric Metaxas, *Bonhoeffer: Pastor, Martyr, Profit, Spy* (Nashville: Thomas Nelson, 2010).

230. Gregg, *For God and Profit*, 140.

231. Anderson, *Christians and Economics*, 22.

232. Martin Luther King, Jr., "Letter from a Birmingham Jail," April 16, 1963.

233. Alexis de Tocqueville, *Democracy in America* (New York: Anchor Books, 1969).

234. Bolt, *Economic Shalom*, 164.

235. Lindsley, *Free Indeed*, 26.

236. Claar and Klay, *Economics in Christian Perspective*, 25.

Chapter 3

237. John J. McCusker, *Mercantilism and the Economic History of the Early Modern Atlantic World* (Cambridge: Cambridge University Press, 2001).

238. Bob Davis and Jon Hilsenrath, "How the China Shock, Deep and Swift, Spurred the Rise of Trump," *The Wall Street Journal*, August 11, 2016, https://www.wsj.com/articles/how-the-china-shock-deep-and-swift-spurred-the-rise-of-trump-1470929543.

239. The Editorial Board, "'I Am a Tariff Man,'" *The Wall Street Journal*, December 4, 2018, https://www.wsj.com/articles/i-am-a-tariff-man-1543965558.

240. Sowell, *Wealth, Poverty and Politics*, 70.

241. Taylor Telford, "A Guide to Trump's Tariffs: What They Are, How They Work and Who They'll Hurt," *The Washington Post*, May 31, 2019, https://www.washingtonpost.com/business/2019/05/31/guide-trumps-tariffs-what-they-are-how-they-work-who-theyll-hurt/?noredirect=on&utm_term=.7b64d70e617f.

242. Gerard Baker, Carol E. Lee and Michael C. Bender, "Trump Says He Offered China Better Trade Terms in Exchange for Help on North Korea," *The Wall Street Journal*, April 12, 2017, https://www.wsj.com/articles/trump-says-he-offered-china-better-trade-terms-in-exchange-for-help-on-north-korea-1492027556.

243. The Editorial Board, "Trump's China Brinkmanship," *The Wall Street Journal*, May 7, 2019, https://www.wsj.com/articles/trumps-china-brinkmanship-11557184406.

244. Adrienne Roberts, "How Higher Tariffs Affect Different Industries," *The Wall Street Journal*, May 11, 2019, https://www.wsj.com/articles/how-higher-tariffs-affect-different-industries-11557513451.

245. Donald J. Boudreaux, "The Elemental Case for Free Trade," Free Market Forum October 14, 2016, https://www.hillsdale.edu/wp-content/uploads/2016/11/FMF-Donald-Boudreaux-Hillsdalespeech-2016.pdf.

246. Bureau of Economic Analysis, International Trade in Goods and Services, https://www.bea.gov/data/intl-trade-investment/international-trade-goods-and-services (retrieved July 5, 2019).

247. Board of Governors of the Federal Reserve System (US), "Trade Weighted US Dollar Index: Broad, Goods (DISCONTINUED) [TWEXBANL]," Federal Reserve Bank of St. Louis, https://fred.stlouisfed.org/series/TWEXBANL (retrieved March 23, 2020).

248. Sovereign Wealth Fund Institute, "What Is a Sovereign Wealth Fund?" https://www.swfinstitute.org/research/sovereign-wealth-fund (retrieved March 23, 2020).

249. Claire Milhench, "Global Sovereign Fund Assets Jump to $7.45 Trillion: Preqin," Reuters, April 12, 2018, https://www.reuters.com/article/us-global-swf-assets/global-sovereign-fund-assets-jump-to-7-45-trillion-preqin-idUSKBN1HJ2DG (retrieved on March 23, 2020).

250. International Monetary Fund, "Total Reserves excluding Gold for China [TRESEGCNM052N]," Federal Reserve Bank of St. Louis; https://fred.stlouis-fed.org/series/TRESEGCNM052N (retrieved March 23, 2020).

251. International Monetary Fund, "Currency Composition of Official Foreign Exchange Reserves (COFER)," http://data.imf.org/?sk=E6A5F467-C14B-4AA8-9F6D-5A09EC4E62A4 (retrieved March 23, 2020).

252. US Bureau of Economic Analysis, "Real Gross Domestic Product [GDPC1]," Federal Reserve Bank of St. Louis; https://fred.stlouisfed.org/series/GDPC1 (retrieved March 23, 2020).

253. The World Bank, "Imports of Goods and Services (% of GDP)," https://data.worldbank.org/indicator/NE.IMP.GNFS.ZS?end=2018&start=1960&view=chart (retrieved March 23, 2020).

254. OECD (2020), "Terms of Trade (Indicator)," https://data.oecd.org/trade/terms-of-trade.htm#indicator-chart (retrieved March 24, 2020).

255. More information on trade between Phoenician cities and Israelites can be retrieved from https://www.metmuseum.org/exhibitions/listings/2014/assyria-to-iberia/blog/posts/phoenicia-and-the-bible

256. R. Mark Isaac, "Does the Bible Condemn Trade?" Institute for Faith, Work & Economics January 8, 2014, https://tifwe.org/does-the-bible-condemn-trade.

257. To read more on the practice of outsourcing, go to https://www.investopedia.com/terms/o/outsourcing.asp.

258. Michael F. Corbett, "The Outsourcing Revolution.. Dearborn 2004, https://www.economist.com/media/globalexecutive/outsourcing_revolution_e_02.pdf.

259. See the chart for predominant jobs outsourced in 2015 at https://medium.com/coderslink/what-is-outsourcing-what-does-it-mean-for-companies-eff73fe60372.

260. Friedman, Thomas L., *The World Is Flat: A Brief History of the Twenty-First Century* (New York: Farrar, Straus and Giroux, 2005), 278.

261. The graph was retrieved from: https://mgmresearch.com/china-vs-united-states-a-gdp-comparison.

262. Organization for Economic Co-operation and Development, Exports: Value Goods for Mexico [XTEXVA01MXQ667S], retrieved from FRED, Federal Reserve Bank of St. Louis; https://fred.stlouisfed.org/series/XTEX-VA01MXQ667S, September 9, 2019.

263. The data were retrieved from https://wits.worldbank.org/CountryProfile/en/Country/USA/Year/2017/SummaryText.

264. To learn more about WTO, go to https://www.wto.org/english/thewto_e/whatis_e/inbrief_e/inbr_e.htm.

265. More details on the MFN clause can be found at https://www.investopedia.com/terms/m/mostfavorednation.asp.

266. The map was retrieved from https://www.wto.org/english/thewto_e/whatis_e/tif_e/org6_e.htm.

267. World Trade Organization, "The Case for Open Trade," https://www.wto.org/english/thewto_e/whatis_e/tif_e/fact3_e.htm (retrieved September 6, 2019).

268. To read more on special and preferential treatment agreements, go to https://www.wto.org/english/tratop_e/devel_e/dev_special_differential_provisions_e.htm.

269. For example, the European Union, Norway, and Switzerland provide duty-free, quota-free market access for all LDC exports. For a more complete list of special provisions applicable to LDCs, go to https://www.wto.org/english/thewto_e/minist_e/min01_e/brief_e/brief03_e.htm.

270. Jacob M. Schlesinger and Alex Leary, "Trump Denounces Both China and WTO," *The Wall Street Journal*, July 26, 2019, https://www.wsj.com/articles/trump-presses-wto-to-change-china-s-developing-country-status-11564166423.

Chapter 4

271. Gregg, *For God and Profit*, 85.
272. Andy Kessler, "Jamie Dimon's Timely Warning," *The Wall Street Journal*, April 21, 2019.
273. Richards, *Money, Greed, and God*, 109.
274. Hazlitt, *Economics in One Lesson*, 123.
275. James Suroweicki, *The Wisdom of Crowds* (New York: Anchor Books, 2005).
276. Richards, *Money, Greed, and God*, 109.
277. Röpke, *A Humane Economy*, 3.
278. Corbett and Fikkert, *When Helping Hurts*, 44.
279. Bradley and Lindsley, *For the Least of These*, 13.
280. Doug Bandow, "Capitalism and Poverty: Economic Development and Growth Benefit the Least the Most," in Lindsley and Bradley, *Counting the Cost*, 213.
281. Hazlitt, *Economics in One Lesson*, 189.
282. Richards, *Money, Greed, and God*, 27.
283. Ibid., 37.
284. Claar and Klay, *Economics in Christian Perspective*, 170.
285. David Henderson, "The Correct Minimum Wage," PragerU.com.
286. Patrick Garry, *The False Promise of Big Government*, 52.
287. Michael Saltsman, "How Many Jobs Would the $15 Minimum Wage Kill?" *The Wall Street Journal*, July 8, 2019.
288. Hazlitt, *Economics in One Lesson*, 120.
289. Ibid., 123.
290. Claar and Klay, *Economics in Christian Perspective*, 172.
291. Hazlitt, *Economics in One Lesson*, 123.
292. Claar and Klay, *Economics in Christian Perspective*, 183.
293. Richards, *Money, Greed, and God*, 39.
294. Claar and Klay, *Economics in Christian Perspective*, 175.
295. Ibid., 175.
296. Eric Morath, "In St. Louis, a Rare Effort to Lower the Minimum Wage," *The Wall Street Journal*, August 27, 2017.

297. Gelinas, "Why Rent Control Hurts Renters."

298. Hazlitt, *Economics in One Lesson*, 192.

299. Ibid., 106.

300. Hay, *Economics Today*, 25.

301. Hazlitt, *Economics in One Lesson*, 102.

302. Ibid., 114.

303. Ibid., 162.

Chapter 5

304. Gregg, *For God and Profit*, 138.

305. Garry, *The False Promise of Big Government*, 40.

306. Ibid., 45.

307. Ibid., 103.

308. Hay, *Economics Today*, 40.

309. Anderson, *Christians and Economics*, 16.

310. Claar and Klay, *Economics in Christian Perspective*, 47.

311. Anderson, *Christians and Economics*, 12.

312. Claar and Klay, *Economics in Christian Perspective*, 203.

313. Röpke, *A Humane Economy*, 5.

314. Hernando de Soto, *The Mystery of Capital: Why Capitalism Triumphs in the West and Fails Everywhere Else* (New York: Basic Books, 2000).

315. Garry, *The False Promise of Big Government*, 16.

316. Anderson, *Christians and Economics*, 30.

317. Claar and Klay, *Economics in Christian Perspective*, 201.

318. Richard Turnbull, "Evangelicals and Poverty: the Voluntary Principle in Action," in Bradley and Lindsley, *For the Least of These*, 123.

319. Claar and Klay, *Economics in Christian Perspective*, 28.

320. Ibid., 201.

321. Gregg, *For God and Profit*, 147.

322. Friedrich August Hayek, *Law, Legislation and Liberty: A New Statement of the Liberal Principles of Justice and Political Economy* (Abingdon-on-Thames: Routledge, 2012), 139.

323. Hazlitt, *Economics in One Lesson*, 136.

324. Ibid., 142.

325. Bradley and Lindsley, *For the Least of These*, xxvii.

326. Ibid., 12.

327. Sirico, *Defending the Free Market*, 51.

328. Bolt, *Economic Shalom*, 126.

329. Sirico, *Defending the Free Market*, 19.

330. Bolt, *Economic Shalom*, 112.

331. R. Mark Isaac, "Markets and Justice," in Bradley and Lindsley, *For the Least of These*, 169.

332. Montero, *All Things in Common*, 50.

333. Lindsley and Bradley, *Counting the Cost*, 67.

334. Paul Heyne, *A Student's Guide to Economics* (Wilmington, DE: ISI Books, 2000), 33.

Chapter 6

335. Lawrence Reed, "Was Jesus a Socialist?" PragerU, July 6, 2019, https://www.prageru.com/video/was-jesus-a-socialist.

336. Robert Whaples, "The Policy Views of Economic Association Members: The Results of a New Study," *Econ Journal Watch*, September 2002, 337–38.

337. Adam McLeod, "Christian Vision of a Free Government," lecture at Acton University, June 19, 2019.

338. Ayn Rand, *Atlas Shrugged*, 6th edition (New York: Plume, 1992).

339. Gregg, *For God and Profit*, 137.

340. Richard Epstein, *Simple Rules for a Complex World* (Boston: Harvard University Press, 1995).

341. Reed, "Was Jesus a Socialist?"

342. Lindsley, *Free Indeed*, 30.

343. Richards, *Money, Greed, and God*, 72.

344. "Ingvar Kamprad," Wikipedia, September 7, 2020, https://en.wikipedia.org/wiki/Ingvar_Kamprad.

345. Arthur Laffer, *An Inquiry into the Nature and Causes of the Wealth of States* (Hoboken, NJ: Wiley & Sons, 2014).

346. Phil Gramma and John Early, "Wealthy Americans Already Pay Their Share," *The Wall Street Journal*, February 25, 2020.

347. Sirico, *Defending the Free Market*, 84.

348. Hazlitt, *Economics in One Lesson*, 21.

Chapter 7

349. Hazlitt, *Economics in One Lesson*, 58.

350. Mankiw, *Macroeconomics*.

351. Gregg, *For God and Profit*, 124.

352. Mankiw, *Macroeconomics*.

353. Sowell, *Wealth, Poverty and Politics*, 268.

354. Wall Street Journal Editorial Board, "A Tale of Two Economies," *The Wall Street Journal*, July 5, 2019.

355. Ibid.

356. Reed, "Was Jesus a Socialist?"

357. Sirico, *Defending the Free Market*, 138.

358. Simon, *The Ultimate Resource*.

359. Sowell, *Wealth, Poverty and Politics*, 7.

360. Sirico, *Defending the Free Market*, 48.

361. Bolt, *Economic Shalom*, 158.

362. Claar and Klay, *Economics in Christian Perspective*, 155.

363. Phil Gramm and Michael Solon, "Tax Reform Unleashed the US Economy," *The Wall Street Journal*, March 4, 2019.

364. Hazlitt, *Economics in One Lesson*, 57.

365. Sowell, *Wealth, Poverty and Politics*, 106.

366. Whelchel, *How Then Should We Work?*, 116.

367. Sirico, *Defending the Free Market*, 30.

368. Claar and Klay, *Economics in Christian Perspective*, 111.

369. Mankiw, *Macroeconomics*, 208.

370. Kessler, "Jamie Dimon's Timely Warning."

371. Bolt, *Economic Shalom*, 106.

372. Mankiw *Macroeconomics*, 254.

373. John Bolt, *Economic Shalom*, 158.

374. Thomas Robert Malthus, *An Essay on the Principle of Population as it Affects the Future Improvement of Society* (London: J. Johnson, 1798).

375. Richards, *Money, Greed, and God*, 8.

376. Sarah Kent, "Could Oil Demand Peak in Just Five Years?" *The Wall Street Journal*, September 10, 2018.

377. Angus Deaton, *The Great Escape: Health, Wealth, and the Origins of Inequality* (Princeton, NJ: Princeton University Press, 2015).

378. Nicholas Kristoff, "Why 2018 Was the Best Year in Human History," *The New York Times*, January 5, 2019.

379. Peter H. Diamandis, "Why the World Is Better Than You Think in 10 Powerful Charts," singularityhub.com, June 17, 2016, https://singularityhub.com/2016/06/27/why-the-world-is-better-than-you-think-in-10-powerful-charts.

380. Andrew McAfee, *More from Less: The Surprising Story of How We Learned to Prosper Using Fewer Resources* (New York: Simon & Schuster, 2019).

381. Stephen Covey, *The Seven Habits of Highly Successful People* (New York: Simon & Schuster, 1989).

382. Stephen Moore, "Happy Earth Day 2015: The World is Doing Just Fine, Thank You," Fox News, April 23, 2015, https://www.foxnews.com/opinion/happy-earth-day-2015-the-earth-is-doing-just-fine-thank-you.

383. Matt Ridley, "The World's Resources Aren't Running Out," *The Wall Street Journal*, April 25, 2014.

384. Ibid.

385. Hazlitt, *Economics in One Lesson*, 51.

Chapter 8

386. Dallas Willard, "Some Steps Toward Soul Rest in Eternal Living," Biola University faculty workshop, August 17, 2011.

387. N. Gregory Mankiw, *Principles of Macroeconomics*, eighth ed. (Boston: Cengage Learning, 2018), 238.

388. N. Gregory Mankiw, *Macroeconomics*, seventh ed. (New York: Macmillan, 2010), 63.

389. Ibid., 207.

390. Ibid., 208.

391. Michael Tanner, "The War on Work," PragerU, July 21, 2014, YouTube video, https://youtu.be/1nN1HqAps4Y.

392. Michael Tanner and Charles Hughes, *The Work Versus Welfare Trade-off: 2018: An Analysis of the Total Level of Welfare Benefits by State* (San Francisco: Cato Institute, 2013), https://object.cato.org/sites/cato.org/files/pubs/pdf/the_work_versus_welfare_trade-off_2013_wp.pdf.

393. Casey Mulligan, "Work Incentives, the Recovery Act, and the Economy," testimony, US House of Representatives, Committee on Oversight and Government Reform, Washington, DC (2013).

394. US Bureau of Labor Statistics, A Profile of the Working Poor, 2017, April 2019, https://www.bls.gov/opub/reports/working-poor/2017/pdf/home.pdf; US Census Bureau, Income and Poverty in the United States: 2017, September 2018, 16, https://www.census.gov/content/dam/Census/library/publications/2018/demo/p60-263.pdf.

395. The Gallup World Poll, https://www.gallup.com/analytics/232838/world-poll.aspx (retrieved March 23, 2020).

396. Jan-Emmanuel De Neve and George Ward, "Does Work Make You Happy? Evidence from the World Happiness Report," Harvard Business Review, March 20, 2017, https://hbr.org/2017/03/does-work-make-you-happy-evidence-from-the-world-happiness-report.

397. Michael Tanner, The American Welfare State: How We Spend Nearly $1 Trillion a Year Fighting Poverty—and Fail (San Francisco: Cato Institute, 2012), 694, https://object.cato.org/sites/cato.org/files/pubs/pdf/PA694.pdf.

398. Michael Huemer, "Is Taxation Theft?" Libertarianism.org, March 16, 2017, https://www.libertarianism.org/columns/is-taxation-theft#_ftnref3.

399. US Bureau of Labor Statistics, "Average Weeks Unemployed [UEMPMEAN]," Federal Reserve Bank of St. Louis; https://fred.stlouisfed.org/series/UEMPMEAN, March 24, 2020.

400. Mankiw, Principles of Economics, 303.

401. Hazlitt, Economics in One Lesson, 188

402. Ibid., 188.

403. Mankiw, Principles of Macroeconomics, 297.

404. BLS Reports, "Characteristics of minimum wage workers, 2018: Report 1078," March 2019, https://www.bls.gov/opub/reports/minimum-wage/2018/home.htm (retrieved March 23, 2020).

405. Mankiw, Principles of Macroeconomics, 308.

406. Jena McGregor, "Why Didn't Hostess Workers Believe the Threats?" https://www.washingtonpost.com/national/on-leadership/why-didnt-hostess-workers-believe-the-threats/2012/11/16/0638138e-302f-11e2-a30e-5ca76eeec857_story.html?utm_term=.e6093eaabd6d (retrieved November 16, 2012).

407. Chris Isidore and James O'Toole, "Hostess Brands Closing for Good," CNN Money, November 16, 2012, https://money.cnn.com/2012/11/16/news/companies/hostess-closing/index.html (retrieved July 23, 2019).

408. For March 2019, total compensation for union workers is $47.27 and for non-union workers it is $33.26; https://www.bls.gov/news.release/pdf/ecec.pdf.

409. Hazlitt, *Economics in One Lesson*, 132.

410. The earliest work on the efficiency wages theory is by G. A. Akerlof, and J. L. Yellen, eds., Efficiency Wage Models of the Labor Market (Cambridge: Cambridge University Press, 1986), and C. Shapiro, and J. E. Stiglitz, "Equilibrium Unemployment as a Worker Discipline Device," The American Economic Review, 74(3) (1984), 433–444.

411. Bosch Global, "Eight-Hour Working Day Introduced by Robert Bosch in 1906," https://www.bosch.com/stories/eight-hour-working-day-introduced-by-robert-bosch-in-1906 (retrieved March 24, 2020). See also Günther Schmid, *Labor Market Institutions in Europe: A Socioeconomic Evaluation of Performance: A Socioeconomic Evaluation of Performance* (Abingdon-on-Thames: Routledge, 2016).

412. Eric Morath and Sarah Chaney, "What the June Jobs Report Tells Us About the US Economy," *The Wall Street Journal*, July 5, 2019, https://www.wsj.com/articles/what-the-june-jobs-report-tells-us-about-the-u-s-economy-11562252400.

413. US Department of Labor, "How Do I File for Unemployment Insurance?" https://www.dol.gov/general/topic/unemployment-insurance (retrieved March 23, 2020).

414. US Department of Labor, Office of Unemployment Insurance, Federal-State Partnership, May 2019, https://oui.doleta.gov/unemploy/pdf/partnership.pdf (retrieved March 23, 2020).

415. US Department of Labor, Monthly Program and Financial Data, updated January 14, 2020, https://oui.doleta.gov/unemploy/claimssum.asp (retrieved March 23, 2020).

416. US Department of Labor, Maximum Potential Weeks of UI Benefits for New Claimants, effective January 6, 2020, https://oui.doleta.gov/unemploy/docs/potential_weeks_map.pdf (retrieved March 23, 2020).

417. Kimberly Amadeo, "ARRA, Its Details, with Pros and Cons," *The Balance*, July 30, 2019, https://www.thebalance.com/arra-details-3306299 (retrieved March 23, 2020).

418. Kelly Evans, "Unemployment Extension Adds Up to 99 Weeks of Benefits," *The Wall Street Journal*, November 6, 2009, https://blogs.wsj.com/economics/2009/11/06/unemployment-extension-adds-up-to-99-weeks-of-benefits.

419. Bureau of Labor Statistics, US Department of Labor, The Economics Daily, unemployment rate in March 2009, https://www.bls.gov/opub/ted/2009/apr/wk1/art01.htm (retrieved March 25, 2020).

420. Bureau of Labor Statistics, US Department of Labor, The Economics Daily, unemployment in July 2010, https://www.bls.gov/opub/ted/2010/ted_20100811.htm (retrieved March 25, 2020).

421. US Bureau of Labor Statistics, "Unemployment Rate [UNRATE]," Federal Reserve Bank of St. Louis; https://fred.stlouisfed.org/series/UNRATE (retrieved March 24, 2020).

422. Mankiw, *Principles of Macroeconomics*, 304.

423. William Horobin, "France Gambles on Jobless Benefits for Those Who Quit," *Wall Street Journal*, November 17, 2017, https://www.wsj.com/articles/frances-macron-gambles-on-jobless-benefits-for-those-who-quit-1510875450.

424. US Bureau of Labor Statistics, "Average Weeks Unemployed [UEMPMEAN]," Federal Reserve Bank of St. Louis; https://fred.stlouisfed.org/series/UEMP-MEAN (retrieved March 24, 2020).

425. US Department of Labor, Office of Unemployment Insurance, Trust Fund Solvency Report 2019, February 2019, https://oui.doleta.gov/unemploy/docs/trustFundSolvReport2019.pdf (retrieved March 23, 2020).

Chapter 9

426. Richards, *Money, Greed, and God*, 140.

427. Ibid., 155.

428. Ibid., 144.

429. Ibid., 156.

430. Gregg, *For God and Profit*, 50.

431. Sirico, *Defending the Free Market*, 37.

432. Hazlitt, *Economics in One Lesson*, 171.

433. Gregg, *For God and Profit*, 56.

434. George Robinson, "Interest-Free Loans in Judaism," https://www.myjewishlearning.com/article/interest-free-loans-in-judaism (retrieved March 23, 2020).

435. Gregg, *For God and Profit*, 34.

436. Board of Governors of the Federal Reserve System (US), "3-Month Treasury Bill: Secondary Market Rate [TB3MS]," Federal Reserve Bank of St. Louis, October 5, 2019, https://fred.stlouisfed.org/series/TB3MS.

437. Board of Governors of the Federal Reserve System, "What Economic Goals Does the Federal Reserve Seek to Achieve Through Its Monetary Policy?" https://www.federalreserve.gov/faqs/what-economic-goals-does-federal-reserve-seek-to-achieve-through-monetary-policy.htm (retrieved March 23, 2020).

438. To read more on the topic, go to "A Closer Look at Open Market Operations," published by the Federal Reserve Bank of St. Louis, stlouisfed.org/in-plain-english/a-closer-look-at-open-market-operations.

439. Sirico, *Defending the Free Market*, 4.

440. Martin Crutsinger, "Ford's WIN Buttons Remembered," The *Washington Post*, December 28, 2006, http://www.washingtonpost.com/wp-dyn/content/article/2006/12/28/AR2006122801002.html (retrieved March 23, 2020).

441. Robbie Whelan, "'Keep de Rates dem Low'—Jamaica Sets Inflation Fight to Reggae Beat," *Wall Street Journal*, October 4, 2019, https://www.wsj.com/articles/keep-de-rates-dem-lowjamaica-sets-inflation-fight-to-reggae-beat-11570199659.

442. More info on the Federal Reserve Act and the goals of US monetary policy can be found at https://www.federalreserve.gov/aboutthefed/fract.htm and https://www.frbsf.org/economic-research/publications/economic-letter/1999/january/the-goals-of-us-monetary-policy.

443. Claar and Klay, *Economics in Christian Perspective*, 135.

444. Ibid.

445. Samuel Gregg, *For God and Profit*, 158.

446. Claar and Klay, *Economics in Christian Perspective*, 139.

Chapter 10

447. Samuel Gregg, *For God and Profit*, 155.

448. Claar and Klay, *Economics in Christian Perspective*, 123.

449. Hazlitt, *Economics in One Lesson*, 161.

450. Ibid., 159.

451. Mankiw, *Principles of Macroeconomics*, 354.

452. Röpke, *A Humane Economy*, 23.

453. Claar and Klay, *Economics in Christian Perspective*, 134.

454. Hazlitt, *Economics in One Lesson*, 156.

Chapter 11

455. Staff, "How the $800B Stimulus Failed," *New York Post*, January 29, 2012.

456. Stephanie Condon, "Obama: No such thing as shovel-ready projects," CBS News, October 13, 2010, https://www.cbsnews.com/news/obama-no-such-thing-as-shovel-ready-projects.

457. Claar and Klay, *Economics in Christian Perspective*, 141.

458. Hazlitt, *Economics in One Lesson*, 188.

459. Garry, *The False Promise of Big Government*, 10.

460. Hazlitt, *Economics in One Lesson*, 159.

461. Gregg, *For God and Profit*, 178.

462. Hay, *Economics Today*, 40.

463. Kate Davidson and Jon Hilsenrath, "How Washington Learned to Love Debt and Deficits," *Wall Street Journal*, June 13, 2019.

464. Hazlitt, *Economics in One Lesson*, 160.

465. Yergin and Stanislaw, *The Commanding Heights*.

466. Claar and Klay, *Economics in Christian Perspective*, 140.

467. Sirico, *Defending the Free Market*, 3.

468. Hazlitt, *Economics in One Lesson*.

Chapter 12

469. Reed, "Was Jesus a Socialist?" PragerU, 2019.

470. UNRV Roman History, "Tax in the Early Days of the Roman Republic," https://www.unrv.com/economy/roman-taxes.php (retrieved March 23, 2020).

471. Anderson, *Christians and Economics*, 46.

472. Bolt, *Economic Shalom*, 136.

473. "PK," "Who Are the One Percent in the United States by Income and Net Worth?" DQYDJ, November 25, 2019, https://dqydj.com/top-one-percent-united-states (retrieved March 23, 2020).

474. Board of Governors of the Federal Reserve System (US), "Share of Total Net Worth Held by the Top 1% (99th to 100th Wealth Percentiles) [WFRBST01134]," Federal Reserve Bank of St. Louis; https://fred.stlouisfed.org/series/WFRBST01134 (retrieved March 24, 2020).

475. Board of Governors of the Federal Reserve System (US), "Share of Total Net Worth Held by the Bottom 50% (1st to 50th Wealth Percentiles) [WFRBSB50215]," Federal Reserve Bank of St. Louis; https://fred.stlouisfed.org/series/WFRBSB50215 (retrieved March 24, 2020).

476. Sirico, *Defending the Free Market*, 102.

477. "PK," "Income Percentile Calculator for the United States in 2019," DQYDJ, https://dqydj.com/income-percentile-calculator (retrieved March 23, 2020).

478. USA.gov, Government Benefits, March 6, 2020, from: https://www.usa.gov/benefits (retrieved March 23, 2020).

479. These programs are: Temporary Assistance for Needy Families (TANF), a straight cash program; Medicaid; food stamps; Women Infants and Children nutrition program (WIC); public housing vouchers; utilities assistance; and the Commodity Supplemental Food Program or CSFP which provides staples such as cheese, milk, canned vegetables, and other basic dietary items.

480. Tanner, "The War on Work."

481. Michael D. Tanner, "Five Myths about Economic Inequality in America," CATO Institute, Policy Analysis No.797, September 7, 2016, https://www.cato.org/publications/policy-analysis/five-myths-about-economic-inequality-america (retrieved March 23, 2020).

482. "PK," "Income Percentile Calculator for the United States in 2019"; and The Census Bureau, PINC-03. Educational Attainment-People 25 Years Old and Over, by Total Money Earnings, Work Experience, Age, Race, Hispanic Origin, and Sex, Current Population Survey (CPS), https://www.census.gov/data/tables/time-series/demo/income-poverty/cps-pinc/pinc-03.html (retrieved March 23, 2020).

483. Tanner, "Five Myths."

484. Michael R. Strain, "The American Dream Is Alive and Well," *Wall Street Journal*, January 31, 2020, https://www.wsj.com/articles/the-american-dream-is-alive-and-well-11580486386 (retrieved March 23, 2020).

485. Daniel Kahneman, Alan B. Krueger, David Schkade, Norbert Schwarz, and Arthur A. Stone, "Would You Be Happier If You Were Richer? A Focusing Illusion," Science 312, no. 5782 (June 2006): 1908–10.

486. William G. Gale, Melissa S. Kearney, and Peter R. Orszag, "Would a Significant Increase in the Top Income Tax Rate Substantially Alter Income Inequality?" Brookings Institution, September 2015, https://www.brookings.edu/wp-content/uploads/2016/06/would-top-income-tax-alter-income-inequality.pdf.

487. Tanner, "Five Myths."

488. "VTD Editor," "Full text: Sen. Bernie Sanders' 2020 Presidential Campaign Kickoff Speech," VTDigger.org, March 2, 2019, https://vtdigger.org/2019/03/02/full-text-sen-bernie-sanders-2020-presidential-campaign-kickoff-speech (retrieved March 23, 2020).

489. "Bernie Sanders Quotes for a Better World," https://www.betterworld.net/quotes/bernie/bernie8.htm (retrieved March 23, 2020).

490. Zach Carter, "Hillary Clinton Calls for 'Toppling' the 1 Percent," *Huffington Post*, April 21, 2015.

491. Tanner, "Five Myths."

492. Ruchir Sharma, "The Millionaires Are Fleeing. Maybe You Should, Too," *New York Times*, June 2, 2018, https://www.nytimes.com/2018/06/02/opinion/sunday/millionaires-fleeing-migration.html

493. AfrAsia Bank, "Global Wealth Migration Review 2018 and 2019," https://www.afrasiabank.com/en/about/newsroom/global-wealth-migration-review (retrieved March 23, 2020).

494. Brittany De Lea, "California Tax Hike Caused 'Significant'' Out-Migration of Top-Bracket Millionaire Residents, Study Shows," Fox Business, October 8, 2019, https://www.foxbusiness.com/money/california-tax-hike-significant-migration-of-millionaires. See also Joshua Rauh and Ryan J. Shyu, "Behavioral Responses to State Income Taxation of High Earners: Evidence from California," NBER Working Paper No. 26349. October 2019, https://www.nber.org/papers/w26349

495. Montero, *All Things in Common*, 56.

496. Hay, *Economics Today*, 54.

497. Robert Bellafiore, "Summary of the Latest Federal Income Tax Data, 2018 Update," Tax Foundation, November 13, 2018, https://taxfoundation.org/summary-latest-federal-income-tax-data-2018-update (retrieved March 23, 2020).

498. Ibid.

499. Sowell, *Wealth, Poverty and Politics*, 410.

500. Ibid., 375.

501. Reed, "Was Jesus a Socialist?"

502. Garry, *The False Promise of Big Government*, 52.

503. Ibid., 63.

504. Robert Sirico, presentation at Acton University, June 21, 2019.

505. Walter Kaiser, "Poverty and the Poor in the Old Testament," in Bradley and Lindsley, *For the Least of These*, 57.

506. Kotter, *Remember the Poor*, 102.

507. Bradley & Lindsley, *For the Least of These*, 102.

508. Bolt, *Economic Shalom*, 155.

509. Doug Bandow, "Capitalism and Poverty: Economic Development and Growth Benefit the Least the Most," in Lindsley and Anne Bradley, *Counting the Cost*, 216.

510. Xavier Sala-i-Martin, *The Disturbing "Rise" of Global Income Inequality*, No. w8904 (New York: National Bureau of Economic Research, 2002), 37.

511. Bolt, *Economic Shalom*, 141.

512. Sirico, *Defending the Free Market*, 25.

513. Pekka Sutela, "The Underachiever: Ukraine's Economy Since 1991," Carnegie Endowment for International Peace, March 9, 2012, https://carnegieendowment.org/2012/03/09/underachiever-ukraine-s-economy-since-1991-pub-47451 (retrieved March 23, 2020).

514. Hay, *Economics Today*, 141

515. Richards, *Money, Greed, and God*, 91.

516. Ibid., 54.

517. Gregg, *For God and Profit*, 134.

518. Mankiw, *Principles of Microeconomics*, 409.

519. Claar and Klay, *Economics in Christian Perspective*, 196.

520. Mankiw, *Principles of Microeconomics*, 409.

521. Sowell, *Wealth, Poverty and Politics*, 411.

522. Ibid., 423.

523. The Editorial Board, "A Tale of Two Economies," *Wall Street Journal*, July 5, 2019, https://www.wsj.com/articles/a-tale-of-two-economies-11562199595.

524. Edward Lazear, "Mind the Productivity Gap to Reduce Inequality," *Wall Street Journal*, May 6, 2019, https://www.wsj.com/articles/mind-the-productivity-gap-to-reduce-inequality-11557181134.

525. Lindsley and Bradley, *Counting the Cost*, 158.

526. Claar and Klay, *Economics in Christian Perspective*, 198.

527. Ibid., 70.

528. Bradley and Lindsley, *For the Least of These*, 219.

529. Lindsley and Bradley, *Counting the Cost*, 144.

530. Ibid., 165.

531. Greg Ip, "Two Capitalists Worry about Capitalism's Future," *Wall Street Journal*, April 24, 2019, https://www.wsj.com/articles/two-capitalists-worry-about-capitalisms-future-11556110982 (retrieved March 23, 2020).

532. Ibid.

533. Sirico, *Defending the Free Market*, 104.

534. Sowell, *Wealth, Poverty and Politics*, 422.

Chapter 13

535. Richards, *Money, Greed, and God*, 55.

536. Hazlitt, *Economics in One Lesson*, 194.

537. Richards, *Money, Greed, and God*, 42.

538. Joe Carter, "Why Christians Support Abortion (And How We Can Change That)," The Gospel Coalition, January 25, 2020, https://www.thegospelcoalition.org/article/why-christians-support-abortion-and-how-we-can-change-that (retrieved March 23, 2020).

539. Becket Adams, "Pete Buttigieg Reaffirms There Is No Room in the Democratic Party for Pro-Lifers," *Washington Examiner*, January 27, 2020, https://www.washingtonexaminer.com/opinion/pete-buttigieg-reaffirms-there-is-no-room-in-the-democratic-party-for-pro-lifers (retrieved March 23, 2020).

540. Gregg, *For God and Profit*, 184.

541. The Editorial Board, "Warren's Free College Time Machine," *The Wall Street Journal*, April 24, 2019, https://www.wsj.com/articles/warrens-free-college-time-machine-11556144467.

542. Jordan Weissmann, "America's Awful College Dropout Rates, in Four Charts," Slate.com, November 19, 2014, http://www.slate.com/blogs/moneybox/2014/11/19/u_s_college_dropouts_rates_explained_in_4_charts.html (retrieved March 23, 2020).

543. Mary Nguyen, "Degreeless In Debt: What Happens to Borrowers Who Drop Out," American Institute for Research, February 23, 2012, www.air.org/edsector-archives/publications/degreeless-debt-what-happens-borrowers-who-dropout (retrieved March 23, 2020).

544. Sean P. Keehan, et al., National Health Expenditure Projections, 2015–25: Economy, Prices, and Aging Expected to Shape Spending and Enrollment, Health Affairs Vol. 35, No. 8 (August 1, 2016), http://content.healthaffairs.org/content/35/8/1522 (retrieved March 23, 2020).

545. The Congressional Budget Office, The 2017 Long-Term Budget Outlook, March 30, 2017, https://www.cbo.gov/system/files/115th-congress-2017-2018/reports/52480-ltbo.pdf (retrieved March 23, 2020).

546. Sirico, *Defending the Free Market*, 138.

547. Ibid., 156.

548. Richards, *Money, Greed, and God*, 199.

549. United States Department of Agriculture, "Agricultural Productivity in the US—Summary of Recent Findings," January 10, 2020, https://www.ers.usda.gov/data-products/agricultural-productivity-in-the-us/summary-of-recent-findings (retrieved March 23, 2020).

550. Ibid.

551. Julian M. Alston, Matthew A. Andersen, Jennifer S. James, and Philip G. Pardey, "Persistence Pays: US Agricultural Productivity Growth and the Benefits

from Public R&D Spending," Natural Resource Management and Policy, Vol. 34 (Berlin: Springer Science & Business Media, 2009), 9–10, http://www.springer.com/cda/content/document/cda_downloaddocument/9781441906571-c1.pdf?SGWID=0-0-45-838614-p173903552

552. Central Intelligence Agency. "United States," The World Factbook 2020, https://www.cia.gov/library/publications/the-world-factbook/geos/us.html (retrieved March 23, 2020).

553. Richards, *Money, Greed, and God*, 188.

554. Sirico, *Defending the Free Market*, 162.

555. Claar and Klay, *Economics in Christian Perspective*, 48.

556. Richards, *Money, Greed, and God*, 202.

Chapter 14

557. Matt Ridley, *The Rational Optimist: How Prosperity Evolves* (New York: Harper, 2010).

558. United Nations, *State of the Future*, 200.

559. Richards, *Money, Greed, and God*, 201.

560. Bradley and Lindsley, *For the Least of These*, 219.

561. Richards, *Money, Greed, and God*, 181.

562. Jonah Goldberg, speech at the Acton Institute, June 21, 2019.

563. Corbett and Fikkert, *When Helping Hurts*, 41.

564. Sirico, *Defending the Free Market*, 120.

565. George Friedman, *The Storm Before the Calm* (New York: Doubleday, 2020).

566. Montero, *All Things in Common*, 61.

567. Garry, *The False Promise of Big Government*, 101.

568. Montero, *All Things in Common*, 104.

569. Sowell, *Wealth, Poverty and Politics*, 9.

570. Garry, *The False Promise of Big Government*, 99.

571. Sowell, *Wealth, Poverty and Politics*, 421.

572. Ibid., 407.

573. Johann Friedrick Hölderlin, "Friedrich Hölderlin Quotes," GoodReads.com, https://www.goodreads.com/quotes/138800-what-has-always-made-the-state-a-hell-on-earth.

574. Himmelfarb, *Lord Acton*, 218.

575. Paul Heyne, *A Student's Guide to Economics* (Wilmington, DE: ISI Books, 2000), 32.

576. Helen Raleigh, "What Socialism Meant for My Great Grandfather," *Wall Street Journal*, July 8, 2019.

577. Reed, "Was Jesus a Socialist?"

578. Ibid.

579. Garry, *The False Promise of Big Government*, 40.

580. Jay Richards, *Money, Greed, and God*, 2.

581. Ibid., 81.

582. Ibid., 217.

583. Hazlitt, *Economics in One Lesson*, 195.

584. Peter Lindert and Jeffrey Williamson, "Does Globalization Make the World More Unequal?" NBER Working Paper #8228, National Bureau of Economic Research, April 2001.

585. Sowell, *Wealth, Poverty and Politics*, 312.

586. Bhalla, *Imagine There's No Country.*

587. Claar and Klay, *Economics in Christian Perspective*, 157.

588. Sowell, *Wealth, Poverty and Politics*, 347.

589. Ibid., 106.

590. Richards, *Money, Greed, and God*, 46.

591. Bandow, "Capitalism and Poverty," 195.

592. Peter Greer, "A Call to Move Compassionately beyond Charity," in Bradley and Lindsley, *For the Least of These*, 231.

593. Sowell, *Wealth, Poverty and Politics*, 125.

594. Hazlitt, *Economics in One Lesson* (Baltimore: Laissez Faire Books, 1962), 173.

595. Sowell, *Wealth, Poverty and Politics*, 107.

596. Claar and Klay, *Economics in Christian Perspective*, 186.

597. Bolt, *Economic Shalom*, 134.

598. Gregory Mankiw, "Global Perspectives."

599. Bolt, *Economic Shalom*, 104.

600. Gregg, *For God and Profit*, 184.

601. Himmelfarb, *Lord Acton*, 218.

602. Röpke, *A Humane Economy*, 13.

Printed in the United States
ker & Taylor Publisher Services